Scoville

How Socrates Became Socrates

How Socrates Became Socrates

A Study of Plato's
Phaedo, *Parmenides*, and *Symposium*

LAURENCE LAMPERT

The University of Chicago Press
Chicago & London

The University of Chicago Press, Chicago 60637
The University of Chicago Press, Ltd., London
© 2021 by The University of Chicago
All rights reserved. No part of this book may be used or reproduced in any manner
whatsoever without written permission, except in the case of brief quotations in
critical articles and reviews. For more information, contact the University of Chicago
Press, 1427 E. 60th St., Chicago, IL 60637.
Published 2021
Printed in the United States of America

30 29 28 27 26 25 24 23 22 21   1 2 3 4 5

ISBN-13: 978-0-226-74633-3 (cloth)
ISBN-13: 978-0-226-74647-0 (e-book)
DOI: https://doi.org/10.7208/chicago/9780226746470.001.0001

Library of Congress Cataloging-in-Publication Data

Names: Lampert, Laurence, 1941– author.
Title: How Socrates became Socrates : a study of Plato's Phaedo, Parmenides, and
    Symposium / Laurence Lampert.
Description: Chicago : University of Chicago Press, 2021. | Includes bibliographical
    references and index.
Identifiers: LCCN 2020039060 | ISBN 9780226746333 (cloth) | ISBN 9780226746470
    (ebook)
Subjects: LCSH: Socrates. | Plato. Phaedo. | Plato. Parmenides. | Plato. Symposium. |
    Nietzsche, Friedrich Wilhelm, 1844–1900.
Classification: LCC B317 .L357 2021 | DDC 183/.2 — dc23
LC record available at https://lccn.loc.gov/2020039060

♾ This paper meets the requirements of ANSI/NISO Z39.48-1992 (Permanence of
Paper).

{ CONTENTS }

Introduction *1*

1 *Phaedo*: The First Stage of Socrates' Philosophic
Education *7*

Prologue: Heroic Socrates as the New Ideal *7*
1. First Words *10*
2. A New Theseus to Slay the Real Minotaur *14*
3. A New Herakles to Cut Off and Bury the Immortal Head of
   Hydra *18*
4. A New Odysseus to Teach the Safe Way to Understand Cause *31*
5. Odyssean Socrates' Report on His Second Sailing in the *Phaedo*
   Measured by the *Parmenides* *52*
6. Odyssean Socrates Ends His Life of Argument *71*
7. Socrates' Last Words: Gratitude for a Healing *82*

2 *Parmenides*: The Second Stage of Socrates' Philosophic
Education *89*

Prologue: A Socrates for the Philosophically Driven *89*
1. First Words *91*
2. At Pythodorus's House during the Great Panathenaia *95*
3. Socrates and Zeno: How to Read a Philosophic Writing *99*

4. Socrates' Solution to What Parmenides and Zeno Made to Seem beyond Us *103*

5. Parmenides the Guide *108*

6. What Is This Gymnastic? *120*

7. Guiding Socrates *124*

8. Last Words *146*

9. The Socratic Turn *148*

3 The *Symposium*: The Final Stage of Socrates' Philosophic Education *152*

Prologue: Socrates' Ontological Psychology *152*

1. First Words *157*

2. Socrates Beautifies Himself for Agathon *161*

3. Diotima's Myth Guides Socrates to the Third Stage of His Philosophic Education *172*

4. Diotima's Logos Guides Socrates to the Third Stage of His Philosophic Education *182*

5. Diotima Teaches Socrates What to Teach *191*

6. Alcibiades Arrives *203*

7. Last Words *206*

Note on the Dramatic Date of the Frame of the *Symposium* *209*

Conclusion: Plato in a Nietzschean History of Philosophy *221*

Works Cited *227*

Index *233*

Socrates, the one turning-point and vortex of so-called world history
— Nietzsche, *Birth of Tragedy*, §15

Did Plato show Socrates *becoming* Socrates? This book is the second of two in which I answer yes. The first of the two, *How Philosophy Became Socratic: A Study of Plato's "Protagoras," "Charmides," and "Republic,"* answered yes by showing how Plato ordered those three dialogues chronologically to give his reader access to Socrates' development in devising a successful *political* philosophy. This second book answers yes by showing how Plato ordered his *Phaedo, Parmenides*, and *Symposium* chronologically to give his reader access to Socrates' development on philosophy's fundamental questions of being and knowing.[1] All three events in Socrates' education in philosophy itself occurred earlier than the *Protagoras*, which Plato set around 434 and which he made the chronologically first of his temporally arranged sequence of dialogues. The three dialogues that treat Socrates' becoming in philosophy proper therefore had to be given more complex structures: each has a frame whose dramatic date is much later than 434 and each reaches back from that later time to a time earlier than 434 in order to recover a stage of Socrates' becoming, back to his youth-

---

1. Seth Benardete speaks of the "three stages in Socrates' philosophical education" ("On Plato's *Symposium*," in *Argument of the Action*, 178). While recognizing the three stages, Benardete never treated them thematically; nor did Leo Strauss, who also recognized them (*Xenophon's Socratic Discourse*, 149). My book owes a special debt to Benardete, the twentieth-century thinker and master of classical thought who opened the tradition of Greek philosophy like no other modern commentator.

ful beginnings in the *Phaedo* and *Parmenides*, back to his young manhood in the *Symposium*.

These three dialogues demand careful attention if one is to recover the proper sequence and learn just how that progress in thinking led Socrates to his ultimate conclusions about nature and human nature. In contrast to that demand for dedicated recovery work, Plato made it easy for everyone to have a pleasing account of how Socrates became himself: Plato's *Apology of Socrates* presents the only speech Socrates ever made to the Athenian public, to the five hundred "men of Athens" who were his judges and the large crowd of interested onlookers at his trial for his life. Socrates tells the Athenian public an autobiographical tale of his becoming, an edifying story that made him the servant of the god at Delphi who assigned him responsibility for the well-being of Athens, particularly its youth. How did Socrates become that odd character that everyone knew him to be, that man of the marketplace talking incessantly of the common things and the public virtues? Apollo made him do it, he says in the *Apology*, commissioning him with a public task to improve public virtue. So a tale of Socrates' becoming the philosopher he became takes its proper place as the most prominent of all the stories Plato related of Socrates. In contrast to that easily accessible pious tale of Socrates' becoming, Plato scattered his other account of Socrates' becoming across three dialogues, leaving it to the reader truly interested in Socrates to recognize that Plato gave three separate installments to the true account of Socrates' becoming, that they fit together chronologically, and that the work of interpreting them opens a route to the truth about Socrates' becoming: he gained a deeply satisfying set of philosophical, that is to say, radical conclusions about human being and beings as a whole.

Plato thus judged that there had to be two accounts of Socrates' becoming a philosopher, different in their content, reconcilable in their intentions. The easily available pious account is literally intended for the whole Athenian public and by extension the public that reads the dialogues. The other account, scattered across three very different dialogues, including the most puzzling of them all, and demanding that work be done to fit them together properly, is intended for those interested enough in philosophy and in Socrates to do that work. For such devoted readers, Plato made it possible to know how Socrates non-mythically became himself as a thinker about nature and human nature and just what he became — what "Apollo" enabled him to achieve through the natural gifts of a passionate drive to understand the causes of all things, and an intellect of genius to generate and sort out rational explanations.

Starting with this premise that Plato gave two accounts of Socrates' becoming a philosopher and that the relation between them is that of a public Socrates and a private one, my book treats only the private account. One reason for this is that the public account is well known and the private account barely visible as a possibility. More importantly, by treating only the veiled account, I aim to show not only that Plato offered such an account, but also that this Socrates is the philosophically fascinating one, beyond his public moral and political concerns. Once that private philosopher is seen, the account of his becoming that Socrates gave to the Athenian public becomes understandable from a new perspective: his public presentation of his becoming at his trial, a presentation consistent with how he had shown himself in the marketplace for thirty years, is a defense of *philosophy*, of what he discovered in private and kept private but what is clearly in need of a public defense. He knows that defense will cost him his life, but it is a cost he is willing to pay, at age seventy, for the sake of philosophy. Philosophy's best-known practitioner died heroically for philosophy of a kind he kept hidden.[2]

The fact that Plato's *Phaedo*, *Parmenides*, and *Symposium* are related in containing sequential accounts of the three major events in Socrates' becoming a philosopher is supported by a structural or taxonomic feature that Plato gave to these three dialogues and to them alone. Among the thirty-five dialogues he wrote, nine are different in being *narrated* rather than simply *performed*; Plato had an identified person speak each of the nine to a given audience, whereas he put all the others before their reader-audience directly, as in a play.[3] Of the nine narrated dialogues Socrates narrates six; each of the other three is narrated by a person identified as its speaker: Phaedo narrates the *Phaedo*, Cephalus the *Parmenides*, and Apollodorus the *Symposium*. That these three dialogues are unique in their being narrated by persons other than Socrates befits that other far more important uniqueness: they are the three dialogues from which Socrates' way to his genuine philosophizing can be recovered. The three share another feature: each is concerned with the *transmission* of Socrates' philosophy. In the *Phaedo*, Phaedo carries the story Socrates told on his last day of his first

2. The public account in the *Apology*, read with careful attention, can itself be seen as harboring Socrates' deeper, philosophic perspective; see Strauss, "On Plato's *Apology of Socrates* and *Crito*," in *Studies in Platonic Political Philosophy*, 38–66; and Leibowitz, *Ironic Defense of Socrates*.

3. Leo Strauss set out the distinction between narrated and performed in *The City and Man*, 58. The *Parmenides* is an exception regarding a "given audience": it is narrated by a Cephalus to an unidentified audience.

beginnings in philosophy to a Pythagorean community outside of Athens, which, as the dialogue shows, gladly welcomes a new philosophic hero to its midst, a hero who saves them from their deepest anxiety—they will treasure the tale of Socrates and keep retelling it, just as they retell tales of their founding hero, Pythagoras. In the *Parmenides*, unnamed "men of Clazomenae" sail across the Aegean Sea in the hope of hearing a conversation between young Socrates and old Parmenides and his disciple Zeno; their hope is rewarded, and they will carry their treasured tale home to the region of Greece where philosophy first began as an investigation of nature. In the *Symposium*, Socrates sees to the preservation of his deepest gains by relating them in Athens to a highly gifted young man whom he singles out from a wider though still private audience of a talented few deeply shaped by the Greek enlightenment; Agathon, a prize-winning tragedian, hears from Socrates what Socrates alleges he heard from fabulous Diotima: will he burn his tragedies and follow Socrates? Each of those responsible for transmitting a piece of the tale, Phaedo, Cephalus, and Apollodorus, treasures what he memorized and relates, but Plato suggests that each of them lacks the kind of interest in Socrates that would allow *them* to assemble the pieces into a whole, an interest in Socrates that is transcended by engagement in philosophy itself, in discovering the truth about all things.

One of the three stages of Socrates' philosophical education that Plato recorded differs from the other two in an important respect. The *Phaedo* and *Symposium* are autobiographical; telling his own tale, Socrates can frame it and shape it in the way that seems best to him in the setting: remember and study my becoming this way, he says in effect to those to whom he is speaking, use it as a guide in understanding who I am and how I may be useful to you. The story of Socrates' becoming in the *Parmenides*, however, is not autobiographical; Socrates played no part in telling it or preserving it.[4] The tale of its recovery, its being saved from oblivion very late by extraordinary effort, shows why it is not autobiographical: those nameless men of Clazomenae recover the event by undertaking a possibly fruitless journey across the sea in the hope of discovering something precious to them, for rumor has it that a conversation some sixty years ago now between great Parmenides and young Socrates may still be remembered by a person in Athens whose very name even their link to the event had forgotten—and they do it because they are "very much philosophers." These philosophically driven men succeed in recovering a tale that Socrates himself could

4. This point is made by Benardete, "Plato's *Parmenides*: A Sketch," in *Archaeology of the Soul*, 230.

never tell to any public because the transcendent forms he introduced in Athens in 429 when he was about forty and "babbled about" till his dying day (*Phaedo* 100b) are, Parmenides showed him when he was young, rationally untenable. Plato did what he could to keep the telling of this explosive report separate from Socrates himself while showing that he intended it solely for those who resemble those men of Clazomenae, future nameless travelers from afar, very much philosophers and willing and possibly able to exercise the intellectual acuity to learn something Socrates learned but was constrained from ever reporting to any public. The *Parmenides* rises as singular among Plato's dialogues on Socrates' becoming not only as especially puzzling but as especially rewarding: this is the central event of Socrates' learning; travel to it from afar if you can.

In my accounts of the three stages of Socrates' becoming a philosopher in the *Phaedo*, *Parmenides*, and *Symposium*, I treat in greatest detail the passages within them that explicitly concern the particular stage of his philosophical education. I also treat the frame of each of the dialogues in detail because the setting Plato chose to give to each of the stages casts light on the stage itself and is indispensable to its understanding. With the *Phaedo* and the *Symposium* this manner of treatment allows the omission of major sections that neither touch on Socrates' becoming nor determine the character of the whole dialogue. With the *Parmenides* each part of the dialogue serves the central purpose of showing the young Socrates the way to think properly about forms, and I therefore treat all of it.

Together, the *Phaedo*, *Parmenides*, and *Symposium* unite to display a young thinker entering philosophy's true radicality. That radicality, when exposed, shows why a public face, a political philosophy, is necessary for philosophy's well-being within a stable social order based on salutary belief. The three dialogues I treated in *How Philosophy Became Socratic* show Socrates learning just what his political philosophy had to teach, while the three dialogues I treat here show Socrates learning what philosophy can come to know, and why, therefore, it is in need of a public shelter. In violating the privacy of Plato's lessons in becoming a philosopher I take permission from the decisive changes in setting between our times and that time, changes set out by Friedrich Nietzsche in the permissions he gave himself to expose the difference between the exoteric and esoteric and to show what a philosopher is in his difference. Like all my books, this book too is an installment in the new history of philosophy made possible by Friedrich Nietzsche.

CHAPTER I

Phaedo

The First Stage of Socrates' Philosophic Education

The dying Socrates thus became the new, never before seen ideal of
noble Greek youth, above all of the typically Hellenic youth Plato.
— Nietzsche, *Birth of Tragedy*, §13

Prologue: Heroic Socrates as the New Ideal

The young Nietzsche's observation captures Plato's intention in his *Phaedo*
exactly: Plato made Socrates the new ideal of Greek youth, replacing the
worn-out, *thumos*-driven heroes of Homer, those models of emulation for
generations of Greek youth, models whose time was now passing. Plato
presents Socrates in his *Phaedo* as the new Theseus and the new Herakles,
the local and Panhellenic heroes of manly action; the new hero of manly
action gave Greek youth new standards of worth and new grounds for vir-
tuous striving. Less obviously, Plato made Socrates a hero modeled on the
Homeric hero whose time never passes, Odysseus, that man of many guiles
who has seen the peoples of many cities and understood their ways, Odysseus, that exemplar of the odyssey to philosophy and of the practice of
philosophy as an art that cannot forgo guile. Nietzsche repeatedly taught
the *Phaedo* to his late-teenaged gymnasium students, and his reasons may
well have included his own familiarity with the aspiration of youth to the
heroic that Plato so successfully tapped in making Socrates immortal.[1]

1. Nietzsche's inaugural public lectures in Basel, "On the Future of Our Educational
Institutions," give a vivid picture of his understanding of the role of hero-worship and

And Nietzsche's study of Western civilization guided that other judgment of his on Plato's success in making Socrates the new hero: "One cannot avoid seeing in Socrates the one turning point and vortex of so-called world history."[2]

The *Phaedo* is also the record of an execution. Socrates' companions in the cell watch as Socrates with heroic resolve faces the death imposed on him by his own city. Watching him as he drinks the death potion and then through to his last seconds when he covered his face and finally uncovered it to speak his last words, Plato's reader watches as Socrates carries out the execution to which his city condemned him, transfixingly heroic to the last moment, in the face of death itself. Socrates' heroic acceptance of his city's judgment against him, his lack of defiance, his apparent submission, are emblems of Socratic philosophy's reconciliation with the city whose fundamental requirements it came to understand. With heroic Socrates, the dying Socrates, philosophy takes up residence in the city. And if Socrates' speech throughout the *Phaedo* provides evidence of how philosophy can best be loyal to the city in tending to the needs of its maturing young men, his speeches point privately to the way in which philosophy is deadly to the city's necessary beliefs.

How remarkable that Plato has Socrates speak of his first beginnings in philosophy on the last day of his life and just before what he knows will be the last argument of his life. Plato has Socrates say that the answer to the last question he faces in his life involves "the cause concerning generation and destruction as a whole" (95e); and then, reporting on his first beginnings, he says he was driven to know "the causes of each thing, why each thing comes to be and why it perishes and why it is" (96a). Plato has Socrates end his life as a philosopher identifying his concern from beginning to end: Socrates' life was a passionate pursuit of the cause of generation and destruction as a whole, of the nature of nature. And the premises of his final argument—he bases it on what he has "never stopped talking about" (100b) since an early point in his life, transcendent forms—shows another continuity in his life, his choice to speak about the fundamental matters by bringing in fixed, unchanging forms that do more than provide a cause

---

emulation in young men. His failure to provide the culminating sixth lecture is a likewise vivid picture, but of his uncertainty at the time about a model *modern* ideal. Ann Hartle pays close attention to the "heroic action" of the *Phaedo* (*Death and the Disinterested Spectator*, 18, 23, 24, 28, 36), noting that Theseus, Herakles, and especially Odysseus serve as Socrates' heroic models.

2. Nietzsche, *The Birth of Tragedy*, §15.

and make it knowable: they order the world morally, founding it on an unchanging good good for human beings.

Plato's framing of the *Phaedo* set Socrates' words on his last day within a Pythagorean setting. Socrates' chief interlocutors, Simmias and Cebes, were trained in the Pythagorean community in Thebes by Philolaus, a Pythagorean teacher about Socrates' age.[3] Philolaus had as a young man of about twenty experienced the destruction of Pythagorean rule in Greek cities in southern Italy around 450; expelled from Italy with the rest of the Pythagoreans, he fled to Thebes, where he established a school. And Plato has Phaedo narrate Socrates' last day in Phlia, a town that was the other center in the Greek homeland in which Pythagoreans gathered after the Italian dispersal.[4] The one member of the Pythagorean community in Phlia to speak in the *Phaedo* is Echecrates, Phaedo's interlocutor in the frame of the dialogue and twice for decisive confessions that begin and end the discussion at the center of the dialogue. Phaedo's narration and its Pythagorean setting indicate that the *Phaedo* is concerned with the transmission, after Socrates' death, of Socrates' teaching through the already constituted schools of philosophy: Echecrates is made a disciple of Socrates by Phaedo's stirring report. It is not only the Pythagorean schools that could aid the afterlife of heroic Socrates: Phaedo himself will establish a Socratic school in Elis, and Plato notes the presence of founders of other Socratic schools in the cell with Socrates.[5]

Another remarkable feature of the *Phaedo* with respect to the transmission of heroic Socrates' philosophy is the youthfulness and foreignness of all of the speakers except the old Athenians, Socrates and Crito. Phaedo of Elis was around nineteen. Simmias and Cebes of Thebes are said to be *neoniskoi* (89a), males who have achieved "adult height [and are] beginning to grow facial hair."[6] Echecrates of Phlia was also very young, perhaps in his

---

3. In his *Memorabilia* Xenophon names Simmias and Cebes twice, both times together (1.2.48; 3.11.17); in his first mention of them he counts them among those who kept company with Socrates in order to become gentlemen and thereby be able to deal in a noble manner with their household, friends, city, and citizens.

4. Phlia lay on the main road between Athens and Sparta and just south of the main road from Corinth to Elis that Phaedo was presumably traveling on his way home from Athens. On all the persons in the *Phaedo* and in all the dialogues, see Nails, *People of Plato*.

5. Antisthenes, about forty-five at Socrates' death, founded the Cynic school; Euclides, aged fifty at Socrates' death, founded a philosophical school at Megara. Other older associates of Socrates were present: Hermogenes was fifty at Socrates' death; Aeschines was about thirty and went on to write Socratic dialogues. Other unnamed Athenians are also present (59b).

6. Nails, *People of Plato*, Glossary, 373; Robert Garland says *neoniskoi* (more commonly *neoi*) "covered the period from the twenties to the early thirties" (*Greek Way of Life*, 200).

early twenties.[7] Present but silent for this last exchange between Socrates and non-Athenian young men are older men, experienced with Socrates. In contrast to the young men made prominent in Phaedo's report, these older associates of Socrates can be expected to know already much of what they hear from him on his last day. They are present in the *Phaedo* like a silent chorus, a counsel of elders listening to what is said, knowing how to judge it, while hearing their master speak for the final time and speak on first things and final things that he had undoubtedly spoken of before with them.

1. First Words

"*Autos ō Phaidōn . . .*" are the first words of the *Phaedo*, "Yourself, Phaedo, were you yourself present with Socrates on the day on which he drank the potion in the prison, or did you hear it from another?"[8] "*Autos ō Echekrates,*" Phaedo answers, "Myself, Echecrates." Openings are of great importance to Plato's artful dialogues, given the evident care he lavished on them. And *autos*, the first word of the *Phaedo*, is repeated as the narrator Phaedo's own first word. Used first for "yourself" and "myself," *autos* is the word for "self," and it opens the dialogue of Socrates' death day, the day on which the continued existence of his self is put to question: What is the self as soul and body both here and now and, in the explicit concern of the dialogue, after death? Does death to Socrates' body, watched so graphically at the end as the poison moves up from his feet, deadening his calves and thighs and slowly reaching his heart, bring death to his *autos*? Or will it live on as the young interlocutors are encouraged to believe about Socrates and themselves? The dialogue itself will suggest that Phaedo's narration preserves the only kind of afterlife available to a human *autos*, preservation in human memory.

Autos is also the word for "itself," as in "soul itself" or "justice itself." The first word of the *Phaedo* is a crucial word for the view of forms that Socrates says he has been babbling about for years and here advocates explicitly as the "safe" way of conceiving of cause. But the *Phaedo* is that special dialogue in which Socrates tells how he first posited transcendent forms as the end of his path of thinking as a young man, a path that led him through

---

7. Nails, *People of Plato*, 138, does not give his dates but says that he was "active 399-mid 4th c." — in the *Phaedo* he stands near the beginning of his career.

8. I use the translation of the *Phaedo* by Eva Brann, Peter Kalkavage, and Eric Salem (1998), with some alterations for greater literalness and consistency of usage.

the existing philosophic tradition to his discovery of what he has now been talking about for so long. And *autos* as the word for "forms" is what the last argument of his life depends on, the argument to prove what the audience in the cell and the audience in Phlia most need to have proven, that their souls are immortal.

And *Autos* was the word Pythagoreans applied to the man himself, Pythagoras, and the *Phaedo* is steeped in Pythagorean themes and Pythagorean personages, making the opening word particularly fitting for the setting Plato chose for the dialogue. The transmission of Socrates' teaching is enacted dramatically by having Socrates transmit his teaching to two young Pythagoreans in the cell and then by having Phaedo transmit it to a Pythagorean school outside of Athens. Will Socrates himself replace Pythagoras himself?

After learning that Phaedo was himself present at Socrates' death Echecrates says why he wants to hear a firsthand report of what famous Socrates said before his death and how he died: "No one from Phlia even visits Athens at all nowadays, nor has any stranger arrived from there in a long time." Phlia, while representing a particularly fertile place for transmitting Socrates' teaching, is emblematic of every place outside of Athens with respect to Socrates' last day: in all places, without such a report, all anyone would ever know of Socrates' last day is that he "drank the *pharmakon* and died" (57b); no one would know "what . . . the man said before his death" or "how he [met] his end" (57a). Phaedo's actual presence gives the authority of an eye- and ear-witness to this singular event, a witness whose devotion to Socrates helps ensure that he will not garble what happened or what was said on that day. Perhaps that is the reason for the title: *Phaedo* is the only dialogue that Plato named for its narrator. Just who Phaedo himself is as a witness carrying the tale of Socrates' last day to distant places will come to light in the center of the dialogue, where his role in preserving the tale will be given a heroic precedent: he will be the Iolaus who aids the hero Herakles in the only deed for which he needed help. And as for Echecrates, the speaker for the Pythagorean school at which Phaedo narrates his tale, he himself becomes important as the kind of auditor to whom and through whom the eye-witnessed tale will be transmitted, for Plato will indicate just who *he* is as well.

The first words have one final significance: Echecrates' words — "Were you yourself present . . . or did you hear it from another?" — do what so many of Plato's first words do: they bring the dialogue into contact with Homer's *Odyssey*. Echecrates' words repeat words Odysseus addressed to the Phaeacian singer Demodocus, praising him for his ability, "whether the Muse taught you or Apollo," to "well and truly . . . sing the fate of the Achaeans . . . as if you yourself had been present or heard it from another."[9] Odysseus had not yet identified himself to the Phaeacians when he praised Demodocus just before inviting him to sing one particular episode in the fate of the Achaeans: "Sing us the wooden horse which Epeius made with Athena helping, the stratagem great Odysseus once filled with men and brought to the upper city, and it was these men who sacked Ilion." Plato opens his *Phaedo* repeating Odysseus's words inviting the song of polytropic Odysseus's greatest ruse, which finally succeeded in bringing down Troy and winning the ten-year war for the Achaeans. Is Demodocus then Phaedo now? The tale he tells will indeed be the tale of an Odysseus performing a memorable and successful deed of conquest. Socrates' deed on his last day, itself a kind of wooden horse drawn into the sacred fortress-city, will save reason, or logos, from the greatest evil. By having his first sentence refer to Odysseus on the island of the Phaeacians, Plato may also be invoking Odysseus's greatest achievement, an achievement of thinking: Odysseus will identify himself to the king of that island, Alkinous, and relate the tale of his odyssey, his coming into his wisdom; he transmits the story of his becoming himself to a wise ruler perhaps fully fit to hear and understand it.[10]

Within the *Phaedo*, Plato utilizes another set of first words, Socrates' first words, as an initial indicator of just who Socrates is. As Phaedo begins his narration in Phlia he describes how he and others were in the habit of visiting Socrates in his cell from early morning till late. They arrived especially early on the last day, knowing it would be the last because they had learned the night before that the ship had returned from Delos. When they were admitted to the cell, they "caught Socrates just freed from his bonds and Xanthippe . . . holding his little boy and seated beside him." The first glimpse of Socrates in the *Phaedo* is as a husband and a father, and near the end of the day he will again be seen as a husband and father (116a-b). The first words of Socrates that Phaedo quotes, "Crito, have someone take her home," mirror the last words Socrates will ever speak: they too address a command to Crito to perform a service for Socrates. At the beginning

---

9. *Odyssey* 8.489–91. See Johnstone, "Homeric Echo in Plato?," 417–18.

10. That Odysseus is Socrates' model for his own becoming in the *Protagoras*, *Charmides*, and *Republic* is part of my argument in *How Philosophy Became Socratic*. In these dialogues too, Socrates' Odyssean character becomes evident only by inference, often through unacknowledged references to the *Odyssey*, itself an Odyssean way of referring to Odysseus, who received his name from his grandfather on his mother's side, Autolocus, Wolf Himself, who surpassed all men, Socrates said in quoting Homer, "in stealing and in swearing oaths" (*Republic* 334b, quoting *Odyssey* 19.495–96).

and at the end of the *Phaedo* Plato calls attention to the close friendship between Socrates and a respected Athenian gentleman. The first words Socrates speaks to his collected friends come after he sits up on his bed, bends his leg, and gives it a good rubbing with his hand (60b). The spot where the shackle had caused him pain thus becomes a source of pleasure for him, and he speaks of experiencing the strange relatedness of pleasure and pain. But that's the very relatedness Phaedo had spoken about in *his* first words about his experience in the cell (58e–59a). Socrates' reaction to a relatedness that both call "wondrous" is different from Phaedo's: Socrates does not stand before it dumbfounded in wonder as Phaedo did (59a); instead, he says: "How absurd (*atopon*) a thing this seems to be, men, which humans call pleasant. How wondrously related it is by nature to its seeming contrary, the painful" (60b). What Phaedo held to be an "unusual blend" and "a simply absurd (*atopon*) feeling" (59a), Socrates holds to be a seemingly absurd relation rooted in nature and open to being understood: while pain and pleasure "are not both willing to be present with a person at the same time," still, "if someone chases the one and catches it, he's pretty much compelled to catch the other one too, just as if the pair of them — although they're two — were fastened by one head." Socrates does not leave his explanation of the wondrous at a natural relatedness; instead, he invents a poetic tale to convey the "one head" natural relatedness of pleasure and pain: "if Aesop had noticed this he would have composed a story," a *mythos*, to give what Socrates noticed a form that would make it understandable and enjoyable by all. A Socratic-Aesopian fable of the natural human experience of the togetherness of pleasure and pain would tell "how the god wanted to reconcile them in their war with each other, but when he wasn't able to do that, he fastened their heads together at the same point, and for that reason, when the one is present with someone, its other follows along later." The one head of human experience becomes two connected heads in a myth to display the experience, a doubling that displays what not even the god could alter in nature: unalterable nature loses a seemingly absurd togetherness when poetized into a tale of divine agency. By giving Socrates and Phaedo opening speeches on a common experience that Phaedo found simply wondrous, but Socrates explained in two ways, as natural and through a pleasing myth, Plato has Socrates display his difference in his first speech: he aims to understand things in their nature and he equips what he has understood with mythic explanation. As Seth Benardete says, "The topic of the *Phaedo* . . . is an account of [Socrates'] own experience."[11]

---

11. Benardete, "On Plato's *Phaedo*," in *Argument of the Action*, 281.

Socrates experienced what all humanity experiences, but he inquired into it and, understanding it, generated poetic explanations of it.

2. A New Theseus to Slay the Real Minotaur

The Athenian hero Theseus enters Phaedo's tale at its beginning when he is forced to explain to non-Athenians an Athenian custom memorializing their local Herakles-like hero. When Phaedo asked if those in Phlia "did not even find out about the way the trial went" (58a), Echecrates said they did learn about that but "kept wondering why" so much time passed between the trial and Socrates' death. Phaedo reports that "chance came to his aid," for "by chance the stern of the vessel that the Athenians send to Delos was crowned on the day before the trial." Naturally baffled by that local reference, Echecrates asks, "Now what one is that?" Because he asked and Phaedo explained, all non-Athenian readers of the dialogue gain access to details necessary for understanding Socrates' circumstances in Athens on his last day and for interpreting what he said and did. The afterlife of Socrates, how well he lives on through reports on his words and deeds, requires some explanation of Athenian customs, like that of sending a ship to Delos to honor Apollo at his birthplace. Through such explanations of uniquely Athenian events, Plato's Socrates can take his deserved place as a more than merely Athenian hero.

Phaedo explains that Athenians say that the vessel they crown and send to Delos is the very one "in which Theseus once went off leading those Twice Seven to Crete, and both saved them and was himself saved" (58b) — Theseus, the agent of *their* being saved, was thereby saved *himself*: the *Phaedo* can be said to display Socrates' action of saving the others, but by its very existence the *Phaedo* is the means whereby Socrates himself is saved as a hero.[12] But Phaedo's explanation of Athenian custom itself employs Athenian shorthand by speaking of the "Twice Seven": those truly interested in Socrates will have to work at recovering and preserving the customs of the city in which he lived his life. For "Twice Seven" refers to a particular event in the distant Athenian past and to the special way in which Theseus took advantage of one of the features of that event: long ago King Minos of Crete imposed on the Athens he had conquered the tribute of sending to Crete every nine years seven youths and seven maidens to be sacrificed to the Minotaur, that monster with a human head on

---

12. See Bacon, "Poetry of *Phaedo*," 152–53, for how "Theseus' Cretan venture" is "emblematic for the whole dialogue."

a bull's body that had been born to Pasiphae, Minos's wife, after Daedalus had fashioned a device allowing her to satisfy her lust for a beautiful white bull. Daedalus also fashioned a labyrinth to house the Minotaur at its center. Young Theseus, son of the king of Athens, delivered Athens from Cretan tyranny by volunteering to go to Crete as one of the seven youths. But he devised a ruse for his particular "Twice Seven": he had two additional youths train and dress to look like maidens in order to help him in his task; his "Twice Seven" was a secret nine plus five.[13] Theseus's plan succeeded because Ariadne, daughter of Minos and Pasiphae, fell in love with him and gave him the sword to kill the Minotaur and the thread to lead him back out of the labyrinth. Every year, at the festival to Apollo called the Delia, the Athenians sent back to Delos, birthplace of Apollo and stopping point for Theseus on his triumphant homecoming from Crete, what they say is the very vessel in which Theseus sailed on his mission of deliverance long ago.[14] Until that ship returned from Delos, this festival for the god of purification required the city to maintain its ritual purity by performing no executions — the chance winds that extended the period of the city's purity by thirty days[15] gave Socrates more time in his cell, including his final day of conversation with his friends.

In an exegetical insight of enduring importance, Jacob Klein showed that the list Phaedo supplied of the Athenians and foreigners present in Socrates' cell (59b-c) resembles Theseus's unique "Twice Seven": it a list of fourteen that mimes Theseus's, for both are not twice seven but nine plus five, in Phaedo's list, nine Athenians, the last two set off from the seven, plus five foreigners.[16] Theseus's saving deed, known in all particulars by every Athenian, is reflected in Socrates' deed on his final day: Socrates will perform a saving deed befitting the hero Theseus's deliverance of Athens from tyranny. What Minotaur does Socrates slay? As Klein says, "The old and true Minotaur is the monster called Fear of Death,"[17] the monster terrorizing young Simmias and Cebes, as Socrates notes (77e). Socrates' argu-

13. Plutarch, *Theseus* 23.2.

14. Christopher Planeaux calculated the date of the Delia, enabling him to affix a date for the trial of Socrates: around May 22, 399. Planeaux, "Appendix F: Socrates' Trial, Imprisonment, and Execution: A Revised Platonic Timeline," in "Apollodoros and Alkibiades." The exactitude of Planeaux's dating of Plato's dialogues is founded in part on his research on the Athenian calendar summarized in *Athenian Year Primer*.

15. Xenophon, *Memorabilia* 4.8.2.

16. Klein, "Plato's *Phaedo*," 377. There are inexactitudes in the fit between Phaedo's list and the myth: Phaedo says "some other locals" were also present; Socrates is not one of the nine Athenians, as Theseus was.

17. Klein, "Plato's *Phaedo*," 378.

ments in the *Phaedo* on behalf of the immortality of the soul are a heroic act that slays that monster for them, putting to rest their fear that their souls may be mortal, a fear seemingly held by all those present in the cell (88c). And Phaedo carries the report of that Athenian act to the wider, non-Athenian world, which also stands in need of it (88c-d).

Satisfied with Phaedo's account of the Athenian vessel sent to Delos, Echecrates asks about "the circumstances of the death itself . . . the things said and done." Not knowing Athenian customs, he asks if any of Socrates' companions were present or if he had to die alone, "bereft of friends." When Phaedo replies that many were present, Echecrates tells him to "put his heart (*prothumētheti*) into" giving them as sure a report as he can (58d). Phaedo's explanation of why he will do that is also a description of just who he is: "To remember Socrates is ever the most pleasant of all things, at least for me, whether I myself do the talking or listen to someone else." Echecrates assures him that he has "for listeners others who are just like you." A devoted follower of Socrates speaks to an audience willing to become disciples, as the *Phaedo* will confirm. And Echecrates urges Phaedo "to go through everything as precisely as you can."

Phaedo begins his report by describing his own experience as "wondrous" in two respects (58e). He experienced no pity that day even though it was the death day "of a man who was my companion": so "fearless and noble" was Socrates' demeanor that day that Phaedo had to think that he "was not going to Hades without divine warrant"—Phaedo makes his piety apparent at the start: the gods themselves consent to Socrates' death. And Phaedo also says that he did not experience on that day his usual pleasure in being engaged in philosophy (59a)—but a confusion creeps into Phaedo's confession when he says he realized "deep down" that Socrates was going to die that day: he experienced the "simply absurd feeling" of the "unusual blend" of pleasure and pain—so on his own testimony he experienced both pleasure and pain. He adds a claim about the others in the cell that he will repeat at other times in his report: he believes that "all who were present were pretty much in this condition." Is Phaedo right in supposing that what he experienced everyone in the cell experienced? Socrates' first words to them declare his difference in precisely what Phaedo claimed all experienced. And when Phaedo later claims that all experienced what he experienced (88c) a subsequent event forces doubt to again arise (103a-c).

Phaedo adds a final feature to his description of his experience that day. Mentioning Apollodorus and his extremes of laughing and crying (59b), he speaks of being "shaken up (*tarassō*)" along with the others. At significant junctures later in the day Phaedo will report important events of being "shaken up" (86e, 88c), and once, late in the day, it matters very much that Cebes not be "shaken up" (103c).

Cued perhaps by Phaedo's mention of the presence of Apollodorus, Echecrates asks who else "happened to be present." And Phaedo begins by listing nine Athenians, adding at its end, "Plato, I think, was sick" (59b10). It is a natural comment for him to make to Echecrates, whose evident knowledge of the Socratic circle would lead him to wonder about the presence of Plato, a man approaching thirty when Socrates was executed and associated with him for some time.[18] Echecrates then immediately asks about the presence of foreigners and after Phaedo lists five (59c) he asks about two others who were well-known associates of Socrates, Aristippus of Cyrene, founder of the Cyrenaic Socratic school, and Cleombrotus of Ambracia. Phaedo reports that "they were said to be in Aegina."[19] When Echecrates asks if anyone else was present, Phaedo says, "I think these were pretty much the ones who were present," and with that Echecrates ends the opening frame of the *Phaedo* by asking about the logoi, the arguments or speeches that Phaedo then began reporting, promising "to go through everything for you from the beginning" (59d).

While Phaedo's brief mention of Plato in the frame of the *Phaedo* is unremarkable in its setting in Phlia it is wholly remarkable within Plato's writings as a whole, for apart from two mentions of his natural presence in the *Apology* this is the only time the author of the dialogues allows his name to appear in them, a mention that suggests his absence. Plato therefore uses this sole appearance of his own name outside the *Apology* to suggest his almost unbelievable absence from what all knew would be Socrates' last day—those accustomed to visit him in his cell learned the night before that last day that the sacred vessel had returned, though his old friend Crito already knew that dreaded fact in the early morning of that previous day.[20] Could Plato really have been absent? A later event

18. As for Xenophon, that other associate of Socrates that the tradition of philosophy singled out as especially worthy, he had been absent from Athens for some time in Asia Minor, where he had gone to observe the younger Cyrus, a trip that Socrates had serious reservations about (see Xenophon, *Anabasis of Cyrus* 3.1.4–7).

19. In Aegina they would have been safe from Athenian persecution; see Ebert, *Phaidon*, 102. On Aristippus, see Xenophon, *Memorabilia* 2.1.

20. Crito had learned very early on the morning of that day before that the ship from Delos had passed Sounion and would arrive in Athens that day. He shared that knowledge with Socrates after he awakened just before sunrise (*Crito* 43d). The two of them then refrained from telling the others that day, for Phaedo says they learned of the ship's return only after they came out of the prison at the end of that previous day of conversation with Socrates and that therefore they came extra early on what would be Socrates' last day (59e).

in the *Phaedo* invites a very close look, for it prompts some doubt about Plato's absence.

Naming Theseus at the beginning in connection with his heroic deliverance of Athens casts an Athenian aura over Socrates' heroic deeds. But Theseus is never named again. Instead, the local hero is replaced by the Panhellenic hero on whom he was modeled, Herakles. At the center of the dialogue Socrates performs an act of affectionate attention that singles out Phaedo and makes a memorable day still more memorable for the one now telling the tale. Having himself introduced Herakles as the hero needed to meet the arguments of Simmias and Cebes, Phaedo is glad to accept the role of Iolaus, Herakles' nephew who aided him in his only labor for which he needed help, for there rises at the center what Socrates himself names the greatest evil, and *its* defeat calls for a heroic act on behalf of the well-being of philosophy itself. It is not the slaying of a Minotaur but a deed of wider import performed by Herakles, the burying of the only head of the Hydra that is immortal, a perpetual danger to philosophy that can only ever be covered up, never slain.

But in the *Phaedo* even Herakles is eclipsed by a different hero, Odysseus, a human hero quietly present since the first words. Odysseus is named only once, just before Socrates begins his preparations for the decisive argument of the day, preparations that include telling the tale of the beginnings of his odyssey to philosophy. And Odysseus is the hero quietly recalled by the last words of the dialogue. Odysseus rises as Socrates' model hero throughout, the Homeric hero of wisdom whom the *Odyssey* shows gaining entry to an understanding of nature through the gift of Hermes. The presence of these particular heroes is no accident: first the local hero and his deed, then the Panhellenic hero and his deed, and throughout the wily hero of thought and action: Plato's Socrates in his deeds and his thinking supplants the traditional heroes for the new generation with whom alone he is reported speaking on his final day.

3. A New Herakles to Cut Off and Bury the Immortal Head of Hydra

A crisis occurs at the center of the *Phaedo* that calls for a Herakles, the Panhellenic hero of mighty deeds. It is a crisis in the argument as Phaedo reports their being "shaken up again," a crisis that breaks out in Phlia too as Echecrates interrupts Phaedo's narrative for the first time, blurting out that they feel the same distress those in the cell felt (88c).[21] The cri-

---

21. The numerical center of the dialogue falls at 88c.

sis arose after Socrates offered arguments and edifying stories to assuage the fears expressed by Simmias and Cebes that their souls would perish when their bodies died. In the first break that Phaedo made in his narration to the Pythagoreans at Phlia, he reported to them that Socrates' first arguments did not satisfy Simmias and Cebes and did not satisfy Socrates either (84c): having invited the two to speak up to express their doubts, Socrates admitted even before hearing their counterarguments that his previous arguments were inadequate "if someone goes through it sufficiently" (84c-d) — but anyone truly seeking a rational argument for the immortality of the soul would insist on going through it sufficiently.[22] Socrates' arguments on the immortality of the soul sort those gathered in his cell into a rank order of the easily trusting, the not so easily trusting, and, perhaps, the never trusting. Simmias and Cebes distinguish themselves at this point as requiring a rational rigor that some of the others did not.[23] Simmias speaks first, setting out what he regards as the three possibilities with respect to "knowing anything sure about such matters" (85c):

> One must learn or discover what's the case, or, if that's impossible, he must sail through life in the midst of danger, seizing on the best and the least refutable of human accounts, at any rate, and letting himself be carried as upon a raft — unless, that is, he could journey more safely and less dangerously on a more stable carrier, some divine account (85c-d).[24]

The "divine account" Simmias and Cebes depended on was the Orphic or Pythagorean doctrine of the soul that they learned in their schooling at Thebes under Philolaus.[25] Their objections show that their schooling had not fully persuaded them. Simmias recognized that the Pythagorean image of the soul as a "tuning" (*harmonia*) of the body implies that it would

22. Socrates planted doubt even in his formulation of the conclusion of one of his arguments: he spoke of the "altogether indissoluble" character of the soul, "or something close to this" (80b) — that is, dissoluble. The dramatic dates Plato assigned to his dialogues give a temporal beginning to Socrates' teaching of the immortality of the soul: he introduced it thirty years earlier, in the *Republic*, which Plato set in 429, shortly after Socrates returned from Potidaea. Socrates said in the *Charmides*, which Plato set a few weeks earlier in 429, that while he was away at Potidaea he learned a new healing medicine from a doctor of the god Zalmoxis, monotheistic teachers who believed in the immortality of the soul. See my *How Philosophy Became Socratic*, 162–70.

23. Socrates said Cebes "is always tracking down some argument or other" (63a); Simmias said Cebes is "the mightiest of men when it comes to distrusting arguments" (77a).

24. On Simmias's statement of the options he faced, see below, n. 88 in this chapter.

25. See Burnet, *Phaedo*, at 85d3; as Burnet points out, Simmias simply says so at 86b-c.

not survive the body it attunes. Cebes recognized that the Pythagorean doctrine of the soul's sequential occupancy of many bodies, its transmigration, does not prove that it survives *all* its bodies: it could perish worn out with the perishing of its last body. To overcome their fears they need something more from Socrates than their Pythagorean training gave them. As for safer or less dangerous "divine accounts," Socrates had in no way challenged the evident piety of these young men; on the contrary, he used that piety to structure his arguments and rhetoric for them: he used Cebes' belief that "we humans are one of the gods' possessions" to argue that suicide is prohibited (62b-d); he told Simmias that he hoped to "arrive among good men" and "among gods who are completely good masters" as a reward for a good life (63c); he spoke of Hades as the place to which his soul would descend when it was freed from his body (80d–81a); and he used their belief in the transmigration of souls to speak of the punishment meted out to the wicked in the next lives they would live (81e–82b).[26]

When Simmias and Cebes nevertheless mistrust Socrates' initial arguments and state their reasons, Phaedo reports that the whole company was plunged into despair: "All of us [had been] powerfully persuaded by the previous argument," but the counterarguments "seemed to shake us up greatly again and cast us back into distrust." Their distrust allowed them to draw an irrational conclusion: not only did they distrust the arguments that had been given but "even what would be said later on" (88c), which of course they could not know. Their fall into total distrust of reason was based on a judgment about their own capacities—"Who knows, we might be worthless judges," and on a judgment about "these matters themselves"—which "might be beyond trust (*apista*)," beyond any trustworthy argument. They despaired of reason itself, the human capacity to know, and they despaired of the knowability of things, despair that may suggest that they had been attracted to philosophy and its reasoning for its capacity to prove these things. Hearing Phaedo's report on their state of being shaken up, Echecrates broke in vehemently—"by the gods"—to

26. In "Why Is Evenus Called a Philosopher?" Theodor Ebert shows that Socrates' question about Evenus being a philosopher at the beginning of their conversation (61c) established that "philosopher" in this dialogue means "Pythagorean"—an important observation because it prepares the discussion of the "true philosopher" as a Pythagorean ascetic who believes in the immortality of the soul and disciplines his body to help prepare for its immortal life as a separable soul. That Socrates is not a "true philosopher" in this sense Plato shows graphically through the presence of his wife, Xanthippe, and their young boys and shows it in the arguments by separating Socrates from Pythagorean images and arguments, however content he is to use them in his initial discussions with Simmias and Cebes.

say he felt the same way they did (88c). And he too reacted with extreme distrust, for he says to himself, "What argument will we trust from now on? The one that was so powerfully trustworthy, the argument Socrates gave, has now fallen into distrust." Echecrates identifies that argument as the tuning argument, the classic Pythagorean image and not an argument at all; but that proves Echecrates to be a very poor listener: the tuning argument was not an "argument Socrates gave" but an image introduced by Simmias to express his doubt after Socrates had given his initial arguments. As for Cebes' "argument" it too is not an argument based on logical premises but a belief based on Pythagorean teachings. Repeatedly, Phaedo and Echecrates use the words *trust* and *distrust* to describe their stance toward arguments, words that betray a less than rational stance toward rational arguments, which are not to be measured by *trust* but tested and judged valid or invalid by reasoning.[27]

Echecrates laments that "what I really need is some other argument which will, from a new beginning," persuade him that his soul survives the death of his body (88d). Not even imagining that he, representative of a Pythagorean school, might himself try to construct an argument for what he wants to believe, he desperately needs to know how Socrates reacted: "Did he too, as you say the rest of you did, reveal in any way that he was distressed or didn't he, and did he instead come serenely to the aid of the argument?" Anything but serene, shaken-up Echecrates craves Socrates' help: "Was his aid sufficient, or did it fall short? Go through everything as precisely as you can." At the center of the *Phaedo*, a member of the Pythagorean school breaks into Phaedo's narrative to look to Socrates in the fervent hope that he might give him a new argument to trust.

The extreme distrust in argument that breaks out among the auditors in Socrates' cell and then again in Phlia is a revelation about them: Why didn't they draw the conclusion that arguments for the immortality of the soul fail not because argument is faulty but because the soul is mortal? These friends of philosophy are ready to despair at reason itself if reason cannot prove that their souls are immortal. David Bolotin clearly stated what their despair betrays: "So powerful . . . is their attachment to the belief in immortality that they would sooner believe that there is no truth in speeches or arguments than that there is no argument for the immortality of the soul."[28] When Socrates detected the despair at reason among those in the cell he initiated a break in the arguments and turned instead to an

27. See Hartle, *Death and the Disinterested Spectator*, 19–20, 25.
28. Bolotin, "Life of Philosophy," 55.

entirely different kind of speaking in order to prepare his now despairing
company for an eventual return to argument, a return to *trust* in argument
that had been shattered. And here at the center of the dialogue a hero is introduced fit to perform that indispensable labor to prepare those who have
fallen into despair at reason for a new argument, for the whole "new beginning" with argument that Echecrates said was necessary for him. With only
a few hours left Socrates is forced to come to the rescue of reason itself.

Responding to Echecrates' desperate hope that Socrates would offer
aid, Phaedo says he "never admired him more" than he did for his response
to this crisis of trust. Phaedo had said that they *all* felt the unease he felt
(88c), but that's not true: Socrates at least did not. The first thing Phaedo
"really wondered at him for" was "how pleasantly and kindly and admir-
ingly he received the young men's argument" (89a): Socrates *admired* what
drove "all" the others to despair at argument.[29] Still, he was attentive to
the plight of the despairing, and that was Phaedo's second reason to really wonder at him: seeing how they suffered, "he healed us." Phaedo gives
Socrates' act of healing a martial cast: the sufferers "were like men who'd
fled and been laid low" — they were like a hoplite army that had broken its
phalanx and turned and ran. Socrates was like a general to the fleeing army:
he "rallied us and turned us about to follow him and consider the argument
with him" (89a). Echecrates, anxious to be healed, asks, "How did he do
it?" He did it in the way appropriate to a fleeing army: he gave them heart
and trust again.

Echecrates remains silent through Phaedo's long narration of how Socrates did it. Only after he has defeated the counterarguments and presented his new way of argument does Echecrates speak up again: "By Zeus,
Phaedo," he says, breaking in for the last time, "a reasonable reply!" (102a).
Phaedo's description of how Socrates healed them, how he brought them
around to trust reason again, is framed by Echecrates' only interventions,
and it depicts a hero of a philosopher performing the indispensable labor for willing followers in Athens, a labor that can be successfully carried
abroad: through Phaedo's account, Socrates becomes the new master of a
Pythagorean school beyond Athens, their new Pythagoras, supplying them
with a whole new form of argument to trust.

"How did he do it?" He did it first by reaching down to his right from
where he sat to where Phaedo was sitting at his feet and caressing Phaedo's
head, gathering his hair at the back of his neck and saying, "Tomorrow,

---

29. Earlier too, after Simmias's objection and before Cebes', Socrates reacted with pleasure to the objection, "with that usual keen look of his and smiled" (86d).

Phaedo, perhaps you'll cut off these beautiful locks of yours," in mourning for Socrates. But "I'll cut mine this very day," bald Socrates says with a remark that had to bring a smile to the suffering, in mourning for logos itself if they cannot bring it back to life. But if he were Phaedo, instead of cutting off his locks, he'd swear an oath, as the Argives did, not to cut his hair before being victorious in the battle against the argument of Simmias and Cebes.[30] Phaedo enters his own narrative of Socrates' last day at its center and enters singled out as the object of an affectionate act by Socrates and then as the recipient of a commission to perform an action in aid of a heroic deed — for Socrates will recruit young Phaedo, turning him, a favored one, into a devoted reporter of the thrilling story of Socrates' healing deed on his last day, a reporter who can include in his report the special affection with which Socrates singled him out, ensuring that "remembering Socrates is ever the most pleasant of all things" for him (58d).

Phaedo protests Socrates' call on him to be victorious against the objections of Simmias and Cebes: "They say not even Herakles could manage against two" (89c). "Then call on me," Socrates says, "as your Iolaus," Herakles' nephew and indispensable aide for his only labor requiring the help of another, burying the immortal head of Hydra while Herakles was also being attacked by a sea monster — the other heads that Hydra grows can be burned off and their roots permanently cauterized, but that one threat alone remains always alive, if buried. Phaedo, a boy of eighteen or nineteen, knows his proper place: "I will call on you," he says, "not as a Herakles but as an Iolaus calling on Herakles." Socrates tacitly accepts the role of Herakles with Phaedo as the indispensable aide he has recruited. Socrates will perform the labor of a Herakles, rallying his fleeing army to stand against the despair at argument that drove them into disarray. Phaedo-Iolaus will be his interlocutor, his aide, for the whole of his discussion at the center, his analysis of what had befallen them, the "greatest evil," he calls it, the threat to philosophy coeval with its flourishing. Phaedo-Iolaus will then retire as an active participant in the day's conversation, having been given his commission as the faithful reporter who will carry Socrates' deed beyond Athens into a philosophic community vulnerable to the same despair. Socrates lives on as the new hero turned immortal by the report of the Iolaus he

---

30. Herodotus 1.82.7. After a disputed battle between the Argives and the Lacedaemonians, the Argives, who wore their hair long, shaved their heads and swore not to let their hair grow until they recovered Thyreae; it was the Lacedaemonians, who had previously kept their hair short, who swore to keep their hair long. It is unclear why Socrates altered the story.

singled out for special favor at the moment of crisis. Echecrates will speak up for the second and final time to affirm that Phaedo's account of Socrates' new way of argument has shown him and those with him in Phlia how to trust argument again: "all who were present" in the cell plus those "who were absent but are listening right now" (102a) are delivered from the crisis by Iolaus's report of the labor of Herakles to restore trust in argument.[31]

Socrates as Herakles "first" calls on them to "be on our guard so we don't undergo a certain experience." He names that experience with a word he may have coined, *misology*, hatred of argument or reason.[32] By having misology break out in Phlia too, Plato indicates that *that* is the immortal head, the condition that always breaks out when reason confronts the need it here confronts, the need to believe that the soul never dies — or when it confronts other such beliefs that expose reason's limits. Socrates-Herakles did not suffer what they suffer, but he can name their condition, analyze its origin and character, and make it the condition most to be resisted. Only after they have been made resolute in this way — ready to trust reason again — can he "enter on the argument again" (91b7–8).

In his very naming of misology, Socrates linked it to a related experience of hatred: we must be on our guard that "we don't become misologists as some become misanthropists; for it is not possible for anyone to experience a greater evil than misology" (89d) — the hatred of argument, of *logos*, is an even worse evil than hatred of humanity, *misanthropia*, perhaps because *logos* is the defining feature of humanity.[33] Each of the two hatreds Socrates understands through its becoming: "Misology and misanthropy come about in the say way," he says, turning first to misanthropy, in order to have its becoming illustrate the becoming of misology.[34] Hatred of humanity arises from "trust," he says, "artless" trust in a person that "holds this person to be in every way true and sound and trustworthy and then a little later discovers this person to be wicked and untrustworthy." One who repeatedly experienced such failed trust, especially at the hands of his

31. On Iolaus and Herakles, see Burger, *Phaedo*, 114–15, 160.

32. Plato's Socrates had used *misology* in *Republic* 3.411d, set in 429, and in *Laches* 188c, e, set in 424/3, the first occurrences in extant Greek literature. See Sulek, "On the Classical Meaning of *Philanthropia*," 401n15.

33. *Misanthropia* is a word that is first referenced in Pherekrates' play *Savages*, where the chorus are *Misanthropoi*; see *Protagoras* 327d-e; in extant writings it appears first in Plato's *Phaedo*, *Protagoras*, and *Laws* 7.791d; see Sulek, "On the Classical Meaning of *Philanthropia*," 401n15.

34. Peter Ahrensdorf's analysis of misanthropy (*Death of Socrates*, 135–39) is especially insightful.

most intimate friends and comrades (89e), "ends up taking offense all the time and hates all human beings and believes there's nothing at all sound in anyone" (89e).[35] Socrates' description of misanthropy deals in extremes, first total trust in one person, then total condemnation of all humanity. Judging it "shameful and clear that such a person was attempting to deal with human beings without art in human affairs," Socrates says that "if he dealt with them artfully, he'd think of them just as they are." How *are* human beings? Socrates says "that both the really good-natured (*chrēstos*) and the really wicked are few, and most are in-between" (90a). Apparently not understanding, Phaedo asks, "What are you saying?" and Socrates gives many examples, saying it's rare to find a really big or really small man or dog or one that's really fast or slow or really ugly or beautiful or really black or white (101a). He pictures the bell-curve distribution of such qualities: "Haven't you perceived that among all such things those at the furthest ends of either extreme are rare or few, while the ones in between are in generous supply and many?" "Of course," Phaedo says, and Socrates gives a last example: "If a wickedness contest were held, those who showed first would be very few" (90b). And he corrects Phaedo's "That's likely," with "Very likely." That ends his description of misanthropy, and he moves on to describe the condition at issue, misology—but what about the other extreme, the few at the furthest end of a goodness contest? When he turned back to misology Socrates said that "arguments are not similar to human beings in that respect"—arguments do not distribute themselves into bell curves with extremes of validity and invalidity or truth and falsity at either end. Why mention that feature of artful dealing with human beings at all then, given that he introduced misanthropy to illustrate how misology comes about? "I was merely following your lead," he explains (90b). No, *he* introduced the issue of how human beings are and how to deal with them artfully; Phaedo asked only that he explain it better. Still, he is following Phaedo's lead in one sense: he took over Phaedo's reference to Herakles, accepting Herakles' role—so he has in fact not omitted the other extreme of the natural distribution of human beings: as Herakles, he accepts the hero's role, the exemplar of the undescribed rarity at the furthest reach of human good nature.

Socrates' introduction of how human beings are, their bell-curve distribution of qualities, is wholly gratuitous, it does not fit the purpose for which he introduced misanthropy, illuminating misology. But it does single

---

35. Being *sound* (*hugiēs*) is a condition that will run through Socrates' explanation of misology and misanthropy to the end. John Burnet (*Phaedo*, at 69b8) gives its origin: "The word *hugiēs* is used of earthen or metal vessels which have no crack or flaw."

him out as one of the rare ones who can deal competently with human hate, the passion that can turn humans into haters of their own kind and haters of the ultimate human trait, rationality. As Herakles, he can lead potential misanthropes to trust in human beings again by trusting in him. His fleeing army, schooled to trust argument but losing their trust because argument seems to point to the opposite of what they most dearly want or need to be true, that fleeing army cannot be turned to argument by argument. Socrates turns his little army by daring to stand as that rare extreme in a virtue contest worthy of trust by those whose relation to argument is always only trust or mistrust. And Plato has Phaedo-Iolaus carry the report of his deed abroad to members of an already constituted philosophic school who are followers by definition. Just here the Iolaus/Herakles likeness shows its full appropriateness: this Iolaus aids this Herakles in burying the immortal head of Hydra, the threat of misology that breaks out whenever those who trust in argument are forced into mistrust by the limits of argument with respect to what humans deeply desire, that they live forever. Philosophy, insurmountably limited with respect to knowledge, always requires heroic defense.

Socrates had another reason for introducing misanthropy. By calling misology the "greatest evil" he flatly contradicted a greatest evil he had introduced only a few minutes earlier: the "true philosopher" held that "the greatest and most extreme evil" is that the human soul is nailed to the human body (83c). Speaking for himself, the philosopher Socrates says that the greatest evil is hatred of the highest capacity of the human, reason. The conflict between the two greatest evils shows that the "true philosopher" dealt with human beings "without art in human affairs" because he did not "think of them as they are" — he took the soul alone to be human and imagined its total separation from the hated mortal body. Socrates seems to suggest not only that the "true philosopher" is wrong but also that he is the paradigm misanthropist, that ascetic who counts himself a philosopher but hates the basic fact about the human: it is bodily existence. The "true philosopher" is a misanthrope teaching misanthropy, while the philosopher Socrates performs an act of careful philanthropy, intimating the truth about belief in the immortality of the soul while teaching that belief, apparently holding it to be salutary if accompanied by belief in reason.[36]

---

36. Plato's twinning of the *Charmides* and *Republic* by dramatic date locates the beginning of Socrates' teaching of the immortality of the soul in 429, upon his return from Potidaea; part of the reason is a crisis facing philosophy; see my *How Philosophy Became Socratic*, pt. 2.

After alleging that he was simply following Phaedo's lead when he introduced a truth about human beings that plays no role in explaining misology, Socrates turns to what does play that role (90b). Trust in humans is like trust in arguments in that both require art, or skill, and "when someone trusts some argument to be true without the art of arguments and then a little later the argument seems to him to be false, as it sometimes is and sometimes isn't, and that happens again and again," then that someone is tempted to fall into misology—and that is precisely what Phaedo and Echecrates reported about *their* trust in arguments (88c-d). Socrates of course could observe only those in the cell with him, but that was enough for him to see that their being shaken up displayed an endemic form of the loss of all trust in argument. Now, having explained that condition and how it arises, he identifies one of its chief causes: "those who have spent their days in debate-arguments (*antilogikoi*)," the sophists (90c). They "end up thinking that they have become the wisest of men and that they alone have come to know that there is nothing sound or stable, not in the realm of either practical matters or arguments"—the human realm—"but all the things that are (*ta onta*) simply toss to and fro . . . and don't stay put anywhere for any length of time" (90c). Socrates' comment expands the field dramatically, from human acting and knowing to all beings simply; the ontology Socrates thus introduces maintains the sovereignty of becoming, a view he assigns to the sophists. What those in the cell and in Phlia experienced as despair at argument leading to misology, the sophists simply advocate in their account of knowing—and in their account of being.[37] Young Phaedo takes himself to be fully acquainted with these views: "Certainly, what you say is true."

The condition of someone who yields to that view of things, Socrates says, "would be a pitiable one if there was in fact some logos that was true and stable and capable of being known . . . and [that person] did not blame himself or his own artlessness but ended up in his distress being only too pleased to push the blame off himself and onto the logoi" (90d). Socrates paints a portrait in which his distressed audience can see themselves, and he completes it with their possible future: "and from that moment on [that person] would finish out the rest of his life hating the logoi and reviling them and being robbed of the truth and knowledge of the things that are"—they would be misologists to the end, never possessing the truth

---

37. In the *Theaetetus* (152c-e) Socrates suggests that the sovereignty of becoming was a view Homer held and passed on to all later Greek thinkers except Parmenides. See below, chapter 3, section 3, "Diotima's Myth," 178–79.

about the beings that they might possess if there were such a logos. "Yes, by Zeus," Phaedo says emphatically, "pitiable indeed." This is the last comment Phaedo makes as Socrates takes over to complete his task of rallying them before facing Simmias's and Cebes' objections. Having shown that their distress could become a never-ending misology, he now tells them exactly how to "be on guard" against it — to be "on our guard against a certain experience" was the very task he gave himself after accepting the role of Herakles (89c): "First of all, let us be on our guard against this and not admit into the soul that the realm of the logoi risks having nothing sound in it" (90e). This is not an argument; it is a command to be resolute against giving up on argument. Instead of giving up, "let us far rather admit that we are not yet sound but must act like real men and put our hearts into being sound" — the real man Socrates shames his frightened, fleeing army put to rout by their own fears, calling on their manliness and their heart, their *thumos*, to stand their ground, "you for the sake of your whole life hereafter, and I for the sake of death itself." Their heroic commander, about to die, lays on them a command to manliness that would be shameful for them to forget or deny.

Having reminded the men he is rallying of his own situation, Socrates turns the focus on himself, treating himself as simply one of them in their manly *thumos*. "I run the risk," he says, "of being not wisdom-loving (*philosophōs*) but victory-loving (*philonikōs*) instead, like the wholly unschooled" (91a): "victory-loving" is the fully appropriate stance for one who is putting his heart into calling them to manliness. As for the wholly unschooled whom he alleges he resembles, when they engage in dispute, they "don't give a thought to the way it is with the things the argument is about, but put their hearts into this: that what they themselves put forward should seem to be the case to those present." Well-schooled Socrates never loses track of the things the argument is about; instead, giving thought to where he stands with his fleeing army, he puts his mind to victory in making what he says persuasive to them while acting as if he is like the wholly unschooled: "At this moment I seem to myself to differ from those in one way only: I won't put my heart into making what I say seem to be true to those present, except as a side effect, but into making it seem so to me myself as much as possible." The one called to be their leader allows himself to be understood as sharing their need to be persuaded that his soul is immortal. But the stance he will take toward the final argument he will give proves he does not share their need: he sees the need to question even that argument and invites them to do so (107b). Socrates put his mind and his heart into questioning arguments; but at this moment he puts both mind and heart into what he alleges is only a side effect: victory in persuading them to be men and never to flag in trusting arguments.

Victory-loving Socrates needs victory in one way only, as he shows in this moment by calling Phaedo "my dear comrade" for the only time: nineteen-year-old Phaedo is seventy-year-old Socrates' aide-de-camp, the Iolaus for the Herakles fighting for victory against misology. Phaedo is Socrates' indispensable aide for victory in the only afterlife available to him; his victory in the cell will become victory in Phlia and beyond through the report of his conscripted aide. By singling out his dear comrade for special affection Socrates assigns him a special role in his victories after his death. In the tale Phaedo loves to tell (58d) Socrates' act of singling him out cannot help but be the most memorable part to him, the most inspiring to his pride, the most imperative in placing responsibility on *him*.[38] In his final address to his aide Socrates presents a form of Pascal's wager: "For I am calculating, my dear comrade — behold how self-servingly! — that if what I'm saying happens to be true, I'm well off believing it; and if there's nothing at all for one who's met his end, well then, I'll make myself so much the less unpleasant with lamenting to those who are present during this time, the time before my death" (91b). Making himself pleasant indeed to those present, the Socrates soon to die calls on his companions to be manly, knowing that he can count on his final conversation being especially commanding to them. Though he will immediately tell them to put the focus on truth, not on him, he was the one who turned the focus on himself, on his resoluteness in facing death as their model of refusal in face of the evil of misology: if the arguments seem to fail, they are to follow him in judging themselves not yet sound. As his last words to his aide before turning back to Simmias and Cebes, Socrates says, "This mindlessness of mine won't continue — that would be an evil! — but will perish a little later."[39] Mindless immortality would be an evil; mortal mindlessness of the sort Socrates possesses is not. On his last day, with a few hours yet to go, Socrates judges *himself* not yet sound rather than judge that the realm of argument has nothing sound in it. Socrates knows his difference, knows he will always be not yet sound with respect to knowledge, but he judges that humans generally cannot bear to live knowing that they will always be

38. Athenaeus (*The Sophists at Dinner* 11.505e) reported six centuries later that Phaedo said he never heard or said what Plato has him hear and say in the *Phaedo*.

39. Burnet restores the *anoia* (mindlessness, folly) of the manuscripts, whereas most modern editors follow Stephanus in reading *agnoia* (ignorance) at *Phaedo* 91b5; see Burger, *Phaedo*, 248n13.

not yet sound, always needing another argument to prove what *they* most need to be true.

Socrates then turns to address the two whose objections moved the company to despair of argument: "Thus prepared, Simmias and Cebes, I enter on the argument"—the resolute commander takes up his task with the two objectors. But before actually entering the argument he issues a command to all of them: "But as for all of you, if you're persuaded by me and give little thought to Socrates and much more to the truth, you must agree with me if I seem to you to say what's true; and if I don't, you must strain against me with every argument you've got, being on guard that I don't, out of eagerness, go off having deceived both myself and you, like a bee that's left its stinger behind" (91c). Will they be on guard against believing in Socrates, giving little thought to Socrates and much more to the truth? In fact, they will show that Socrates has left behind, in them, the stinger of belief in him; insofar as they are like Cebes, whom Simmias believes to be "the mightiest of men when it comes to distrusting arguments" (77a), they will believe that the final argument Socrates gives for the immortality of their souls is a trustworthy proof, a proof they welcome that will enable them to continue to trust argument.

The *Phaedo* is the record of an execution. The Socrates who accepts the death sentence voted by his fellow citizens acts heroically in his last hours on behalf of philosophy to ensure that his exact words will be faithfully carried forward by a devoted disciple. His words are wise words in which the threat of misology built into philosophic inquiry with its questions about the stability of both arguments and beings is defeated by an art of arguments that will entail an ontology of permanence. The dying philosopher, always not yet sound, holding an ontology of eros, retails an imaginary soundness of both arguments and beings.

Socrates' injunction to "be on guard" brings the central part of the *Phaedo*, his Heraklean action of rallying his army, to a fitting end:[40] "But we must get going," he says, a reminder that his time is limited in the most final way possible. Socrates' Herakles-like deed at the center makes it clear that the presence of the heroic in Plato's *Phaedo* is no literary ornament. The philosopher Socrates performed genuinely heroic deeds, extraordinary achievements of insight and action. But philosophy is a rare appearance in the world and in the radicality of its insights it discovers truths that it recognizes to be deadly to the social order while recognizing too the frailty of its own social power. Without the actions of a Socrates this

---

40. Socrates uses "be on guard" (*eulabeomai*) twice more: 99d, 101c.

thing of highest worth, human understanding of nature and human nature, could perish with his perishing. The hero of the *Phaedo* is a philosopher-ruler in action, acting on behalf of philosophy; in coming to rule the minds of Phaedo and the rest, Socrates does so in a way they welcome because it does them good, saving their hopes while securing them against the harmful distrust that leads to misology. Plato has Socrates' heroic actions come to sight as the actions of a Theseus and a Herakles, but Socrates' essential model proves to be the figure who now emerges as the most important Homeric hero throughout the *Phaedo*, including in the actions just performed — Odysseus.

4. A New Odysseus to Teach the Safe Way to Understand Cause

Of that polytropic man, tell me, Muse, who was driven far journeys after he had sacked Troy's sacred citadel.

> —Homer, *Odyssey* 1.1–2

The great sweep of life has always shown itself to be on the side of the most unscrupulous polytropoi.

> —Nietzsche, *The Gay Science*, §344

Polytropic is the word Homer chose to describe unnamed Odysseus in the first line of the *Odyssey*. *Polytropic* is the word Nietzsche chose for life's most successful figures while adding *unscrupulous*. No wonder Plato made Socrates' appropriation of Odysseus less visible in the *Phaedo* than his appropriation of the Hellenic action heroes Theseus and Herakles: in addition to their public face, Socrates' heroic qualities include some that are best kept muted. Life was on the side of unscrupulous polytropic Odysseus in the conquest of Troy and in the twofold success the *Odyssey* relates, his odyssey to philosophy and his refounding rule in Ithaca. And life was on the side of polytropic Socrates as he set out to advance the life of philosophy in the world through his own wise thinking and acting.

Plato affirmed the heroic qualities of Odysseus in his *Lesser Hippias*, a dialogue unwelcome to some precisely because of Socrates' elevation of unscrupulous polytropic Odysseus. Plato knew what he was doing: he has his Socrates claim irrational seizure for his argument praising polytropic Odysseus as "voluntarily going wrong and [doing] what is shameful and unjust" and for saying that such a man "would be no one else than the good man" (*Lesser Hippias* 376b). Straight Hippias, that morally strict sophist, is appalled at Socrates' judgment and argues that Achilles is superior to

Odysseus because he is morally straight; and he can cite the outspoken revulsion Achilles directed at wily Odysseus:

> One must surely speak out without regard to consequences,
> Just as I am going to do and as I think it will be fulfilled;
> For that one is as hateful to me as the gates of Hades
> Who hides one thing in his mind but says something else.
> (*Lesser Hippias* 364e–365a; *Iliad* 9.308–14)

Socrates shows in his argument with Hippias that Odysseus's success depended upon his always speaking with a view to consequences, hiding one thing in his mind while saying something else. His reason is that unlike Achilles he did not trust the outcome to how he "thinks it will be fulfilled"—by moral gods seeing to the moral outcome.[41] In his *Lesser Hippias* Plato practices his own polytropic means of preserving the moral uprightness of the model Socrates, but for him as for Homer the wise man is polytropic *because* he is wise. Beyond good and evil, the wise act with a view to consequences because they know they inhabit a world with none of the transcendent moral enforcers an Achilles looks to. In the *Phaedo*, Socrates embodies two kinds of hero, one deserving public fame for his easily recognized achievements in what everyone can admire as worthy, the other avoiding public notice for acts that are far less evident in their necessity and worth, dubious even, or shocking, yet in the end required for the advancement of the things of enduring worth. Plato's Socrates is Heraklean in his public achievements, Odyssean in what he can share only with his like.

Plato made evident in the first words of the *Phaedo* that polytropic Odysseus would play an important role. Echecrates' opening words repeat words that Odysseus, veiled as a rescued traveler, addressed to the Phaeacian singer Demodocus, inviting him to sing Odysseus's own ruse of the wooden horse, the stratagem responsible for the fall of Troy. The opening words of the *Phaedo* raise a possibility that the rest of the dialogue confirms: an Odysseus acts here, a wise man whose guile serves great ends. The last words of the dialogue also refer to the *Odyssey*: Phaedo ends his tale

---

41. Plato supplies the *Lesser Hippias* with a frame in which the father of the young man responsible for there being an exchange between Hippias and Socrates is shown to have taught his son to favor moral Achilles over devious Odysseus: the moral uprightness that noble fathers pass on to their sons supports Hippias and not Socrates. See my "Socrates' Defense of Polytropic Odysseus."

by saying that Socrates was, "among those we'd come up against, the best and, yes, the wisest and most just," words almost identical to Telemachus's words praising Nestor, the man he regards as the wisest of the Achaians.[42] And in the *Phaedo* Plato names Penelope, Odysseus's faithful wife (84a), to recall her wise and successful act of secrecy and guile, her nightly unweaving of the shroud for Laertes, whose completion would signal that it was time for her to give up Odysseus for dead and marry one of the suitors.[43] The *Phaedo* confirms what Plato often indicated in his dialogues: Odysseus is the Homeric hero from whom we can learn the most in understanding Socrates.[44]

Plato names Odysseus only once in the *Phaedo* but at the perfect point. Socrates has just completed his dismantling of Simmias's objection, his annihilation of the Pythagorean cliché of the soul as a tuning, the "argument" Echecrates had trusted that is no argument at all but an image that invites doubt by suggesting that the soul dies with the death of the body it attunes (91e–92d). To conclude his argument against Simmias's objection and prepare for his far more demanding task of refuting Cebes' reason for doubt (94d), Socrates summarized the image of the soul that replaces the tuning image: the soul is the inner master ruling the many drives of the body, disciplining and admonishing them as if it "were other than they and had a task other than theirs." Then he names Odysseus: "As Homer too has put it poetically in the *Odyssey* where he says of Odysseus, he struck his breast and reproached his heart with this word: 'Bear up my heart, for at other times you've borne things even more fit for a dog.'" Odysseus's reason must master his passion to punish the slave girls as they pass him on their way to what will be their last rendezvous with the suitors. One thing

42. *Odyssey* 3.244. On these opening and closing references to the *Odyssey*, see *Phaedo*, trans. Brann, Kalkavage, and Salem, 13n.

43. Plato's reference to Penelope is itself polytropic: Penelope is named by the "true philosopher," that Pythagorean ascetic of Socrates' "apology" for Simmias and Cebes who hates the body and disciplines his soul to leave it. But he misreads Penelope's wise action to fit his bias: he criticizes her "endless task," taking it to be the model for a pointless repeated binding of the soul to the body through indulging the pleasures of the body and never achieving the goal of deliverance from it. But Penelope's unweaving is not endless; it ends when Odysseus returns. When she recognizes that the beggar is her returned husband she performs another act of successful guile: she sets up the contest of the bow that will arm her husband for his fight with the suitors. The "true philosopher" failed to read Homer properly and found in him lessons for his own prejudice; he misunderstands philosophy just as he misunderstood Penelope.

44. The Odysseus that Socrates recovered from Homer's poems has been recovered through Plato for contemporary readers by Seth Benardete, particularly in *The Bow and the Lyre*.

only makes his task of rational control necessary, the great task looming at that moment: still masked as a beggar, Odysseus must control his impulse on this night because the next day he must perform the signal task of his return; he must kill all 108 suitors, that is, wipe out the future of the old regime in order to found the new. That moment in "Homer, the Divine Poet" (95a) perfectly fits the one Plato has arranged: Socrates' great task is now looming, his preparation and deployment of the decisive argument basic to *his* new founding. Successful as a Heraklean general, Socrates moves from that trans-Athenian hero of deeds to polytropic Odysseus, the trans-Athenian hero of thought. After refuting Simmias, a task as easy as killing the slave girls would have been for Odysseus, Socrates prepares to refute Cebes' objection, a far more difficult task because it will involve "the whole question of the cause of coming-to-be and destruction" (95e), the fundamental question of philosophy. How philosophy's deepest question can best be handled with a "philosophic" audience like Simmias and Cebes requires the polytropic wisdom of an Odysseus. In the last argument of his life, Socrates will deploy his most characteristic philosophic innovation, transcendent forms, for an argument aimed at securing as his own a central Pythagorean innovation in philosophy, the immortality of the soul. He will do so only after he has told a tale of his own odyssey: his beginnings in philosophy as a youth that led to his own main innovation in philosophy, the "second sailing" that he has sustained from that early point on to the end of his life. At the end of his life of reasoning, his argument deploying forms wins the victory for him, the regime-changing victory that will aid in establishing culture-wide rule by the Socratic, replacing culture-wide rule by the Homeric.[45] But Socrates' story of his beginnings for Cebes, and for Phaedo and for the transmission of his philosophy, is deeply Odyssean in being radically truncated: he hides his true identity by neglecting to say that shortly after he invented his transcendent forms at age nineteen Parmenides showed him that they were rationally untenable.

Before turning directly to Cebes' fears, Socrates cites an additional mythic image: likening the two young Thebans to the pair who founded their city, he turns from Harmonia, the Theban goddess, daughter of Ares

---

45. Plato made the need for a post-Homeric teaching clearest in the *Republic*. Young Glaucon and Adeimantus display their learned distrust in the foundational Homeric civic virtues of justice and piety, and Socrates not only provides them with new grounds for justice and piety but does what is necessary with the old grounds: he goes out of his way at the end to reintroduce poetry in order to destroy Homer's authority and help establish his own. He does so with Homer's blessing: his Odysseus knew that he had to kill all 108 suitors. See my *How Philosophy Became Socratic*.

and Aphrodite, to Cadmus, Harmonia's Phoenician husband, the brother of Europa and the bringer of writing to Greece (95a). Cadmus/Cebes is confident that Socrates will defeat "the argument of Cadmus" as easily as he defeated Harmonia/Simmias's, but Socrates warns against boasting: "We don't want some witchery to rout the argument we're about to make" (95b). Cebes' argument in fact demands far more of Socrates, and, leaving any jinxing of the argument "to the god's care," he brings in Homer again to prepare his final argument: "As for us, let us, in Homeric fashion, come to close quarters and try to see if there's anything to what you're saying." "Homeric fashion" brings individual Achaian heroes into close quarters with individual Trojan heroes: the coming tale belongs to the acts of the new hero, who turned his fleeing army to face argument again by his own heroic, single-handed battle.

Socrates begins his battle telling an autobiographical tale of how he first began in philosophy, a tale that differs from the one he told the Athenian public in his public defense a month earlier. His Homeric tale here has two parts, dividing at the point of his "launching" himself on a "second sailing," his reverting to oars or to his own effort after weighing and abandoning the efforts of his philosophic predecessors (99d). Socrates' first sailing was his impassioned thinking through of philosophy's first sailing, the gains its individual thinkers had made up to his time: Socrates divides philosophy into two sailings, a first sailing with which he came to close quarters early and then, after discovering its limitations, his own second sailing that the first somehow implied or required.

When Socrates restates Cebes' fears he employs Cebes' words, deathless (*athanaton*) and imperishable (*anōlethron*) (88b), the two words on which his argument will end: "You demand that our soul be shown to be both imperishable and deathless" (95c). Without proof of both, a "philosophic man" would be "mindless and stupid" to face his death believing he will do well in the afterlife, as Cebes charged very early in the day's discussion, leading to Socrates' "apology" (62d-e). This restatement[46] repeats the letter of Cebes' view — the soul's superiority to body and its surviving many bodies are no guarantee that it will survive its present body. But Socrates adds something Cebes did not say, though it is part of his Pythagorean view: the soul's entering a body is "like a disease, the beginning of its perishing," and it "lives this life wearing itself out in misery and ends up perishing in what's called death" (95d). Socrates says of his restatement that he purposely kept "going back over things often so that nothing may escape us and so that, if

46. It is Socrates' second restatement of Cebes' fears; see 91d.

you want, you may add or take away something" (95e). Cebes does not take away what Socrates added but says, "That's just what I'm saying." Socrates' addition that this life is a kind of curse is fully in the spirit of what Cebes said; it faithfully expresses the Pythagorean view of life to which Socrates is attaching his own philosophy for these young Pythagoreans.[47]

At this point silence fell over the whole company as Socrates "paused for a long time and considered something within himself" (95e), heightening the drama that precedes the last argument of his life. When he does break his silence he says that an adequate response requires consideration of "the cause concerning generation and destruction as a whole" and that, if Cebes wants him to, he can recount "my own experiences about them for you" so that if anything he says "appears useful to you, you can use it for purposes of persuasion in the very matters you're talking about." Socrates has explicitly told Cebes how to use his report on his beginnings: use it to persuade yourself not to be terrified at the prospect of dying without knowing that your soul is deathless. His report plus the argument it prepares succeeds in persuading Cebes not to be terrified. But a report on his beginnings by Odyssean Socrates can be presumed to contain more than the mere persuasion for which it is useful to Cebes.

This then is the wholly remarkable setting for the earliest glimpse Plato ever gave of Socrates' experiences: it is approaching evening on Socrates' last day; having only a few hours left, he determines that he must pause to make a detour before mounting the last argument of his life; the detour takes him and his audience back to the very beginnings of his philosophic life and to the first steps he made in thinking through his great predecessors; when it comes, his argument concerns the grounds of generation and destruction as a whole and the possible place within this whole of a thing that is imperishable and deathless; the audience for his detour and his argument has been shown from the beginning to believe in the immortality of their souls and underway to be more committed to the indestructibility of their souls than to reasoning itself; and Socrates, with these young followers of Pythagoras, has cast himself as a general responsible for saving his fleeing army—and he will speak like an Odysseus, speak with a view to consequences. By deciding to lay out the beginnings of his philosophic life, Socrates at the end of his life ties his end to his beginnings, leaving

---

47. Ebert shows that Socrates' addition actually allows an easier kind of counterargument than Cebes' objection does (*Phaidon*, 336–38): it is necessary only to argue that *death of the body* does not entail the death of the soul, whereas Cebes' objection required demonstrating "that the soul can have its existence ended by no means at all and at no other time."

his audience with the impression that they have seen the whole arc of his becoming: a satisfying wholeness to Socrates' career completes his self-presentation in the last hours of his life. But those most drawn to him will find that the stinger this bee left behind impels them to see that this impression of seeing his philosophic life whole is false.

Odyssean Socrates Tells the Tale of the First Stage of His Philosophic Education

To begin his tale, Socrates tells young Cebes that when he was young, he was "wondrously desirous of that wisdom they call 'inquiry into nature'"[48] (96a). "Have any of you ever heard me conversing about such things?" — about the inquiry into nature? Socrates had asked his jurors and the Athenian public that question a month earlier: sustained public silence was the best defense he could offer the public at his trial against the charge that he was a thinker who inquired into nature (*Apology* 19d, 18b). Now, "beyond the reach of those who condemned the study of nature as wicked,"[49] and speaking privately to young Pythagoreans, he can say that a passion for such study fired his beginnings as a thinker, for it was a wisdom that seemed "glorious[50] — to know the causes (*aitia*) of each thing, why each thing comes to be and why it perishes and why it is" (96a): Socrates began with the fundamental question, the causes of the coming to be and passing away of all things.[51] The *Phaedo* gives no indication of how old Socrates

48. Burnet notes that *peri phuseōs historia* "is the oldest name for what we call 'natural science'. . . . Heraclitus (fr. 17) said that Pythagoras had pursued *historia* further than other men, and it appears that even geometry was called by this name in the Pythagorean school" (*Phaedo*, at 96a8). The phrase therefore has resonance for Socrates' Pythagorean audience in the cell and for Phaedo's audience in Phlia. Burnet argues for the historicity of Socrates' report on his early views, tracing them to their sources in the thinkers whose written words would have been available to him. Burnet adds that "the state of science here indicated is quite unlike any we know to have existed either at an earlier or a later date. It belongs solely to the period to which it is here attributed" (at 96b9), that is, around 450. Moreover, such scientific views "correspond closely with the caricature of Aristophanes in the *Clouds*, which was produced in 423 B.C." (Burnet, *Phaedo*, at 96a2).

49. Strauss, *Xenophon's Socratic Discourse*, 164.

50. According to LSJ, *hyperēphaneō* usually carries the sense of "overweening" and only rarely the good sense of "magnificent" or "splendid"; it cites this passage as one of the latter instances.

51. Translating *aitia* as "cause" is called by David Gallop a "hallowed mistranslation" that is "particularly unfortunate here" because what Socrates is concerned with here is not always subject to causal explanation in the usual sense. Gallop uses "reason" instead because the question Socrates asks — "Why is a thing what it is?" — sometimes requires a causal

was when he began posing the question of becoming, but the *Parmenides* does: it reports a conversation between Socrates, Parmenides, and Zeno at the Great Panathenaia in 450 when Socrates was about nineteen and had already gained the view of transcendent forms that he will present in the *Phaedo* as his early and lasting achievement.[52] Plato's Socrates began his life in philosophy as a teenager with a passionate interest in natural philosophy.

To begin reporting the first questions he asked about nature, Socrates says, "Very often I cast my thought this way and that"—he began in an unsystematic manner—"looking first of all into questions like these," and he identifies four fields of his early questioning. One concerned the origins of life, how elements transform into organisms: "Is it when hot and cold bring about a certain fermentation as some say?" From the beginning, his questioning is clearly informed by positions already argued by previous natural philosophers, especially those already resident in Athens.[53] His next question concerned the origins of "what we think with" (*phronoumen*) (96b4): Is it blood, or air, or fire, all of which had been posited in the poetic tradition as well as by previous natural philosophers?[54] Or is what we think with itself active in what we think—does the brain produce the senses of hearing and seeing and smelling, and do memory and opinion (*doxa*) arise from them with knowledge being memory and opinion come to a state of rest?[55] Along with these questions on the coming to be of life and of knowledge Socrates says he also looked into "the processes by which these things pass away." The fourth and final matter he mentions as a subject of his early inquiries concerns "the things that happen to heaven and earth"—

---

explanation and sometimes a conceptual explanation (it is what it is because of this or that feature). The word *aitia* has roots in moral and legal judgment where an *aitia* is a charge, blaming or accusing someone. Nevertheless, it seems preferable to use "cause" here because Socrates is reporting his first inquiries into nature as a question about the coming into being and passing out of being of things, a question that looks for a causal explanation in the customary sense. See Sebell, *Socratic Turn*, 166n4: the word "cause" "is the least misleading translation."

52. That Plato set the *Parmenides* in 450 is generally agreed by scholars.

53. As Burnet notes, what "some say" is the view of "Archelaus, the disciple of Anaxagoras and . . . the teacher of Socrates" (*Phaedo*, at 96b3). Both Anaxagoras and Archelaus were resident in Athens; see below, n. 67.

54. Blood—Empedocles; air—Anaximander and Diogenes of Apollonia, who lived part of his life in Athens; and fire—Heraclitus. Aristophanes has Socrates claim air as the source: *Clouds* 230.

55. Burnet reports that this view of the basis of knowledge in memory and opinion stems from Alcmaeon of Croton, born c. 510, a natural philosopher and theorist of medicine (*Phaedo*, at 96b5).

immediately adding that he "ended up with the opinion that my natural fitness for this 'looking into things' was next to nothing" (96b). Socrates thus joins to his investigations into "the things aloft and the things under the earth" the avowal of natural incapacity for such investigation; those were the very investigations that led easily to charges of atheism and the denial of Hades by the pious many: they are the most immediately suspicious of philosophy's topics, and to deny any natural fitness for them aligns Socrates' speech in the cell with his public speech.[56]

Socrates offers what he calls "sufficient proof" of his natural unfitness for this kind of inquiry, proof that concerns what he "had sure knowledge of even before, in my opinion at least and in the opinion of others." He was so "intensely blinded" (96c) by this looking "that I unlearned even what I thought I knew before about many other things and about why a human being grows."[57] His first example of what he unlearned concerns generation: he "used to think" that how a human being grows "was clear to everyone: that a human being grows through eating and drinking"; in the food eaten "amounts of flesh are attached to flesh and amounts of bone to bones" (96d) and similarly with other parts of the body; thus, what "was little has become a lot and in this way the small human being becomes big" (96d) — what he used to think about eating and growth is what Anaxagoras thought.[58] What led him to unlearn this, proving his natural unfitness? Instead of simply stating that, Socrates looks to Cebes' reaction: for the first time in his report on his past he invites a response from him. Emphasizing that "that's what I used to think then," he asks, "Don't I seem sensible to you?" And Cebes adds his assent to what was clear to everyone.

Socrates never refers again to this first example of becoming bigger by eating, but all the other examples he gives he will refer to later, after setting out his own view of cause: each of these later examples he will refer to as "the other causes, the wise ones" (100c) that he tells Cebes to ignore and even to shout down. His first such example concerns measures of size: he

56. Burnet says with respect to Socrates' denial of such cosmological investigations in the *Apology* 19b-d: "We may be sure that he never talked about these matters in public. Plato is consistent on this." His silence "is not in any way inconsistent with his having at one time been attracted by [science] or even to his having studied [it] in the company of his [companions]" (*Euthyphro, Apology of Socrates, Crito*, 163) — or to his studying it in that company to the end.

57. I follow Sebell on just what Socrates is referring to in what he thought he knew before: his earlier scientific views, not his prescientific opinions, as is customarily thought; see Sebell, *Socratic Turn*, 30–31, 159n11.

58. Graham, *Texts*, 282–85.

used to think that when a big man appeared standing next to a small one "he was larger by the head itself," by that material part of a man, and he adds "a horse of a horse" — one horse is bigger than another by the same kind of measure.[59] Socrates' other two examples of what he used to think are "even more lucid" and concern the becoming of two and of one. It used to seem to him that ten things were more than eight "because two were added to the eight" (96e), and it seemed to him that a two-foot length was larger than a one-foot length "because it exceeded it by half of itself." But at this point in Socrates' report on what he used to think, Cebes interrupts: "And now, how do these things seem to you?"

Now? Privileged to hear how the philosopher they had sought out began his life of thinking about these things, Cebes interrupts to ask what he thinks about them *now*. Anyone interested in Socrates' becoming, how he became what he is, would have asked, What did you think *then*, back then when you were first thinking through these questions of cause? But Cebes asks about *now* — Cebes' interest only in what Socrates thinks now seems to indicate that he wants to learn from Socrates what *he* should think now. Socrates responds to Cebes' disinterest in his past by reporting what he now thinks but he will not stay for long in the present to which Cebes called him: once he has given Cebes a brief report on what he thinks now about the addition of ones to make two, he will return to his beginnings, first, in order to report very briefly that back then he threw together a way of his own, and second, to report one other early attempt of his to explain cause: he must want Cebes to hear those things and learn from those things despite his expressed lack of interest in Socrates' past. But a direct result of Cebes' interruption is that Socrates' promised "sufficient proof" of his natural unfitness for "looking into things" remains unspoken.[60] Still, his brief report on his skepticism about knowing the most basic mathematical operation fully befits the more general skepticism he now, in his maturity, holds, the *human* natural unfitness for knowledge of causes in nature that Plato shows him learning through the exercises Parmenides set out for him.

Socrates responds to Cebes' interruption by uttering his last oath, "By

---

59. "By a head": as the Trojans and Achaians battled before the walls of Troy, Priam asked Helen the name of the Achaian leader who stood out for grandeur even though there were "others taller by a head than he is"; after she identified him as Agamemnon, he asked who that man was who was "shorter by a head" than Agamemnon. She replied that it was "resourceful Odysseus . . . [who] knows every manner of shiftiness and crafty counsels" (*Iliad* 3.163, 193, 200–203).

60. See Sebell, *Socratic Turn*, 46–47.

Zeus,"[61] and stating what he now thinks: "I seem to be far from thinking, I suppose, that I know the cause (*aitia*) concerning any of these things."[62] Cebes has brought into the present Socrates' report on puzzles that arose for him fifty years ago and his description of what he now thinks separates him completely from his scientific ways of attempting to explain cause back then. His statement has two parts, the second elaborating the first. First, he describes what he no longer permits himself to say: "I don't even allow myself to assert that whenever someone adds a one to a one, the one added to or the one that was added has become two; or that the one that was added and the one to which it was added became two by the addition of the one to the other." Having given these three alternative and distinct ways of understanding ones becoming two, the most basic of all mathematical operations, Socrates elaborates what he finds problematic in them. "Here's what I wonder about" (97a), he says, and goes back to spell out his example of addition: "When each of the two was separate from the other, each was one and the pair were not two but when they came close to each other, this became the cause of their becoming two, the *concourse* that comes from their being placed close to each other." Then he opposes to this action of making two—bringing together—a different action for making two: "Nor again can I yet be persuaded that if someone splits a one apart, this, the splitting, has in turn become the cause of their having become two." He states the obvious: these two causes are the contraries of one another, but it is not the contradictory character of the two causes, bringing together and splitting apart, that are the grounds for his difficulty in understanding the becoming of two: each of the two procedures, by itself, failed to account for the becoming of two. What is at issue then is not accounting for the becoming of two things, two units, this plurality. Instead, the problem is accounting for the two*ness* of two, its own being a unit or a one of a particular kind or form; neither of the contradictory ways of becoming two account for the idea of twoness.[63]

The different ways Socrates gave of accounting for two can be viewed as combinations of material cause and efficient cause; neither separately

---

62. Dustin Sebell notes that Socrates' vocabulary undergoes a significant shift after Cebes' interruption: having earlier used "cause" (*aitia*) only once and in the plural, when first speaking of his desire "to know the *causes* of each thing" (96a9), he used only *dia* (by, through, because of) when giving examples from his early experiences; but as soon as Cebes shifted the focus to "now" Socrates began using *aitia* in the singular with great frequency (*Socratic Turn*, 57–58).

63. Stern, *Socratic Rationalism*, 112; Sebell, *Socratic Turn*, 66–67.

nor together can those two kinds of cause account for the being of the unitary, of the oneness that two is. What Socrates does in his brief account of what he now thinks about these things prepares what he is planning to present to Cebes, his discovery of transcendent forms as the only proper or adequate way to understand cause; or, more generally, he is preparing his discovery that what is at work in cause are "operations of the mind."[64] But first, he moves from these examples of wonder to the most comprehensive possible statement about the necessary ignorance he now sees built into this way of supposed knowing: he no longer even persuades himself that he could know "why a one comes to be nor why, in a word, *anything else* comes to be or perishes or is by this way of proceeding" (93b3–6). After that to-talizing judgment against the failure of this way of understanding cause, Socrates says, "I've randomly thrown together (*phurō*) another way myself, and that former one I don't tolerate at all" (97b). From the start Socrates' effort seems to be directed at immunizing Cebes against the investigation of nature and persuading him to follow the way he threw together.

Socrates ended the report Cebes forced on him about what he thinks now by briefly mentioning his new method, and Cebes or the reader might, as Paul Stern says, "expect to hear Socrates' new method at *this* point."[65] Instead, Socrates moves from now back to his past again in order to report on his first hearing Anaxagoras being read. What he heard is made singular by his insistence on returning from Cebes' interest in now back to his own beginnings, and by the fact that of all the philosophers before him that he might have named and discussed he chose only one, Anaxagoras. He chose not to mention the philosopher he most honored,[66] the one Plato made most important to his development, Parmenides. And he chose to discuss only one of the chief points for which Anaxagoras had become well known. He thus makes his encounter with Anaxagoras's writings seem indispensable to his early thinking about cause, or at least to what he wants Cebes to hear of his early thinking.

Socrates' report on first hearing Anaxagoras being read is remarkably vague at its start: he says he once heard someone reading from a book that that person said was by Anaxagoras. Anaxagoras was from Clazomenae, one of the Greek colony cities in Asia in which natural philosophy began and flourished. But he left Clazomenae and spent thirty years in Athens and was said to be the first to bring philosophy to Athens. He was there-

64. Benardete, *Socrates' Second Sailing*, 1.
65. Stern, *Socratic Rationalism*, 114.
66. See *Theaetetus* 183e–184a.

fore in Athens for all of Socrates' youth up until he was about twenty; at that point Anaxagoras suffered a dramatic fate that ended his long stay in Athens.[67] His name would have been well known to everyone in Athens at that time because he was part of Pericles' intellectual circle over many years as Pericles rose to become Athens' leading citizen. But Anaxagoras's fame became infamy for many: his view that the sun was a mass of red-hot metal led the Athenians to put him on trial for impiety and convict him. He was either banished as some reports say or imprisoned and released only because Pericles was able to persuade the demos to permit it. As Socrates was first being taken over by philosophy he not only heard Anaxagoras being read, as he mentions, but he would also have known that this philosopher whose view attracted him was convicted of impiety by an Athenian court, as he does not mention.[68]

The single thing Socrates reports hearing from the book by Anaxagoras was that it "said that it is in fact mind (*nous*) that puts the world in order and is responsible for (*aitios*) all things" (97c). Socrates had said that his first and overarching concern was knowing the causes of all things; given that concern, he "was pleased with this sort of cause (*aitia*) and it seemed to me in some way good that mind should be responsible for all things." His expectation was that if mind was responsible for all things, then "mind, in ordering the world, would order all things and position each thing in just the way that is best." He does not say that he wondered about the nature of such a mind or the manner of its agency; he says only that "if someone wanted to discover the cause concerning each thing, in what way it comes into being or perishes or is"—which is what he said he very much wanted—"he would have to discover *this* concerning it, in what way it's

---

67. For the surviving ancient reports of Anaxagoras's life and teaching, see Graham, *Texts*, 271–325. The generally agreed-upon dates for his life are c. 500–428, but just when he spent his thirty years in Athens is disputed and depends on which of two archonships Diogenes Laertius meant when referring to Anaxagoras's arrival in Athens: was it that of Callia<de>es (480) or Callias (456)? The earlier date seems more plausible, given the extant information about Anaxagoras in Athens (the arguments are summarized by Graham, 313–14). The "someone" Socrates heard reading could have been Archelaus, an Athenian: according to Diogenes Laertius, Socrates was a student of Archelaus, the outstanding student of Anaxagoras. Archelaus became head of the school after Anaxagoras was forced to leave Athens (Diogenes Laertius 2.4.16–17). Diogenes Laertius also preserved the remark of a fifth-century poet, Ion of Chios, that Socrates and Archelaus visited Samos together, perhaps in 441–440, when Athens was blockading Samos and Socrates was about twenty-nine years old (2.5.16, 19–23).

68. The Athenians were particularly active in prosecuting philosophers during Socrates' lifetime; see Ahrensdorf, *Death of Socrates*, 10.

best for it either to be or to undergo or do anything whatsoever." His expectations were extreme: with this account of cause it would befit "a person, in this matter and in all others, to look to *nothing but* what is most excellent and best" (97d). As the final point in his list of expectations, he says
that knowing that, one "necessarily knows what is worst as well; for the
knowledge concerning these is the same." Socrates thus pictures himself as
a young man "reasoning these things out" by himself and drawing extreme
conclusions about what Anaxagoras must have meant, saying finally that it
gave him "great pleasure" to think that he had discovered in Anaxagoras "a
teacher after my own mind (*kata nous*) concerning what is" — his little pun
on *nous* makes his mind accord with Anaxagoras's mind in making mind
the sole cause of every event in nature, thus making nature perfect in the
whole and in each of its particulars. No wonder this view pleased him.

Socrates reported that on hearing a single thought of Anaxagoras's
being read he leapt to the conclusion that he would find in Anaxagoras a
comprehensive cosmic mind that knew what is best and was the sole causal
and ordering force behind every fact and event in nature. His youthful
expectations included specific examples of what mind would order and
cause, and they concerned exclusively cosmological entities and events,
beginning with the earth and whether it was flat or round and why it is
better that it be such (97e).[69] He believed Anaxagoras would then tell him
the placement of the earth in the cosmos and if he put it in the middle
he would show just how "it is better for it to be in the middle." If Anaxagoras could persuade him of such things, he was prepared "to yearn no
longer for any other form of cause" (98a). He also anticipated finding out
from Anaxagoras about the sun and the moon in the same way, and about
the rest of the heavenly bodies, expecting Anaxagoras to tell him "their
speeds relative to one another" and their "turnings" and the other changes
they underwent.[70] And he imagined that Anaxagoras would not impute any
other cause for these cosmic events than that it is "best for them to be in
just the condition they're in" and that he would "take me through what is
best for each and the common good for all" (98b). With these exacting and

---

69. Anaxagoras (and Archelaus) held that the earth was flat (Graham, *Texts*, 294–97),
whereas the Pythagoreans held that it was round. Burnet states that "this was still a living
problem in the days when Socrates was young, but not later" (*Phaedo*, at 97d8). Anaxagoras
also held that the earth is suspended in air and that the sun and moon rotate around it;
despite his flawed cosmology he was the first to give a correct account of lunar and solar
eclipses (Graham, *Texts*, 294–99), further demythologizing the sky.

70. According to Burnet, "turnings" refers to "the annual movement of the sun from the
'tropic' of Capricorn to that of Cancer and back again" (*Phaedo*, at 98a4).

all-encompassing hopes, Socrates turned to the writings of Anaxagoras. He got hold of them, he says, "in all haste" and read them "as speedily as I could so that I might know as speedily as possible the best and the worst."

What has Socrates just reported about his reading back then? That he began reading Anaxagoras in the worst possible way: in utter haste with precisely defined expectations of what he wanted the writing to say. His report on his reading displays the impetuous, headlong rapidity and self-assurance in judgment typical of a brilliant youth accustomed to seeing solutions immediately and imagining total solutions: everything in nature becomes explicable in one fell swoop by one sole cause. It is just this youthful, confident, headlong rush that Plato put on display in the *Parmenides*, the parallel account he gave of Socrates at nineteen, his first meeting with Zeno and Parmenides just after he had come up with his own solution to the problem of cause, transcendent forms. In that encounter Socrates would learn that he misread their writings, but Zeno favored him by telling him that he had to read his writings differently, with a view to their intention, and asking himself why Zeno would wonder about whether he should publish them at all. Plato's dialogues show that Socrates did learn how to read the philosophers, and not only them but the foundational poets of the Greeks as well, Homer and Hesiod, Hesiod being the poet who said he was told by the Muses that they speak lies like the truth and that they also tell the truth when they wish.[71] In the *Phaedo* Socrates' report on his youthful fervor shows that he had no appreciation either of the enormity of the problem of cause or of the subtlety with which earlier philosophers had expressed their views.

After describing how he approached reading Anaxagoras, Socrates reported that "from this wonderful hope, my comrade, I was swept away," for reading Anaxagoras showed him that he "didn't employ mind at all and didn't hold any causes responsible for putting things in order, but instead put the blame on air and ether and water and other things many and absurd" (98c).[72] Before embarking on his account of his philosophic beginnings, Socrates had intimated that Odysseus was the genuine philosophic hero (94d–95b) and here, in saying he was "swept away" from his first hope for an easy solution to understanding cause, he intimates an Odyssean parallel: Homer described Odysseus being "swept away" in his easy first

---

71. Hesiod, *Theogony* 27–28.

72. Socrates does not mention that Anaxagoras used mind (according to Diogenes Laertius) to give the initial impetus to the original state of the cosmos in which "all things were together" (Graham, *Texts*, 274–75).

attempt to fulfill his hope of homecoming.[73] Odysseus's hope had been arranged by Aiolos, keeper of the winds for the gods, for he sewed up in a bag all the winds but Zephyr, who then aided Odysseus and his crew in their nine-day sail home, bringing them so close to Ithaca that they could see the night fires burning. But after his nine days of forced wakefulness, Odysseus could not help falling asleep, and his comrades opened the bag in which Aiolos had trapped the winds, which then swept Odysseus's ship away from Ithaca, blowing it back to Aiolos's island. This experience caused Odysseus to lose all trust in divine or quasi-divine guidance, for Aiolos, seeing Odysseus's ship blown back to his island, cursed him as an object of enmity to the immortals — and from that point on Odysseus no longer imagined that divine guidance might aid him in achieving his home-coming.[74] In a similar way, Socrates, "swept away" from a first "*wonder*-full" (*thaumastēs*, 98b7) hope in some guiding cosmic mind, no longer looked explicitly for such a cause — while leaving Cebes to believe that he blamed Anaxagoras for *not* using mind as explanatory cause.

Young Socrates, that reader in a rush, misread Anaxagoras by failing to ask about his intention, for Anaxagoras seems to have intended mind to play a different role in his writings from that of a causal agent. Knowing that writings are open to everyone who can read or even listen to his books being read, and that almost all are unlike Socrates and will never want to read his writings, Anaxagoras seems to have intended mind as causal agent to leave just that pleasing impression that Socrates experienced: he put his statement about mind ordering things in the first sentence of his treatise,[75] knowing it would garner the most attention right there. Even those who did read him but were less demanding about cause than Socrates had been, not expecting mind to be the total causal explanation of every entity and event in the cosmos, could have been satisfied that along with causal expla-nations like air and ether and water there was a ruling causal mind pleas-ingly ordering all things for the best. As a member of Pericles' intellectual circle and a longtime resident in democratic Athens, Anaxagoras was cer-tainly aware of the gap between their way of thinking as an enlightened minority and the way of thinking of the population at large, for Pericles'

---

73. See *Phaedo*, trans. Brann, Kalkavage, and Salem, 78n18.

74. *Odyssey* 10.1–66. Benardete, *The Bow and the Lyre*, 80–82, calls attention to Odys-seus's "complete self-reliance" from this point of the *Odyssey* on, as indicated by the six straight days of rowing that followed. Benardete uses this occasion of rowing to speak of "the proverb 'second sailing'" and thus to link this event in the *Odyssey* with Socrates' account of his first experiences in philosophy in the *Phaedo*.

75. As Diogenes Laertius reported; Graham, *Texts*, 274–75.

effective rule depended in part on his speaking in a way that pleased the demos—and Socrates said that it was Anaxagoras who made the natural orator Pericles into a perfect one.[76] Anaxagoras, knowing the principles of rhetoric, would not have ignored in his own writings one of the conditions of successful public speech in a democracy where his books would be available for purchase in the marketplace.[77] Young Socrates' failure with Anaxagoras was the same failure Plato showed him making with Zeno and Parmenides, a failure to understand the intentions of philosophic authors. The old Socrates' intention in making a show of his young self to young Cebes dictates that he speak of his search for the causes of all things in the appropriate way for those in danger of falling into misology. Socrates' Odyssean intention in choosing to single out Anaxagoras in reporting his own becoming resembles Anaxagoras's: blame Anaxagoras for failing to employ the teleology of mind he seemed to promise; imply that he himself endorses a teleological directedness of all things but never say he does.[78]

To show Cebes the reason he was disappointed with Anaxagoras's actual explanations of cause, Socrates does what Cebes had done, jump from his beginnings fifty years ago to now, right now, his sitting there with his legs bent, conversing. He says that Anaxagoras as an explainer of cause is "most like"[79] someone who says Socrates does everything he does by mind, but when actually giving the causes of "each of the things I do" assigns the causes of his "sitting there" to his bones and sinews, letting mind fall away entirely. And Socrates gives a detailed explanation of how the bones and sinews of his legs work in his sitting there right now with his legs bent (98d). From that example and its causes, he moves to his second example, his conversing with them, and imagines someone assigning similar causes to that: "voices, and air, and sounds and a thousand other such things." Reverting to his sitting there, Socrates gives its "true causes" (98e): "to the Athenians it seemed to be better to condemn" him, while to him "it seemed better to sit here and more just to stay put and endure whatever penalty they command" (99a). Both the Athenians and Socrates who has been sitting there for a month awaiting death judged it better that he sit

76. See *Phaedrus* 270a; he also said there that Anaxagoras taught Pericles "the nature of mind and lack of mind."

77. See *Apology* 26d.

78. Benardete showed in his late writings on Homer and Hesiod and Heraclitus and Parmenides that the practice of exoteric sheltering was standard by Anaxagoras's time.

79. The exactness Socrates claims for his comparison is emphasized in different ways in looser translations: "in exactly the position of someone who" (Gallop), "very much as if one should say" (Fowler).

there, but only of his own judgment does Socrates say justice was its basis: had he not judged it more just to sit there, "by the Dog!" his "bones and sinews" would "long ago have been in Megara or Boeotia,[80] swept off by an opinion about what is best, if I didn't think it more just and more noble, rather than fleeing and playing the runaway, to endure whatever penalty the city should arrange" (99a). Socrates' decision not to do what Anaxagoras of Clazomenae had done came from weighing his opinion about "what is best" against what he thought more just and more noble. That Socrates thought that saving his life was best is a revelation, as Ronna Burger argued: facing death in a few hours, Socrates declares that life and its preservation are best.[81] But at that point in his life, at age seventy and as it were before the eyes of all his countrymen, his view of justice and nobility overrule his judgment of what is best. Socrates defined his view of justice thirty years earlier in the *Republic* as doing good for friends and not harming anyone";[82] as for his view of the noble, it must include at its peak his understanding of the most admirably human, the heroic; *his* justice and *his* nobility dictate that he accept the judgment of his fellow citizens and sit there, surrendering what is best in favor of a heroically memorable act on behalf of philosophy. Socrates' sitting there is an affirmation of a philosopher's life affirmed in a philosopher's way: while encouraging the city, that condition of the possibility of the philosophic life, to judge this philosopher loyal, a law-abiding if different citizen whose way of life is not a threat to their common life, Socrates' choice of sitting there will elevate him as a heroic model of philosophy's supreme worth.

Socrates gave the true causes of his sitting there; he does not give the true causes of his conversing.[83] Unlike his sitting there, his conversing—*dialegesthai*—seems not to have a city-shared basis in moral choice, in justice and the noble. Although his conversing is itself an artful mix of the public and private that shelters what he is by nature, what drives his conversing can be seen as twofold, the deeply experienced force driving him to inquire and a derivative force driving him to share what his primary drive led him to discover. Socrates' display in the *Phaedo* does not provide the guidance necessary to understand the nature of that primary drive

---

80. In Socrates' cell, Euclides and Terpsion are from Megara, and Simmias and Cebes from Boeotia.

81. Burger, *Phaedo*, 143. Burger calculates that Socrates' statement about what is best (99a2) is the "displaced center of Plato's labyrinth," according to the complex acts of centering that she sets out on pp. xii–xvi of the foreword to the second edition of her book.

82. Implied by *Republic* 335b–336a.

83. See Sebell, *Socratic Turn*, 104–5.

to understand the causes of all things. By leaving open the true causes of Socrates' conversing, the *Phaedo* implicitly poses the question that Plato's three-part scattering of Socrates' becoming is set up to answer. For just as the account Socrates will give of his second sailing invites comparison with the parallel account Plato records in his *Parmenides*, so too Socrates' leaving open the true causes of his conversing, the core of his life, invites comparison with the report Plato has Socrates give in the *Symposium* of Diotima leading him to understand the fundamental cause of the beings through knowing himself.

Socrates had introduced his condition as an explainer of the causes of his sitting there and conversing as "most like" Anaxagoras's condition as an explainer who says mind is the cause of all things yet omits it entirely regarding the causes responsible for the placement of earth, sun, and moon. The causes of Socrates' sitting there and conversing involve end-directed, teleological choice made by reasoning minds judging what is best—they can be "most like" Anaxagoras's examples only if there is a corresponding cosmic mind weighing and choosing what is best. Socrates makes no effort whatever to prove that possibility, to justify his "most like." Instead, as Paul Stern says, "Socrates' treatment of teleology indicates the existence of a distance between humanity and the whole of nature."[84] Socrates' refusal to close that distance between his human examples and Anaxagoras's cosmic ones suggests, as Stern says, "that in his treatment of Anaxagoras's thought lies a reason to think that a teleological account [of nature] is unavailable."[85] Socrates leaves latent the reason to think that, while being completely open in blaming Anaxagoras for not using teleology to explain cause: Cebes can naturally conclude that Socrates thinks Anaxagoras should have. Could "most like" then have a more appropriate application? *Most like* are two philosophers attempting to parry the suspicions of the city but failing and being condemned; *unlike* are Anaxagoras's brief appeal to mind and his flight and Socrates' coming appeal to transcendent forms and his sitting there conversing—plus his eventual success.

To call such things as bones and sinews and voices and air and sound *causes* of his actions is "too absurd," Socrates says (99a) as he introduces the distinction with respect to cause that characterizes his own view or the view he will display. If someone were to say that he would not be able to do what seemed best to him without such things as bones and sinews "he would be speaking the truth"; but if that someone said "it was through

84. Stern, *Socratic Rationalism*, 117.
85. Stern, 114.

(*dia*) these things that I'm doing what I'm doing, engaging in these acts by mind" (*merely* mind, unexplained, vague mind) "but not by choice of what is best" (as the Athenians chose in condemning him, and he chose in sitting there) "the thoughtlessness of his speech would be large and deep" (99b). Anaxagoras engaged in thoughtless speech, failing to give mind its proper role in events like Socrates' sitting there and conversing: "Imagine not being able to distinguish that it's one thing to be genuinely the cause and another to be that without which the cause would not be a cause!" Failure to make that distinction left "the many groping around as if in the dark" when they applied the name of cause to the mere conditions for the cause's effecting something. *These* many are Anaxagoras and the other investigators of nature: one says the earth stays put under heaven because it's the center of a vortex, as Empedocles did; another props it up on a pedestal of air, as Anaxagoras had. What Socrates demands is not some more accurate material or efficient cause but instead "the power of placing things as they are now situated—in the best way possible—this power they don't search for, nor do they think it has any divine (*daimonian*) strength" (99c). The investigators of nature are blamable as strict materialists and all-too-apparent atheists, whereas Socrates' distinction between mere conditions and actual cause seems to demand a non-material power or force that causes material events—here, seemingly a mind-force causing material actions on the basis of a judgment of what is best. A chronological reading of Plato's dialogues looks to the *Symposium* to interpret this account through a very different ontology, an ontology of eros that lacks the permanences Socrates will here suggest. For here his audience is Cebes, a young man with fears about the permanence of his soul, and Socrates speaks with a view to consequences.

Socrates ends his critique of the investigators of nature by suggesting that he will supply what they failed to supply. They "believe that someday they will discover an Atlas stronger and more deathless than this one," the Atlas we all grew up with and know, Homer's and Hesiod's divine Atlas, their way of accounting for the placement of the earth below the heavens and above Hades.[86] The godless power the investigators of nature search for, a stronger and more deathless supporter of the earth, they have not been able to find. And "they don't at all suppose that it is" in some way like "this one," our old divine one, some "good and binding that in truth binds and holds things together. For *that* sort of cause, how it works, it

---

86. Homer, *Odyssey* 1.52–54; Hesiod, *Theogony* 517–20.

would be a pleasure to become anyone's student." But Socrates found no teacher able to teach him an Atlas like our old one: "I was robbed of this and never became capable of discovering it myself or learning it from another" (99c8–9). This is as close as Socrates comes to denying outright a divine mind as the cause of the whole of things, deliberative as a human mind is and choosing what is best. By going only this far Socrates can leave Cebes with the impression that his main criticism of Anaxagoras is that he failed to use the teleological explanation he suggested and that he should have. While Socrates denies that he discovered or was taught an Atlas like our old one, he just spoke about a good and binding that holds things together, and when he immediately goes on to mention again the way of proceeding that he put together on his own (99d; cf. 97b), it seems that the newfound enthusiasm for Socrates' past that Cebes will express has been kindled by his hope that Socrates' new way will in fact be some new Atlas like our old one.

For at this point Socrates calls in Cebes again, ending the long speech he made after Cebes interrupted him to ask what he now thinks, a speech in which he returned to his past, despite Cebes' seeming disinterest, and introduced Anaxagoras and mind. His speech moved back to his present and ended on the problem of cause and the possibility of some new Atlas more like our old one in not being a merely material or efficient cause. Now he can call on a properly primed Cebes, a Cebes made enthusiastic about this aspect of Socrates' past, for he asks, "Do you want me to make a display (*epideixis*) of the way by which I've busied myself with the second sailing in search of the cause?" (99d). *Epideixis* is the word for the prepared speeches sophists gave to present their case in the most persuasive manner, a way of speaking Socrates typically refused.[87] For him to call what he is about to report an *epideixis* suggests that this too is a speech bent on persuasion; with his display Socrates will in fact give Cebes a more adequate way of making mind seem to rule the whole than Anaxagoras's was, a way more like our old Atlas and not that wholly material Atlas the investigators of nature searched for in vain. Does Cebes want him to make a display about that? "'Extraordinarily so,' Cebes says. 'Yes, I want you to." Literally, Cebes says, "*Supernaturally* (*huperphuōs*) so," a fitting word for what Socrates implicitly promised and goes on to give. Socrates' display sets out the way of transcendent forms that he has already employed in his arguments in the *Phaedo*. What he already said and what he will now say about his sec-

---

87. As he did in *Protagoras* 334c–335c and *Hippias Minor* 369c; cf. *Gorgias* 447a-c.

ond sailing make it almost explicit: transcendent forms replace the gods as causes of everything, ordering them teleologically. Socrates did discover a new Atlas more like our old one.

5. Odyssean Socrates' Report on His Second Sailing in the *Phaedo* Measured by the *Parmenides*

Socrates chose a dramatic way to prepare his display for Cebes on the decisive turn in his philosophic experiences as a young man, his turn away from direct consideration of beings to what he called a second sailing: he made it seem as if his turn back then resulted from the incapacity of natural science to account for the causes of his sitting there and conversing right now. But by choosing to focus on the causes of events in the present to explain his turn in his distant past, he left the actual causes of this great event fifty years ago completely unaddressed. A few minutes earlier, when he first mentioned that he had thrown together a method of his own (97b), he there too tied his past to what he thinks now, in the present to which Cebes had called him. Both of Socrates' references to his own method leave out his actual reasons back then for first devising it. Were his reasons then similar to the reasons he gives now, the incapacity of natural science to explain human actions like his sitting there and conversing? Plato's *Phaedo* offers no answer to the question its silence opens about Socrates' actual reasons for his turn in his youth. But his *Parmenides* does.[88]

---

88. Socrates' second sailing is sometimes taken to be his reverting to the options Simmias set out just before he stated his objection at 85c-d. (Kanayama, "Methodology of the Second Voyage," 92; Sebell, *Socratic Turn*, 173n7). But the options a Simmias depends on are not the options of a Socrates. Simmias said that "if one cannot learn or discover what's the case, he must sail through life in the midst of danger, seizing on the best and least refutable of human *logoi* . . . letting himself be carried upon it as on a raft," and he added a final option, "unless, that is, he could journey more safely and less dangerously on a more stable carrier, some divine account" (85c-d). Socrates has in no way abandoned discovering what is the case himself: his second sailing is an attempt to do just that. Nor has he abandoned learning what is the case from another — after inventing the forms and hearing Parmenides demolish them, he is eager to learn from him. But most decisively, Socrates never shows himself willing to seize on any of the human logoi and let himself be carried along by it as on a raft: Simmias is willing to be passive in accepting some raft, Socrates is not; he turns to the logoi not to sail through life in the midst of danger but to examine them with a view to discovering the truth of the beings. As for the hope Simmias holds out that there may be some reliable divine account, Socrates just indicated that as a young man he rationally abandoned trust in any divine account however much he found it desirable to seem to trust in such accounts. In taking Socrates to be referring to Simmias's options both Kanayama and Sebell take him to be likening his second sailing to Odysseus's attempt to sail home on his well-

The report in the *Phaedo* on Socrates' early becoming is autobiographical; the report in the *Parmenides* is not. As Seth Benardete noted, that means that the report in the *Parmenides* lacks the "framing" by the mature Socrates that the other two Platonic reports on Socrates' beginnings have.[89] Because Socrates exercised no control over that report, and because Plato presents it as a literal, memorized transmission of what was actually said, the *Parmenides* report tacitly claims superior historical authority, inviting its reader to recognize the priority owed to a report given by a firsthand witness who memorized it and taught it to another. And Plato supplied a special audience for that report: he prefaced it with an introduction that showed its singular importance for one audience only, foreigners from far-off Clazomenae, "very much philosophers," whose keen interest in a conversation the young Socrates reportedly had with Parmenides and Zeno drove them to sail across the sea in the hope of confirming a rumor that the report of that conversation might still be remembered by a person in Athens to whom it had been taught.[90] The *Parmenides* offers a privileged view on Socrates at nineteen not framed by the intentions that guide Socrates in the *Phaedo*, his need to defend philosophy against misology and to transmit his own teaching through an Iolaus. The *Phaedo*, on its surface, is for fans and potential fans of heroic Socrates who will find their already existing beliefs confirmed by Socrates' arguments: he could become their hero too, and they would help carry his teaching forward. The *Parmenides* is for those few profoundly driven by philosophic desire and the hope that they might learn about a conversation between a young Socrates and the great Parmenides and his companion Zeno that could have contributed to the essential becoming of a philosopher they admire, and thereby to their own philosophic becoming.

A chronological reading of Plato's dialogues thus offers a special opportunity to readers who resemble those foreigners at least with respect to wanting to know how the philosopher Socrates became the philosopher he

---

constructed raft from Ogygia, the island of Calypso the Concealer, the raft sailing Poseidon thwarted with a storm that wrecked the raft. But this misapplies Homer's tale: Odysseus's failed effort to sail home on his raft has nothing to do with his voyage of discovery to gain the fundamental truths of human nature and nature, and what Socrates is now displaying is his version of *that* voyage as a young man — Odysseus's comparable voyage in the *Odyssey* occurred seven years earlier, as Odysseus tells the wise king of the Phaiacians.

89. Benardete, "Plato's *Parmenides*," 230.

90. *Parmenides* 126b. The *Parmenides* thus employs its own devices of distancing from historical directness; these features of the remarkable singularity of the *Parmenides* will be treated in detail in the next chapter.

was. It cannot be accidental that Plato so arranged his dialogues that two of the three narrated by someone other than Socrates report on the same decisive event—Socrates' turn!—in very different ways. When the settings of the two reports are compared it becomes clear that the *Parmenides* gives the more direct report, making it the means by which to measure the display of his turn that Odyssean Socrates framed for the audience in the cell and for his Iolaus to spread abroad. From the perspective supplied by the *Parmenides*, Socrates' account of his beginnings in the *Phaedo* comes to light as his salutary teaching for young men who view philosophy as a tool for confirming the edifying beliefs they already hold: the dangers of mathematical natural science should strike fear into your hearts and help you to abandon such efforts at explaining cause. For this audience Socrates offers a view of cause that he presents as safe, a view that can cure them of potential misology and help them trust reason.

The account in the *Parmenides* with its transmission of an essential aspect of Socrates' turn can at certain points be mapped onto the steps Socrates reports to Cebes and his audience in the cell. And in the *Parmenides* there is no fear and no need for a safe view; it records a private conversation among inquirers, one young but having already made an important turn, the two others mature and seasoned and, as their writings attest and their words in the *Parmenides* confirm, looking to the future well-being of philosophy. The shared passion of these three is inquiry, their prime goal understanding, and their sole instrument reason—and their proper audience is restricted to those who are very much philosophers. The account of Socrates' beginnings in the *Parmenides* confirms the already evident truth that Socrates was Odyssean to the end and Plato Odyssean throughout.

In the *Phaedo*, to begin to satisfy Cebes' strong desire to hear his display speech on his second sailing, Socrates sets out an elaborate image about a certain fear that led him, after he renounced any direct looking into beings, to follow a new way of his own. "It seemed to me, after these things, since I had renounced looking into beings, that I had to be on guard so as not to suffer the very thing those people do who look into the sun during an eclipse. For surely some of them have their eyes destroyed if they don't look at the sun's likeness in water or in some other such thing" (99d). Applying this image of the possible loss of sight, he says, "I feared that I might be totally soul-blinded if I looked at things with my eyes and attempted to grasp them by each of the senses." Socrates' emphasis on looking and being blinded links this preparatory statement on his own way to his earlier statement about a looking that led to blindness (96a-c).[91] There, he offered his blindness as "proof" that his "natural fitness for this looking into things was next to nothing" (96c), a proof that led him to his first mention of a new way of proceeding that he "randomly threw together" (97b). Here, his reference to blindness leads to his elaboration of that new way, and it intimates that humans as such are naturally unfit for any direct "looking into things"; the human way of knowing blocks direct acquaintance with things as they are, as the *Parmenides* will confirm.

"So it seemed to me that I should take refuge in logoi and look in them for the truth of beings."[92] *Taking refuge* fits the fear Socrates just expressed about being blinded and implies a second best way, with the best way being simply too dangerous. Fear rhetoric dominates Socrates' whole *epideixis* with its eventual deliverance into the "safe" way ultimately endorsed enthusiastically by those present in the cell and in Phlia (102a). But the word Socrates uses for "taking refuge," *katapheugō*, also means "to have recourse to," and that fear-free action fits far better the process of inquiry that the young Socrates actually followed as recorded in the *Parmenides*. For the nineteen-year-old inquirer on view there showed no need to take refuge in a safe view; instead, he had recourse to the logoi in order to find a more rational, non-contradictory way of achieving his goal of understanding the truth of beings, a better way than the supposedly direct way of examining what appear to be the beings themselves, for that way was blocked by insurmountable puzzles. And that turn to the logoi was exactly what Parmenides praised in the young Socrates; twice he told him that he admired him for his "zeal for the logoi" (*Parmenides* 130b1–2, 135d3), zeal that drove him to find a rational way to deal with the puzzles present in "the visible things" (135e2), like the puzzles of many-ness that Zeno made as arresting as possible in order to point to Parmenides' superior way of the one, a way that Parmenides himself had also made deeply puzzling. Parmenides praised the young Socrates for not investigating the "perplexities among the visible things, nor even in reference to them," but instead "only in reference to what most of all one should grasp by logoi" (135e4). Young Soc-

91. Socrates' use of *skopeō* (to look at, contemplate, inquire) and *skeptomai* (to look carefully at, to examine) grows particularly dense in this passage, six times in eleven lines from 99d5 to 100a2; he also uses *blepō* (look, look at) (99e3).

92. I leave the capacious term *logoi* untranslated in order not to narrow its broad applications; Brann, Kalkavage, and Salem (*Phaedo*, 102) give a brief statement on the latitude of the word *logos*, listing "sentence," "account," "argument," "reason," and "ratio" as possible translations.

rates accepted that praise, saying that "this way there seemed no difficulty in showing what beings are like and unlike." His new way overcame the particular difficulty that Zeno put first in his treatise, the contradiction of the same thing being apparently both like and unlike at the same time. "Beautiful!" Parmenides said in response to Socrates' brief statement of why he moved to the logoi and to the forms.

In the *Phaedo* Socrates tells Cebes that he turned to the logoi in order "to look in them for the truth of beings." But before telling him what that turn to the logoi entailed for him, he warns of a misunderstanding built into his image of looking at the eclipsed sun in its "likeness" in water: "I don't at all concede that someone who looks into beings in logoi looks at them in likenesses to a greater extent than one who does so in actions (*ergois*)" (100a). The eclipsed sun is not simply the perceived object moving across the sky that it appears to be while its reflection in water is a likeness: the perceived sun in its action is, in some unspecified way, itself a likeness. Socrates could have arrived at this comprehensive view of likeness in both logoi and actions only as a result of his turn to the logoi — and not immediately: that conclusion could come only after considering the implications of his turn to the logoi; this is therefore a look back at his turn to the logoi from the standpoint that that turn made possible. The conclusion states that looking at things in their actions, seeming to see individual things as they are, is in fact no less mediated than looking at things in logoi. Socrates' image of the *eclipsed* sun is therefore an exact fit for the point he is making: human awareness as such, even of "actions," *eclipses* the beings, causes them to be in principle unavailable for direct examination as they are.[93] And the *blinding* that his image refers to is also an exact fit: to examine perceptions simply, as if they presented the beings as they are, is to be blinded to the active role of mind in all human awareness. Just here a trace of Anaxagoras's cosmic mind finds expression: there *is* an ordering by mind in all experienced things, not a cosmic mind but the human mind active in ordering all of its awarenesses and in that action universally causal.

In the *Phaedo* Socrates simply declares in explaining his eclipsed sun image that all human awareness is mediated; he folds that declaration, that

93. A solar eclipse is also a fitting image for Socrates to use here for the two reasons Sebell and others give: first, it intimates a continuing interest in the "things aloft," things investigated by natural science; and second, an eclipse of the sun is an event that "was almost universally said in Socrates' day . . . to be a god-sent or divine sign" (*Socratic Turn*, 112).

radical philosophic conclusion about the limits on human knowing, into his account of his turn without showing how or why he came to that view. Plato left it to the *Parmenides* to show that this was a conclusion to which Socrates was led by Parmenides, but only after Socrates had turned to the logoi and arrived at his view of forms on his own. And Parmenides did not teach him this radical conclusion by any direct statement on his part but instead guided him to draw it based on the immense puzzle of reasonings that he presented to Socrates as the gymnastic training he needed. Parmenides offered *guidance*; he did for Socrates what he presents the goddess doing for him in his poem. Socrates would have to prove himself worthy of true understanding, just as Parmenides had done; he would have to reason his way through the logical maze Parmenides left him with and earn its conclusions by his own efforts in reasoning.[94]

In the *Phaedo*, having clarified his image of the sun's likeness, Socrates says, "In any case, that's how I launched myself" (100a). He then describes in a single sentence just what he did in launching himself into the logoi: "On each occasion I put down as hypothesis whatever logos I judge to be mightiest; and whatever seemed to me to be consistent with this, I put down as being true, both about cause and about all the rest, while what isn't I put down as not true." Just what the criteria of *might* in a hypothesis are, or just how he measured consistent and inconsistent, or just what "all the rest" in addition to cause could be Socrates does not say, for he stops himself at this point, saying to Cebes that he will "tell him more plainly" what he means because Cebes seems not to have understood.[95] No indication is given of just why Socrates might have perceived in Cebes a reason for stopping his description of how he launched himself and for moving instead from that turning point in his past to the present. For telling Cebes "more plainly" how he started out entails a statement on what he "has never stopped talking about at other times and in the account that has just occurred as well," a statement on the forms, which he can easily speak about here because he had already employed forms in his earlier arguments

---

94. After following Parmenides' guidance to its end, could Socrates have wondered whether Anaxagoras's declaration about mind and cause was not itself a mere pointer to the true view, a rhetorical device by a knowing guide that also serves as a salutary opening?

95. Paul Stern singles out "consistent with" (*sumphōnein*) as the focus of "the widely recognized ambiguity of this passage": Does it mean "be consistent with" or "is deducible from"? But Stern judges, with Gallop, that the more important issue is "that neither interpretation offers a solid ground for thinking a proposition true or false" (*Socratic Rationalism*, 125).

and Simmias and Cebes had exhibited their familiarity with them and with the use Socrates put them to.[96]

By stopping his autobiographical display of his beginnings at just this point and returning to how he argues right now, Socrates again opens the gap that has characterized their exchange, the gap between back then and right now. The *Parmenides* shows that Socrates breaks off with Cebes at a point where, fifty years ago, Parmenides led him onward to an essential step in the process of reasoning about beings through logoi. For immediately after praising the young Socrates for refusing to deal with the visible things and instead investigating the logoi and considering forms (*Parmenides* 135e), he told him that he had failed to take a further step indispensable to advancement in reasoning about beings: "Do not investigate only the results of a hypothesis if each hypothesized thing *is*, but also hypothesize that this same thing *is not*. Do that if you want to get more gymnastic training" (136a) — gymnastic training being what Parmenides had just told Socrates he had to undergo if he was to advance in philosophy (135d). Parmenides encouraged that advancement for one reason only: he had closely observed Socrates' philosophic reasoning on at least two occasions and had judged that he was a young inquirer worthy of being guided to the next steps — whether Socrates would be capable of using that guidance for further advancement Parmenides left entirely to him. In the *Phaedo*, Socrates, having closely observed Cebes' uses of philosophy, stops at just that point where Parmenides had guided *him* to the way forward, to also positing "is not." And the gymnastic training that Parmenides chose to set out for the young Socrates reveals, if only through the most careful and patient practice, that systematically positing "is not" generates the most radical philosophic negations, skeptical conclusions about the knowability of beings and about the existence of the commonly supposed peak of the hierarchy of beings. Parmenides gave the young Socrates the means, puzzlingly difficult though they be, to reason himself forward to radical conclusions that he can prove himself worthy of only by attaining. The autobiographical display of his becoming that Socrates is offering Cebes and that his Iolaus will retell to whoever will listen stands in need of supplement for one audience only, the philosophically driven.

In the *Phaedo* Socrates now moves on to a direct setting out for Cebes of

---

96. Socrates introduced *eidē* into his argument on recollection at 73a, d, and when he mentioned the equal *itself* (74a), Simmias reacted, saying, "By Zeus, we certainly shall claim that, wondrously so" (74b). Socrates employed forms while speaking with Cebes at 79a-d, with Cebes himself contributing to the argument by introducing the form visible (79b6).

"the form of the cause with which I busied myself," namely, transcendent forms (100b), "busied myself" being a neutral term that does not betray any particular stance toward those forms. The action he had briefly described of positing hypotheses he now enfolds into "those much babbled-about things," the forms, and he says he takes his "beginning from them," thus making the forms, already familiar to Cebes, his alleged beginning point, what he "puts down as hypothesis," hypothesizing that "there is some beautiful itself by itself and a good and a big and all the others."[97] *Are* there such forms? He says to Cebes, "If you give me those and grant that they are, I hope, from them, to show you the cause and to discover how soul is something deathless" (100c). That is exactly what Cebes wants most, proof from a philosopher he honors that his soul is deathless: of course he says, "By all means, take it as given, don't let that stop you from finishing the account." Socrates asks Cebes to grant a second point: whether he is of the same opinion as Socrates "about what comes next after" positing forms: "If anything else is beautiful besides the beautiful itself, it's not beautiful because of any other single thing but this: because it participates in that beautiful. . . . Do you grant such a cause?" Cebes grants that too, and because he grants both points — that transcendent forms are and that participation in them is the sole cause of particulars having the qualities they have — Socrates can continue with his account, having eliminated all other kinds of cause, "those wise ones" (100d).[98] Socrates can put those other kinds of cause completely aside in his display speech because of Cebes' willingness, based on his hope that by these means Socrates will prove that his soul is deathless and imperishable.[99]

Positing forms as cause is the final step in his autobiography that Socrates reports in the *Phaedo*. And it is here that the biographical report in the *Parmenides* maps most arrestingly onto the autobiography in the *Phaedo*, for in turning to forms here in the *Phaedo* Socrates alleges an unbroken continuity in his talk about them: forms "are the very thing I've never stopped

97. Socrates had referred to forms of beautiful and good earlier (74d) and spoke of "babbling" about them (76d); he earlier spoke of the poets "babbling" about the things of sight and hearing (65b).

98. As Sebell says, "The concession to dogmatism, to irrationality is startling" (*Socratic Turn*, 121) — though not for Cebes.

99. As commentators have suggested, the distinction Socrates makes between forms and the things that participate in them resembles the Kantian distinction between concepts and percepts, between the sorting actions of the mind into kinds or classes and the seemingly passive reception of individual entities and events by the senses, which are themselves subject to the categorizings of mind. See Stern, *Socratic Rationalism*, 119–20, 112–13; and Sebell, *Socratic Turn*, 109–10.

talking about at other times and in the account that's just occurred as well"
(100b). But in his *Parmenides* Plato portrayed a proud, swaggering nineteen-
year-old Socrates announcing that his view of forms — precisely the forms
as set out in the *Phaedo*[100] — is the solution to the problems of the one and
the many made so prominent by the famous Parmenides and his famous
follower Zeno. The Athenian who was the host for these philosophers in
Athens, the man who memorized the whole exchange in order to preserve
it, thought Parmenides and Zeno would be angered by his young countryman's performance, but he noticed them exchanging frequent glances with
one another and "smiling as if admiring him" (*Parmenides* 130a). Admire
him they did, as Parmenides told him directly, speaking up for the first
time in the dialogue (130b). The smiles of Parmenides and Zeno and the
admiration Parmenides expressed show that this, exactly this, is what their
writings were intended to do: provoke a gifted young inquirer to face up
to the problems of perception that philosophic inquiry uncovers, like the
problem of the one and the many, and to try to solve those problems with
inventive solutions like the one young Socrates had just advanced. It was
not the solution, transcendent forms, that they admired: after expressing
his admiration of Socrates, Parmenides mercilessly destroyed that view
with a battery of well-thought-out and increasingly devastating arguments
that suggest that he too had once entertained this possible solution. Socrates tried to counter Parmenides' arguments but soon saw that they were
both rational and unanswerable. After bringing his arguments to their
most arresting conclusion, Parmenides looked to young Socrates' reaction,
seeing to it that he not leave him bereft but encourage him to keep at it.
Socrates' reaction confirmed his philosophic disposition: he was not cast
into despair at being deprived of his vaunted solution but instead, clearly
in awe of old Parmenides' keenness of insight and mastery of argument,
asked for help when Parmenides suggested that he needed more training. And Parmenides provided help — the gymnastic exercises that, when
memorized, practiced, tenaciously worked through, could lead Socrates, if
he proved able, to the proper way of understanding beings, or more exactly,
to the proper way of understanding understanding, the knowledge Socrates would eventually use as a public trademark: knowledge of ignorance,
which put positively is knowledge of the nature of knowing.

In his *Parmenides* Plato shows Parmenides destroying the young Socrates' view of the forms that in his *Phaedo* he shows Socrates still advocating fifty years later and using in the last argument of his life. Plato's *Par-*

100. As I will show in detail when I treat Socrates' speech in the *Parmenides*.

menides does not *simply* contradict Plato's *Phaedo*; instead, the way Socrates advocates the forms in the *Phaedo* shows just how to interpret the massive contradiction Plato set up by his two treatments of Socrates at nineteen. What Socrates says to Cebes about forms advances his already initiated intention of destroying for him the kind of cause employed in natural and mathematical science. Danger and safety rule Socrates' *epideixis*; Cebes and the rest can be spared misology by assigning cause to transcendent forms. Transcendent forms belong to the politics of philosophy.

Setting these passages in Plato's *Phaedo* alongside parallel passages in Plato's *Parmenides* — doing what Plato's prominent chronological indicators in these dialogues suggests be done — shows that the way to understand Socrates' definitive view of the forms is not to compare the forms in the *Phaedo* to the forms in the *Republic*, say. Socrates' final view of forms is found in the *Parmenides* and — the chronological ordering suggests — their political utility is found in both the *Phaedo* and the *Republic*. In the *Phaedo* the forms are a teaching intended to be the stopping point for Cebes and all the rest who, in great relief, embrace it as true. It is in fact only useful in showing that philosophy of a certain kind can prove to the satisfaction of Cebes and the others that the soul is deathless and imperishable, and save them from misology. A similar use of the forms is central to the *Republic*, the dialogue that chronologically marks the occasion, thirty years earlier than the *Phaedo*, on which Socrates introduced them as his public teaching. There, the forms are useful to Socrates for persuading Glaucon and the rest that there is a secure foundation for justice, for the life of moral decency that they want to live, but only if they can believe that it is rationally grounded.[101] Montaigne said that with respect to philosophy's long-standing practice of veiled or exoteric writing Plato played that game with his cards pretty much on the table.[102] Plato put his cards on separate tables in the *Parmenides* and the *Phaedo* in order to communicate a salient fact about Socrates' becoming: the irrational view refuted for him by Parmenides proved supremely useful in his maturity as part of his public defense of always suspicious inquiry.

After Cebes granted that the forms exist and that the cause of all events and qualities in the particulars is participation in forms, Socrates says that he is no longer able to recognize the other causes, "the wise ones" (100d).

101. For the significance of Plato's chronological placement of the *Republic* in 429, shortly after Socrates' return from his two-and-a-half-year absence with the Athenian army besieging Potidaea, see my *How Philosophy Became Socratic*.

102. Montaigne, *Essays*, ii.12; "Apology for Raymond Sebond," trans. Frame, 379.

He makes an example of himself: if someone tried to explain to him why a thing is beautiful by referring to color or shape or anything else of that sort, "I bid farewell to all that, because I'm shaken up by all these things." Is Socrates ever "shaken up" (*taratto*) by an attempt to explain cause? *Taratto* in all its other uses in the *Phaedo* describes what others experience but he does not.[103] Feigning being shaken up by an argument, Socrates shows what those who are shaken up by arguments should do: hold close to themselves, "simply and artlessly and perhaps naively, . . . that nothing makes a thing beautiful but its communion with that beautiful itself"—simple, artless, and naive is an artful way for Odyssean Socrates to describe himself. Similarly, he states that he holds tight to this view of cause without being able to say how participation occurs: "however and in whatever way you say it happens; as for that, I don't yet make any assertion."[104] Could Socrates *not care* about his inability to explain participation? When Parmenides questioned him in his youth about his view of forms it was precisely the puzzles of participation that Parmenides raised as his first two objections to the view: if Socrates used participation in forms to explain the just, beautiful, and good things, then logic compelled him to use participation in more problematic cases and posit forms for humans or fire or water (130b-c), and for "hair and mud and dirt" (130d). Parmenides went on to raise an even more telling objection to participation: logic requires Socrates to *extend* his positing of a form to explain a thing's qualities: to explain the likeness between a particular and its form he must posit their participation in another

---

103. Phaedo was "shaken up" by the blended experience of pleasure and pain that he and the others had during the conversations on Socrates' last day (59b); Socrates by contrast spoke in his first reported speech of the "wondrous" (*thaumasiōs*) relatedness of pleasure and pain (60b), which he then explained. Socrates reported that the soul of the "true philosopher" is "shaken up" by the close relation between soul and body (66a and 79c)—as he himself never was. Socrates speaks of Cebes being "shaken up" by the failure of the previous arguments to meet the objection Cebes then raised (86e). And, most tellingly, Phaedo reported that the whole company was "shaken up" by the persistent objections of Simmias and Cebes (88c), whereas Socrates clearly was not. Finally, after Socrates set aside a late objection that threatened his whole argument, he sought assurance that the objection did not "shake up" Cebes, and Cebes assures him it did not but that many other things do "shake me up" (103c).

104. Stern lists other times that Socrates uses the word "assertion" (*diiskhurizomai*): earlier he said he would not assert with certainty the account he was about to give of what awaited him in the next world (63c2); later he will say that the myth he just told about the fate of the souls in the next world could not be asserted with certainty (114d) (*Socratic Rationalism*, 123). Burnet says that the phrase Socrates used—"however and in whatever way you say [participation] happens"—is the formulaic phrase that "arose from fear that the gods [might] be addressed by the wrong name" (*Phaedo*, at 100d6).

form and so on infinitely (132a-b). In the *Parmenides* Socrates' inability to explain participation is part of the reasoning that forces him to abandon transcendent forms. In the *Phaedo*, however, Socrates makes his inability to explain how participation works a model: Cebes and the rest should not let their inability to explain it bother them—it doesn't bother *him*. Unable to make a definite assertion about just how participation works, Socrates does assert "that it's by the beautiful that all beautiful things are beautiful" (100e), and he says why he asserts that: "because that seems to me to be the safest way to answer both for myself and another." Safety, not truth, is the only criterion Socrates applies, and he applies it repeatedly. Is *safe* also *true*? Socrates seems to take as given that what he advocates as safe Cebes will understand as true.

"Safe for both myself and another"—the Socrates who says that is the Socrates who will be executed in a few hours. His sitting there and conversing is a demonstration of how unsafe philosophy proved to be even for him, the philosopher who had been advocating transcendent forms for thirty years. How safe is that view? Socrates, hero and model though he is, is nevertheless a singularity; Plato's *Apology of Socrates* and its attendant dialogues, *Euthyphro* and *Meno*, show that the complex mix of practices, particularly with respect to politics, that Socrates engaged in across many decades of a public life in Athens were the true causes of his execution despite his advocacy of a safe view of cause. Sitting there and knowing why he is being executed, inviting it even, Socrates can converse about transcendent forms as the safe view for those acquainted with philosophy, both the rare genuine philosopher like himself and those like Cebes and Simmias and the rest who amuse themselves with philosophy as a tool for confirming what they already believe. The history of Western philosophy with its long dominance by Platonism as a public philosophy shows that Socrates was not wrong about philosophy's safety.

Socrates then describes for Cebes and the rest a very odd way to treat philosophic debate: "By holding tight to this," he says, "I think I won't fall down but it will prove safe for myself and for anyone else to answer that beautiful things are beautiful by the beautiful." Holding tight in order not to fall down is the opposite stance, as the *Parmenides* shows, to that of an inquirer like Socrates toward a hypothesis however dear: in that barely saved access to the young Socrates, instead of holding tight to the forms he is so proud of, he abandoned them immediately upon being shown their illogic by Parmenides. In the *Phaedo*, however, looking to the safe view, Socrates asks Cebes with respect to holding on tight, "Or doesn't that seem so to you?" When Cebes answers, "It does seem so," he could be thought to be conceding only that, yes, it seems safe, while withholding judgment about whether it's a proper stance toward a proposed explanation of cause. And the same could be thought about his response to Socrates' subsequent questions: he assents to the safety of what Socrates advocates but not to its truth. However, at the end of Socrates' presentation, Cebes and Simmias answer in unison that "what you say is very true" (102a), and in the only argument left in the dialogue, Cebes will hold tight to transcendent forms as cause in proving his soul deathless: he does in fact hold tight to Socrates' safe way as the truth.

With forms as the sole explanation of cause Socrates shows Cebes how he can simply rule out, one by one, each of the instances of cause he had introduced earlier, both the ones that he "used to think" (96d-e) and those that he doesn't allow himself to assert now (96e–97b): "You would not allow it if someone should claim that one man's bigger than another by a head and that the smaller man's small by this very same thing but you'd call gods and men to witness that you're not going to say anything else but this" (100e–101a) — and he dictates the formula Cebes is to use: everything big is big by the form bigness, and everything small by the form smallness. And he ratchets up the fear factor: "I suppose you'd be terrified that some contrary argument would come at you if you claimed someone's bigger or smaller by a head." The terror lies in puzzles like a thing's being bigger or smaller "by the same thing," or "the bigger being bigger" by something small: "It's surely a monstrosity that something be big by something small" (101b). At this point he asks, "Or wouldn't you be terrified by these things?" Bursting into laughter, Cebes says, "I sure would." His laugh seems to betray his sense that Socrates' emphasis on fear is comic and inappropriate for settling the philosophic issue of cause. But Socrates simply continues, running through his previous puzzlements about mathematical or scientific explanations of cause. Cebes "would be terrified to assert that ten things are more than eight by two" (96e) and instead would say it is by "multitude," and he would be terrified to assert that "the double foot is bigger than the single one by half but not by bigness" (96e). "For I suppose there's the same terror." "Of course," Cebes says in his last comment before Socrates' long speech brings his presentation of the safe way to its end and Cebes judges it all "very true."

Having spoken of *terror* three times, Socrates adds a different action to how Cebes is to respond: "When a one has been added to a one or divided up" Cebes would beware of saying that addition or division is the cause of its becoming two (cf. 96e–97a) and instead "would *shout* that you don't know any other way each thing comes into being except by participating in the particular being of each form that it participates in." To terror and shouting he adds a third action: "You'd bid farewell to such dividings and addings and other such fancy stuff leaving them to others wiser than you." Young Cebes, trained in a Pythagorean school, is told by Socrates to fear, shout down, and abandon the most basic operations of mathematics and the most fundamental explanations of cause offered by natural science. Instead, "in fright at your own shadow, as the saying goes [you would] hold tightly to the safe hypothesis and answer" as Socrates just did, clinging to the form (101d).[105]

But oddly, Socrates then introduces the proper response to someone else clinging to a hypothesis: "If, on the other hand, someone should hold tightly to the hypothesis taken all by itself, you'd bid him farewell" (101d). *This* holding tight to the hypothesis and bidding farewell is different from the one Socrates just pictured: there, you bid farewell to other explanations of cause, "leaving them to others wiser than you" and hold onto the safe hypothesis that posits a transcendent form (101c8–d2). Here, you bid farewell to a person who holds onto the hypothesis "taken all by itself."[106] This is not a farewell to other ways of explaining cause but to a person who fails to apply the method of hypothesis properly because he simple holds onto his posited hypothesis—and does nothing more. In the presence of such a person, Socrates says, what you are to do is bid *him* farewell in order to think the hypothesis through on your own. Bidding farewell in this case means engaging in a private consideration of the adequacy of that hypothesis, examining for yourself "the things that spring forth from the posited hypothesis" in order to determine if those things "are consonant or dissonant with one another." This whole situation is different: terror is gone, there's no shouting—and no mention of transcendent forms. Instead, in the quiet solitude of your own fearless thinking you carry on a conversation with yourself—the dialogic monologue, it seems, that Socrates in the *Theaetetus* defined as the essence of thinking (189e–190a). Unobtrusively, and beginning with a confusing repetition of stubborn holding

---

105. Xenophon shows Socrates making a similar effort to steer young men attracted by philosophy away from mathematical or scientific explanations of cause. "The 'What is . . .' questions are meant to dispose of the questions regarding the 'material and efficient causes' of the natural species" (Strauss, *Xenophon's Socratic Discourse*, 98). And Xenophon's Socrates directs his auditors to what Strauss called a "teleotheology," a view that the gods govern human and earthly things and direct them to ends that are good. See my *Enduring Importance of Leo Strauss*, 97–101.

106. This move on Socrates' part has been taken by some commentators to be simply a contradiction: first he says, cling to the hypothesis; then he says, don't. See the discussions in Burnet, *Phaedo*, at 101d1–3; Gallop, *Phaedo*, 188–91, 235n67; and Stern, *Socratic Rationalism*, 125–27. I use some of Stern's wording in the translations here.

onto a hypothesis, Socrates seems to have inserted into his display speech for Cebes a brief indication of the proper procedure after the turn to the logoi and the positing of a hypothesis: here, a private dialectical method of hypothesizing posits a plausible hypothesis, and examines what the hypothesis implies in search of possible contradictions that it might either generate or presuppose. Only here does Socrates suggest, and then only inferentially, what he left unspoken when he first described how he launched himself (100a): a criterion for *might* in a hypothesis. And he supplies the next step too: "And should you have to give an account of that hypothesis itself" — *have to*: the compulsion stems from the private examination of the hypothesis, not from some other person — "You'd give it in the same way, by hypothesizing in turn another hypothesis, whichever of the higher ones appeared best" — where higher seems to mean more general, and appearing best requires the same examination for consonance and dissonance (101d5–7). You would follow this process "until you came to something sufficient" (101e1). What constitutes sufficiency? It can only be provisional completion of the examination already described, for Socrates does not say anything more but instead turns to what you would *not* do. Does sufficiency ascend to some comprehensive claim like the form of the good that Socrates taught Glaucon to affirm in the *Republic*? Nothing in Socrates' brief account in the *Phaedo* account suggests it, perhaps because nothing in this account of privately positing and examining hypotheses suggests positing transcendent forms — or a form of forms.[107]

At the end of his exhibition speech, replete with commands directing Cebes to a non-philosophic holding onto the safe way, Socrates thus returns to what he said first in his report on how he launched himself in turning to the logoi, the positing of a hypothesis and the examination of it (100a). At its end as at its beginning Socrates' report supplies brief pointers to the authentic method of dialectic, incomplete but seeds planted perhaps, meant to arrest one of those trained to shout in fear that transcendent forms are the only cause. Such brief pointers could suggest to such a person that the shouted forms doctrine is different from the quietly held method that one who had bid farewell to simply holding on could apply in his solitude with a view to arriving at a more satisfactory understanding of cause. That the guidance here is incomplete can be recognized most easily by turning to what Parmenides told Socrates to do fifty years earlier, if only after testing him: "Do not only investigate the results of a hypothesis if each hypothe-

107. I thus agree with Sebell in interpreting 101d3–102a as an intimation of Socrates' genuine method (*Socratic Turn*, 127–32). See also Stern, *Socratic Rationalism*, 128.

sized thing is, but also hypothesize that this same thing is not" (*Parmenides* 135e). Hypothesizing "is not" leads, in the dialectic gymnastic, to a more adequate understanding of forms and thereby also of cause, but even with the guidance he does give, a Parmenides leaves its steps and its consequences for a Socrates to figure out. As for form and the character of form as cause, they remain crucial to Socrates' becoming, not form as he babbled about it but form as Parmenides' gymnastic guided him to think about it.

Socrates ends his display speech by telling Cebes not to do what the "debaters" (*antilogikoi*) do.[108] They "jumble together the beginning and what emerges out of it" (101e1–3). As a result, "for them, perhaps, this isn't a matter of the least thought (*logos*) or concern; their wisdom enables them to mix everything together, yet still be pleased with themselves." Twice in his description of what not to do Socrates tells Cebes what would qualify him to be a genuine inquirer compared to the *antilogikoi*: "if you wanted to discover something about the things that are (*to onta*, 101e3)" and "if in fact you are one of the lovers of wisdom (*philosophoi*)" (101e6). If you meet those two conditions, Socrates says to end his whole display speech, "you would, I think, do as I say" (102a). Does Cebes meet those conditions? Does he truly want to discover the things that are and thereby exhibit that he is one of the philosophers? If so, he will do as Socrates said at both the very end and the very beginning of his description of how he launched himself. But doubts have been raised about Cebes' being driven primarily by a drive to know, doubts confirmed by his response to Socrates' final argument: he will hold tight to the transcendent forms the argument depends upon and not examine them; he will be persuaded by Socrates' final proof of the deathlessness of his soul even though the argument is flawed in a way that can be seen by anyone who placed rational rigor above the need for a proof of his soul's indestructibility.

When Socrates ends his display speech Cebes and Simmias together express their emphatic affirmation: "What you say is very true." Their affirmation draws in Echecrates for the second and last time: starting again with an oath he says, "By Zeus, Phaedo, a reasonable reply." Phaedo has now done what Echecrates asked him to do when he intervened the first time — he has gone "through everything for us as precisely as you can" (88e), and he has as well answered the question Echecrates asked, "How

---

108. Socrates previously spoke of the *antilogikoi* when describing "the art of arguments" and the great danger in practicing argument without that art: one could end up like the *antilogikoi*, who think they are "the wisest of men and that they alone have detected that there's nothing sound or stable" (90b-c).

did he do it?" He did it as a Heraklean general turning around his dispir-
ited army of those who take themselves to be philosophic but are ready
to despair at argument if it cannot prove the immortality of their souls.
With trust in reason restored through his appeal to irrational transcendent
forms Socrates can continue in the way Echecrates describes, thinking it
the highest praise: "For it seems wonderful to me how lucid that man made
all this, even to someone who didn't have much of a mind." Precisely. What
Echecrates finds wonderful is in fact an essential tool of a philosopher's
exotericism: Socrates made the mysteries of being easy to understand by
those who lack a philosopher's mind.[109]

The final exchange between Phaedo and Echecrates brings unanimity
in Athens and Phlia to the relief at being cured by Socrates' efforts. "Of
course, Echecrates, and so it seemed to all who were present," says Phaedo.
"And to us too who were absent but are listening right now," Echecrates
replies. Believing in the lucidity of the forms whose irrational implications
Parmenides demonstrated to Socrates fifty years earlier, the turned army
can now trust an argument based on forms that Socrates will give, believing with Cebes that it proves their souls immortal. No further reports on
the Phlia audience will be given, but the avowed universality of agreement
in the cell will be contradicted, quietly enough, when someone, "I don't
remember who," Phaedo says, speaks up to raise a fundamental objection
at the beginning of Socrates' final argument.

Socrates' long pause to consider how best to answer Cebes' objection (95e) can now be seen to be his preparation for a complex answer:
he told the tale of his becoming in order to set out the double rationale
for transcendent forms, which he had already successfully employed that
day. Transcendent forms replace — for all but the most driven inquirers —
philosophy's dangerous search for some material or efficient Atlas that
could account for all causal events in nature; the few philosophers know
that form will have to be accounted for in some more adequate way. And
transcendent forms help replace the gods, the dying Homeric gods, by giving an Atlas-like understanding of a mind-full, end-directing cause of all
things, believably edifying and community serving — and thereby a service
to philosophy itself.[110]

---

109. The word translated "lucid" in Echecrates' sentence is *enargōs*, whose root is *argos*
(shining, bright), a fitting Greek word in that it names a clarity in visibility without implying
the rational rigor English implies by "lucid."

110. Socrates' most extensive observation of the death of the Homeric gods and his
action of replacing them with moral gods — and quasi-divine transcendent forms — is in the
Republic; see my *How Philosophy Became Socratic*, 286–89, 402–3.

Plutarch understood what it meant for Socrates to provide a shelter for a science of nature, and he could report the success of the Platonic strategy four centuries later.[111] He set his report in a telling context: the superstition of the Athenian general Nicias. As leader of the Athenian expeditionary force in Sicily, Nicias refused to escape with his army from its exposed position after a battle because an eclipse of the moon seemed to him an ominous divine sign — Nicias's superstition led directly to the final disaster for the Athenian expedition, the annihilation of the army and of the fleet supporting it. Saying first that it was Anaxagoras who "put in writing the clearest and boldest of all doctrines about the eclipse of the moon," Plutarch says that the Athenians could not tolerate such reduction of divine agency to "blind forces and necessary events" and consequently persecuted the philosophers, of whom he names Protagoras, Anaxagoras, and Socrates. But the Athenian persecution of philosophers came to an end: "The radiant reputation of Plato, because of the life he led and because he subjected the compulsions of the physical world to divine and more sovereign principles, took away the infamy of such doctrines as theirs and gave their science free course among all people" —*free course*, that is, sheltered within the pious exterior Plato supplied.[112] Plato saved Greek natural philosophy by seeming to subject natural necessity to divine causes.[113]

Writing late in the first century CE and at the opening of the second, Plutarch attests to the success of the Platonic Socrates' strategy for philosophy as viewed from a standpoint in the Roman Empire some five centuries after Socrates' death and two centuries before Christianity came to rule the Roman polity.[114] Plutarch attributes that success to Plato, Plato who chose to present Socrates as a model in the *Phaedo*: an exemplary life could be modeled on the heroic life Socrates lived to his last moment, with his apparent or exoteric subjection of strictly natural causes to divine principles. Socrates' safe way for Cebes and company, already being carried abroad by Phaedo shortly after Socrates' death, turned out to be the

111. For the purposes of this book I ignore here as elsewhere the distinction between Socrates and Plato in order to speak simply of the Platonic Socrates. Any such distinction depends on comparing Plato's Socrates with the Socrates of Xenophon, Aristotle, and Aristophanes and on distinguishing within Plato's dialogues Socratic and Platonic elements.

112. Plutarch, *Nicias* 23. Strauss referenced Plutarch's account in *On Tyranny*, 206. According to Benardete, this is one of only three references in all of extant ancient literature that refers to "the principles of Platonic writing" (*Argument of the Action*, 407), principles that were known and as a result not widely publicized.

113. David Bolotin shows that Aristotle employed a similar strategy in his physics and cosmology; see *An Approach to Aristotle's "Physics."*

114. Plutarch's dates are commonly given as 46 to 119+ CE.

historically successful safe way for philosophy within Greek and Roman civilization. That strategy of the Platonic Socrates held for some seven centuries, giving natural science space to proceed and giving the social order a teleological, gods-directed cosmos within which moral virtue could appeal to firm, unchanging foundations.

But viewed from a standpoint in northern Europe some seventeen and a half centuries after Plutarch that success looked very different to Nietzsche. Plutarch's report with its two facets of morality and cosmology/ontology accords well with Nietzsche's view of the transformative effect of Socrates and Plato on Greek morality and Greek philosophy except that what Plutarch praised Nietzsche blamed. Nietzsche judged the strategic success of Socrates and Plato in Western culture after the millennium and a half during which Christianity rose to absolute power and then suffered decay, Christianity being what Nietzsche called "Platonism for the people."[115] What was praiseworthy to a philosopher in a Roman world little touched by Christianity became blameworthy to a philosopher in a European civilization infused with the values of Christianity but in the process of abandoning belief in the Christian tale of redemption—a time of the death of God, and in that regard not unlike the time of Socrates. A Nietzschean history of philosophy employs the art of reading that Plato will show Socrates learning in the *Parmenides* as part of his philosophic education. Read with the help of that art and its distinction between exoteric and esoteric, well known to Nietzsche,[116] the history of Western philosophy comes to light as a sequence of culturally transformative events in which philosophers intervened with history-making teachings on behalf of the well-being of philosophy in the world. The most transformative philosophic event within Christianized Platonism was the reintroduction of a public science of nature by Francis Bacon and René Descartes in particular, a reintroduction made advisable by the Europe-wide wars of the Christian sects that threatened to end the renaissance of Greek and Roman thought and practice. Their Plato-informed advancement of learning made inexorably public the natural science that the Platonic Socrates had found it necessary to shelter within a teaching of moral gods and transcendent forms.[117] The philosophic strategy for science adopted by the early modern philosophers required that they explicitly attack the Socratics Plato and

---

115. *Beyond Good and Evil*, Prologue.

116. *Beyond Good and Evil*, §30.

117. On the transformative role of Bacon and Descartes, see my *Nietzsche and Modern Times*.

Aristotle and openly advocate the advancement of natural science, making science one of the chief instruments with which to fulfill their intention of crushing imperial Christianity, which had come to rule even philosophy.[118]

As for the *Phaedo*, it presents the first stage of Socrates' philosophic education as a turn to the logoi and then, apparently immediately after that, an embrace of transcendent forms as the timeless cause of the beautiful and good, and of the big and small and the one and two, leaving no apparent place for an actual science of nature, dangerous as it is to piety. Those two steps of philosophic development described by Socrates in the *Phaedo* as the essentials of his philosophic autobiography appear again in the *Parmenides*, where a nineteen-year-old Socrates believes he can refute Parmenides and Zeno on the basis of his turn to the logoi and the transcendent forms. But Parmenides' response to young Socrates' refutation proves that what Socrates presented of his turn or his second sailing in the *Phaedo* was in fact only a first stage. Socrates moved on, driven forward by Parmenides' refutation of transcendent forms and, decisively, by Parmenides' gift of a deeply challenging gymnastic that could train him in philosophy if he proved able to understand it. The *Parmenides* shows that the first stage of Socrates' philosophic education in the *Phaedo* was of permanent importance as a turn to the logoi, but as a turn to transcendent forms it proved to be a false step, although one that became useful in his subsequent philosophic life, useful in its seeming to be true to Cebes and his like. That aspect of the first stage of Socrates' philosophic education could become the last stage of theirs.

6. Odyssean Socrates Ends His Life of Argument

The chief fascination of the last argument of Socrates' life for a chronological reading of the dialogues is its dependence on the forms that Parmenides refuted for him fifty years earlier. But the argument is also note-

---

118. Nietzsche's most extended indictment of Christianity for its effect on Greek and Roman science is found in *Antichrist*, §§59–60: it cheated us out of the harvest of ancient culture where "all the presuppositions of a scientific culture, all scientific *methods*, were already there; the great and incomparable art of reading well had already been established — that presupposition for the tradition of culture, for the unity of science." As for Nietzsche's criticism of Socrates and Plato, he followed the philological convention making Socrates responsible for the reduction of philosophy to moral counsel in the Socratic schools and Plato responsible for the theological cosmology that prepared the way for Christianity; e.g. *Beyond Good and Evil*, §§190–91; *Twilight of the Idols*, "How the True World Finally Became a Fable."

worthy for the objections raised and not raised against it: an unidentified person in the cell and then a someone Socrates invents object to it underway, but when Cebes ends it no one objects despite an obvious objection. Both the *Parmenides* and the objections measure the last argument of Socrates' life and help to show that it is a model of Socrates' mature art of argument: even in private, even in the last hours of his life Socrates speaks with a view to consequences.

Socrates' last argument must counter Pythagorean Cebes' fear that his soul may eventually wear out and perish with its last body; it must show that his soul is both "deathless and imperishable," the two words that Cebes introduced early (88b) and that Socrates emphasized (95c). Socrates' argument carries those words through to its end (105b–106d), proving first that the soul is deathless and then ending when Cebes states his reason for not needing another argument to prove that his soul is also imperishable. There is no need to rehearse all the details of the last argument. Instead, I will concentrate on the role of transcendent forms and on the objections as models of how to object to the argument. As for Cebes' final satisfaction, it is a model of just who would find the argument successful and why.

The pedantic repetition and detail with which Socrates makes his first point leads him to say "with a smile, 'I seem to be even on the verge of book-speak'" (102d) — a remark worthy of a smile by a famous thinker about to die never having written a book but having learned profoundly from the books of others, a famous thinker now arguing with "Cadmus," the legendary Phoenician who introduced writing into Greece. He indulges in book-speak because he "wants the very thing that seems to me to be the case to seem so to you." Book-speak characterizes his whole argument with its frequent repetitions and its exhaustive examples: memorize this, Socrates says in effect, treat it as something you can always call on like a lesson in a book.

Socrates begins by introducing the key premise of his coming argument: the presence *in us* of the form. Instead of abiding the small, he says, the big in us will do one of two things: either "flee and get out of the way when its contrary, the small, advances toward it, or else it must already have perished" (102d-e). Either *get out of the way* or *perish* — this is the decisive distinction, stated twice more and then again after the argument is over (103d, 104c, 106e). Socrates generalizes what he wants Cebes to think, saying that none "among the contraries is willing . . . ever at the same time both to become and be its own contrary; instead, it either flees or else perishes in this experience" (103a). Cebes emphatically agrees — he thinks what Socrates wants him to think. But where Cebes agrees, an unnamed objector — "Who it was I don't remember for sure" — breaks in: "By the gods!" he says and calls attention to what looks to him like a contradiction, for he recalls the first argument (70d–72e), the curiously pre-Socratic argument that dealt with "all things that have a becoming" (70e), just as the argument Socrates is now launching deals with "generation and destruction as a whole" (95e). "By the gods," he says, "wasn't what we agreed to in the previous arguments the very contrary of what's now being said?" (103a). He summarizes Socrates' earlier argument: "Wasn't it that the bigger comes to be out of the littler and the littler out of the bigger and, simply, that this is the coming-to-be for contraries — out of contraries?" He ends his outburst forcefully, concluding, "But now it seems to me it's being said that this could never come to be."

Socrates and the nameless objector seem especially attentive to one another, for Phaedo says that each "listened" to the other (103a4, 11) and that Socrates turned his head toward the objector and afterward looked back to Cebes (103a, c). Socrates singles out the objector by congratulating him for the "manly" way in which he recalls what had been said (103b), linking the objector's manliness to his ability to recollect: he kept in mind what had been said before,[119] and he is willing to strain against Socrates (91c) by daring to say in the most forthright way that he is guilty of contradicting himself. Just by breaking in, the manly objector exhibits his singularity, for after Simmias and Cebes very gingerly raised their earlier objections (84c-d), Phaedo reported that "all" in the cell fell immediately into despair at argument (88c-e). For someone to object now, the sun that much lower in the sky, and to object after Socrates successfully rallied his fleeing army and called on them to hold on tight to the form and shout down opposition, shows that Socrates is not the only exception in the cell to Phaedo's statement that "all" were shaken up by Simmias's and Cebes' objections — to object now calls for a manliness that looks to the validity of the argument, not to the fate of his soul.[120] Socrates must act quickly to forestall a renewed outbreak of collective despair at argument; he cannot do what he did when Simmias and Cebes objected — with a gentle smile invite them

---

119. So far in the final argument Socrates had twice used the word "opposite" (*enantion*), the word he used repeatedly in his first argument, and his first example in that first argument was also big and little (70e).

120. Helen Bacon notes "how much courage it takes at this moment to confront any weakness in the argument" ("Poetry of *Phaedo*," 155).

to ask whatever they wish in the time allotted (85b). No wonder Socrates turned his face toward the objector and looked straight at him: his singular manliness could ruin everything.

Socrates tells the objector, "You're not noticing the difference between what's being said now and what was said then." *Now* is after Socrates described his turn from the beings to the speeches and his use of transcendent forms as the only cause: "Then it was said that a contrary *thing* comes out of a contrary thing, but now it's being said that the contrary itself" — the form — "would never become contrary to itself." *Now* is also just after Socrates emphasized not just the form itself but the form in the thing, the bigness or smallness "in us." In his response to the objector Socrates focuses on that: "For then, dear friend,[121] we were speaking of things that have the contraries, and we named these things with the names of those contraries; but now we're speaking about those contraries themselves, which, being in the things named, give them their names." *In* the things named and *giving* them their names, yes, but in being in the things and giving them their names do the forms continue to share all the qualities supposed of the form itself? How does the form in us respond to the coming of *its* contrary? Does it flee? Or does it perish? That will be the issue to which this argument will remain vulnerable. Socrates' response to the objector says in effect, Pay close attention to the forms and the form in us. He ends his explanation for the objector by rewording the statement that had drawn his objection: "And we claim that those very contraries would never be willing to receive a coming-to-be from one another." So what will happen to the relevant contraries in us — the dying and the undying, the perishing and the unperishing? The manly objector, singular and fearless judge of arguments, will be measuring the last steps of the last argument and the role of forms.[122]

Having turned his head toward the manly objector for their whole exchange, Socrates then "looked hard at Cebes" and asked, "But you, Cebes, I suppose none of what this man said shook you up . . . did it?" (103c). He is right to be concerned about Cebes being *shaken up* — he used the

121. Socrates called Cebes "dear friend" at the end of the first argument (72c), the only other time he used the term.

122. There is a symmetry to all the arguments: the first (70d–72e) matches the last (both with Cebes), the second (73b–77e) the second last (both with Simmias), and the "argument" from the soul's nature or "the chants for children" (77e) with Cebes (78a–84b) is matched with the myth Socrates tells Simmias at the end of the day's arguments. The two arguments with Simmias make use of the same Socratic principle, recollection, whereas the two arguments with Cebes move from the "pre-Socratic" argument to Socrates' forms.

word for the condition that moved Cebes to state his objection (86e) and for the condition that befell the rest of the company when Simmias's and Cebes' objections robbed them of their trust in argument. By using that word here Socrates shows where the singularity of the manly objector lies: not shaken up, his intellect is alert to contradiction. Cebes confirms what Socrates invited as his reaction: "This is not my condition at this time, although I don't say that many matters don't shake me up" (103c). By glancing away and putting *this* question to Cebes, Socrates seems tacitly to tell the observant objector, That's enough; Cebes is satisfied; shaking him up with doubt about the argument is not desirable. As for objections, Socrates will state one himself at just the time and in just the way *he* wants.

Socrates can now resume the final argument of his life, continuing in a highly didactic manner—"Go back and recollect," he says at one point, "it does no harm to hear it often" (105a). He employs numerous examples, among them the forms hot and cold and the particulars fire and snow, which prove especially illuminating. Having set things up to his satisfaction Socrates initiates Cebes into the new way of answering by having Cebes "imitate" him in supplying the answer to questions Socrates poses (105b). Socrates can say that he will "now give an answer beyond the first one I spoke of, that safe one, because I see another safety coming out of what we're saying right now" (105b). The old safe way with transcendent forms as the only cause had rallied and sheltered those who despaired at argument in the cell and in Phlia, but to answer Cebes a new safe way is needed, a more refined way of considering forms with the focus placed on the form in us. To encourage Cebes to imitate him, Socrates mimes an exchange in which he answers Cebes' questions: "If you should ask me what comes to be in the body by which that body will be hot, I won't give that safe and unlearned answer and say that it's hotness; instead I'll give the fancier one coming out of what we're discussing just now and say that it's fire" (105c). With two additional examples Socrates sets up Cebes to follow him in rote imitation.

So begins the last series of questions Socrates will ever pose. He asks, "What comes to be in a body by which that body will be living?" Having constructed his question in the precise way in which he structured his examples, Socrates hears Cebes answer as a mimic: "It's soul." That is exactly right: Cebes is learning how to give the new safe answer, superior to the less fancy *aliveness* because it focuses on the way the form aliveness is in us—and it's *Cebes' soul* and its fate that count here. Socrates' next question secures the point that this is always the case and he can then ask: "Does soul always come on the scene bringing life to bear on whatever it itself occupies?" (105d). Cebes can answer, "Of course." And is there a contrary to life or not? "There is." Asked what that contrary is, Cebes naturally gives the one-word answer, "Death" (*thanatos*). Socrates can count on the previous examples when he then asks if "soul will absolutely never admit the contrary of what it always brings to bear on something." "That's surely the case," Cebes says. Socrates now prompts Cebes to a series of repeated negations, each of which employs the common Greek form of negation, an alpha-privative whereby the letter alpha placed in front of the word negates it; repeated negations using alpha privatives prepare the desired final negation. "Well, that which doesn't admit the idea of the even — what were we just now naming it?" "Uneven (*anartion*)," Cebes answers.[123] "And what doesn't admit the just, and what doesn't admit the musical?" — examples that Socrates had not used but that fit the pattern of negation that permit Cebes to answer with single words: "unmusical (*amouson*)," "unjust (*adikon*)" (105e). Finally Socrates asks the question toward which he has been building: "Alright, so what do we call whatever doesn't admit death?" Cebes answers with the only word possible, "Undeath (*athanaton*)," in English, "undying." "And soul doesn't admit death?" Socrates asks, insisting on repetition. "No," Cebes says. "The soul is undying," Socrates states. "Undying," Cebes repeats. Triumphant repetition of the word leads Socrates to a satisfied conclusion: "Alright, shall we claim that this has been demonstrated? Or how does it seem to you?" "Very sufficiently demonstrated indeed," Cebes says.

But to demonstrate that the soul is undying (*athanatos*) is not enough, and Socrates pushes on to the other matter requiring proof, that the soul is "imperishable" (*anōlethros*). Again, he is extremely didactic, running through a series of examples that follow the new safety, the "fancier" one — and are all counterfactual. "If it were necessary for the uneven to be imperishable" — though in fact, "the uneven is not imperishable" (106c3) — "would three things be anything but imperishable?" (106a). Cebes answers correctly, "Why of course not." Socrates' second example is the nicely telling one of snow: "If it were necessary that the unhot be imperishable as well, whenever anyone brought hot upon snow, wouldn't snow slip away safe and unmelted? For surely it wouldn't have perished, nor again would it have endured and admitted hotness." "What you say is true," Cebes answers, however hard it may be to picture snow slipping away safely escaping advancing heat. After the final example of the uncold with fire taking

---

123. "Just now" refers to Socrates employment of an alpha-privative negation just before he described his new safe way: "So threeness is uneven (*anartios*)" (104e5).

off and going, "safe and sound," Socrates turns to the undying: "Isn't it a necessity then, to talk that way about the undying? If the undying is also imperishable, it's impossible for soul to perish when death comes at it" (106b). And he runs briefly through his examples, this time omitting snow.

But right here Socrates interrupts his own argument and just before the end of his final argument does what he did so often on other days: supply a "someone" to raise an objection. The last objection ever to an argument by Socrates is raised by Socrates himself, raised in the midst of concerns about safety that he himself emphasized. It is a deeply radical objection this late in the day by an exemplary objector who remembers and adheres strictly to the agreements already arrived at: "'But,' someone might say, 'what prevents the odd, not from becoming even when the even comes at it—we agreed this couldn't happen—but rather from itself perishing when the even has come into being in its place?'" (106b-c) Socrates states the difficulty: "We wouldn't be in a position to contend with someone who made this point by saying that the odd doesn't perish, because the uneven isn't imperishable." And the same goes for the other examples: "If we had agreed on that, we could easily have contended that when the even came at them the odd and the three take off and go away. And we could have made this contention about fire and hot and the rest, couldn't we?" Called upon to give the obvious answer, Cebes acknowledges that if they had made that argument they could "certainly" contend that. So Socrates applies the point to the case that matters: "So now, concerning the undying: if we agree that the undying is also imperishable, then soul, in addition to being undying would be imperishable too. But if not, we'd need another argument"—they'd need it because of the deficiency in the argument for undying: for the soul in us, instead of "getting out of the way" by leaving the body and remaining intact, the soul in us, while being undying, could perish as the supplied objector contends, perish as snow does, for while always being unhot, it does not "get out of the way" at the approach of hot and remain intact as snow but perishes by melting into water. So Socrates rightly says to Cebes, "We'd need another argument"—the argument proving the undying is imperishable.

"But we don't need it," Cebes said (106d). And he knows why we don't or why *he* doesn't: "Because hardly anything else could fail to admit destruction if the undying, which is everlasting (*aidios*), will admit destruction." Cebes *knows* there are other things that fail to admit destruction, and Socrates jumps in, seemingly eager to identify the most obvious "anything else" that makes Cebes' response correct for the world of firm opinion in which he dwells: "And the god, I think, and the form itself of life—and anything else if it's undying — would be agreed by all never to perish." As he had from the beginning, Socrates assumes Cebes' piety, seeming to share it himself. *All* agree that the god is imperishable, and Socrates is careful to put his forms right there alongside the god. Cebes adds a touch of humor in what must be relief at feeling the argument to be over, the proof secured: "By all human beings of course, by Zeus, but even more, as I think, by the gods" — the immortals themselves agree they're imperishable. It is Socrates who affirms the necessary final extension to this cast of undying things: "Now, since the undying is also indestructible (*adiaphthoros*), what else could hold but that the soul, if it turns out to be undying would be imperishable as well?" (106e). "It is a great necessity," Cebes adds, attesting to his own assurance. Socrates provides the summary, using the vocabulary of his examples and the Pythagorean perspective in which Cebes and Simmias were raised: "Therefore, when death comes at a human being, his deathbound part, as is likely, dies, but his undying part takes off and goes away safe and undestroyed, having gotten out of death's way." He completes the picture with the traditional destination of the soul: "Therefore more than anything else, Cebes, it's the case that soul is an undying and imperishable thing and that our souls really will be in Hades" (107a).[124]

In the final argument of his life Socrates accedes to the piety that had been a part of the Homeric and Pythagorean training of young Simmias and Cebes: he's satisfied when they're satisfied. And Cebes expresses full satisfaction, saying he does not "in any way distrust our arguments." *Trust* is what makes him satisfied. He calls attention to their situation late on Socrates' last day: "But if Simmias here or anyone else has something to say, he'd do well not to remain silent — I don't know to what better occasion someone could put off the discussion than the one before us right now." Simmias speaks and speaks of his trust: "I'm certainly not in a position to be at all distrustful any longer about what's being argued." Yet Simmias congratulates himself for withholding full assent: because of "the bigness of what our arguments are about and because I hold our human weakness in dishonor," he is compelled "to have some lingering distrust within myself about what's been said" (107b). But Simmias has shown himself to be less rigorous than Cebes and willing to raise silly objections (76d) — the

---

124. There is humor in the agonies expressed over this final argument by Plato scholars who believe that it is *Plato's* argument and not the argument his Socrates constructs for his Cebes. Robert Hackforth, for example, says: "It is only if we allow that the appeal is to faith that we can avoid deep disappointment in this matter, inasmuch as from the standpoint of logic the argument has petered out into futility" (*Plato's "Phaedo,"* 164).

dishonor in which he holds human weakness including his own ensures that he will continue to trust this argument for the same reason Cebes will: he knows the gods are undying and imperishable.

Socrates, even at the end, proves himself different, for while assenting to what Simmias said, he is willing to add that "our very first hypotheses, even if to all of you they are trustworthy, must nevertheless be looked into for greater surety." At the end of his life of argument Socrates invites inquiry into their first hypotheses — the hypothesizing of transcendent forms (101d). He is careful to point to limits in possible inquiry: "If you sort them out sufficiently, you will, as I think, be following up the argument as much as it's possible for a human being to follow it." Socrates well knows the limits on possible human inquiry into the nature of things for Parmenides led him to that knowledge decades ago. Socrates' life of arguments comes to an end with this: "And should this very thing become sure" — should their first hypotheses prove trustworthy to them — "you'll search no further." To search no further is to be done with philosophy; trust in Socrates' arguments for forms replaces philosophy for the trusting. Socrates anticipates that his audience of trusters in philosophy will continue to regard themselves as philosophers — they will employ the safety devices he supplied them with — but the "philosophy" they trust in will be only a showy residue of philosophy that comforts them as it comforts those exposed to it.

But what of the manly objector? Why didn't he speak up when Cebes invited anyone with doubts about the final argument to speak up? Perhaps he refrained from speaking up because he saw that Socrates himself had raised the fatal objection and then shown himself content with their trust in a flawed argument. If so, the manly objector doesn't speak up because he has learned to seem satisfied if Cebes is satisfied. Had he spoken up to insist on what Socrates made it possible to see, why they need another argument, Socrates would go to his death leaving his little company of followers experiencing the need for another argument, or, for almost all of them, shaken up and prone to a misology that would be terminal with no Socrates present to cure it. The silence of the unnamed manly objector suggests that his learned discretion now overrules his manliness. His silence completes the exemplary exoteric character of Socrates' final argument: knowing the need to stay silent, he in his singularity embodies the other audience of all of Socrates' arguments. Generated in the interests of philosophy to make philosophy safe both for its auditors and for the philosopher himself, Socratic rhetoric speaks to human beings as they are: for the most part they are like Simmias and Cebes and all the others present except one, vulnerable to misology if reason is unable to prove what they most need to be true. But Socrates' art of argument makes allowance for the presence of a singularity, one who is able to fearlessly follow the logic of the argument to its proper conclusion, one who learned that it belongs to that art of argument to maintain an edifying silence in the interests of a collective safety. Plato made Socrates' final argument a salutary use of forms proving the soul immortal, but he made it possible for a reader alert to objections to conclude that the form of the undying in us perishes, melts like snow, and as for the transcendent form of aliveness as its only cause, Plato made it possible for a reader to learn that Socrates has known since he was younger than Cebes that such forms are irrational.

So Who Might the Unnamed Manly Objector Be?

It is extremely odd for Phaedo to say he can't remember who the objector was: he can remember that Socrates moved his head to fix his eyes on that person and that after their exchange with one another he looked hard at Cebes. And he can remember what each said to the other. And his memory is almost infallible: his "narrative omniscience"[125] falters only rarely, here at the end and near the opening, just after he stated that Apollodorus was present and Echecrates asked him who else was present: he answered with a list that began with nine Athenians and ended with five non-Athenians. Between the nine and five, he said: "But Plato, I think, was sick" (59b10). While his "I think" expresses uncertainty, it clearly implies that Plato is not to be counted among the Athenians present because sickness forced him to be absent. Almost immediately after that Phaedo is again inexact about who was there and who was not: "Pretty much, I think, these were the ones present" (59c6).

But it would be an astounding absence. Plato, already thirty years old, Plato, who devoted his genius to the memory of Socrates, absent on what everyone who cared knew would be Socrates' last day? Plato allowed his name to appear in his dialogues on only one other occasion: a month earlier at Socrates' trial he had Socrates speak his name twice, confirming his presence at the trial (*Apology* 34a, 38c). And he was absent on the day of Socrates' death? Because he was, Phaedo thinks, *sick*? That Socrates declares Plato present at his trial is nothing to wonder at; his implied absence on Socrates' last day certainly is. I wonder, Is the unnamed manly objector Plato?

125. Burger, *Phaedo*, 14.

Of course, wondering about Plato's presence or absence on Socrates' last day is of no importance for the things that matter most in the *Phaedo*, Socrates' heroic actions on behalf of philosophy employing his novel theory of being and becoming to make philosophy safe for himself and others, a theory he knows to be irrational. Still, it is of interest in light of the character of Plato's dialogues: how fine and fitting it would be of Plato as an author to suggest his absence while keeping inferentially open his own presence among Socrates' auditors on this last possible occasion. He is present in the *Phaedo*, if he is present, in the same way all the others are present yet differently: surreptitiously present as the singularity who proved himself capable of doing what no one else present could do, compose Socratic dialogues in which he is always present as the author of every word but not evidently present. And if Plato is present while keeping his presence hidden except to a certain process of inference, then his presence in the *Phaedo* also mimes the presence of truth in Socrates' exoteric teaching: that truth, sheltered within uplifting untruth, makes itself present only through exercises of inference that take time and effort and can be plausible and pleasing only to a few.

A final consideration may also suggest Plato's presence. Socrates' last words are, "Crito, we owe a cock to Asclepius; so pay the debt and don't be careless."[126] These words express Socrates' gratitude to the god of healing for the cure of a sickness; they point back to words that open the center of the dialogue, Phaedo's statement to Echecrates that Socrates "healed us" (89a) — healed them of the condition that shook them all up and made them doubt all future arguments, the misology Socrates judged to be the greatest of all evils. But near the beginning of the dialogue Phaedo had said that he thinks Plato was *sick* and therefore needing a cure. Could the cure for *Plato's* sickness overlap the cure for the greatest evil, the cure of a man, that very special man who saw to the transmission of the cure of the worst sickness that can beset humankind?

Wondering about the manly objector, and considering the possibility of Plato's presence on Socrates' last day, suggest that something remarkable occurred in the moment in which Socrates turned his head toward the objector before turning it back to Cebes: a brief face-to-face dialogue between Socrates and the author of all the dialogues. And what was the topic of their dialogue? The difference between viewing cause in nature without transcendence as the coming to be of contraries out of contraries and viewing cause in nature as exclusively explained by participation

---

126. I treat other aspects of Socrates' last words in the next section.

in transcendent forms. Their single topic was the opposition between a scientific-mathematical approach to nature and a salutary approach employing impossible transcendent forms. Their topic was the advantage for philosophy of exoterically suppressing a science of nature in favor of what came to be called "Platonism." In their one exchange Socrates commissions Plato to do what he did.

7. Socrates' Last Words: Gratitude for a Healing

"Crito, we owe a cock to Asclepius. So pay the debt and don't be careless" (118). Phaedo insists that there be no mistake that these last words of Socrates really are his *last* words: not only does he say so before quoting them; after quoting them he says Crito asked Socrates if he had anything else to say and "when he asked him this he no longer answered." Socrates uttered his last words at the last possible moment, for with his feet and legs already growing cold he lifted the shroud from his face in order to say them and then covered his face again to die. Socrates' last words are no afterthought, some postscript added hurriedly as an addendum to a life. They are what he kept to say last, and they attest to what is deep and lasting in Socrates' life as a thinker. His last words precede a last deed displayed retrospectively by the executioner lifting the shroud moments later: "He had composed his countenance."[127] Socrates' soul composed his body's final look, devoid of agony or terror, with open mouth and open eyes — the now wordless mouth of a speaker, the now sightless eyes of an observer, both closed now by Crito. The composure that allowed Socrates to compose his countenance composed his last words. What can they mean?

Socrates' addressed his last words to Crito, informing his oldest friend of a debt and commanding him to pay it. Why Crito? The question gains weight when one considers that Socrates' first words in the *Phaedo* are also addressed to Crito and also command him to perform a deed, to see to it that Xanthippe be taken home (60a). Crito's prominence in the *Phaedo* carries to the very end his prominence in Plato's corpus as a whole. Plato named a dialogue after him that portrays a private conversation between Crito and Socrates in the early morning of the day before Socrates' death; to Crito, Socrates defends his decision to obey Athenian law despite Crito's urging to escape, as he helped arrange. Another whole dialogue, set some thirty years earlier, consists of Socrates narrating to Crito a conversation with sophists that had taken place a day earlier and that Crito

---

127. See the translators' comment in *Phaedo*, trans. Brann, Kalkavage, and Salem, 23n.

found shameful (*Euthydemus* 304d–305b) but that Socrates defended as necessary. Crito is also present in the *Apology*, where he is named as one of the fathers with no complaint about his son's association with Socrates (33e), and as one of the four (along with his son Critobulous, and Plato and Apollodorus) who proposed that Socrates offer to pay a larger fine that they will guarantee (38b). Crito is Socrates' old friend, but this alone is not enough to explain his prominence in the *Phaedo* and other dialogues. His importance lies in his friendship with Socrates as a model of the friendship possible between this Athenian philosopher and an Athenian gentleman, a man of standing, who, in his very person, refutes the decades-old charge against Socrates that he is a corrupter of the young: this old and intimate friend is as grateful for Socrates' services toward his son Critobulous as the fictitious Strepsiades is resentful and vengeful toward a fictitious Socrates for his corruption of the fictitious Pheidippides. Crito's devotion to Socrates is a refutation of the *Clouds*.

Socrates' last words are a request given as a command to Crito who assures him that "it shall be done." No doubt Crito performs the sacrifice that pays the debt to Asclepius for the healing that has been accomplished. But however much Crito honors Socrates and is grateful to him, his payment of the debt will have little to do with philosophy, of which he understands little, as Socrates again made apparent after the completion of the arguments of the *Phaedo* (115c-d, 116e). Why have Crito pay the debt?

Answering the question requires looking closely at the exact wording of Socrates' final request—and seeing that it is odd. The first, indicative part of Socrates' sentence is in the plural, *we* owe, and it is natural to suppose that the friends Socrates and Crito mutually owe that debt. But the second, commanding part is also plural, and the plural *you* who are to pay the debt and not be careless cannot be the same as the *we* because it cannot include Socrates. Crito and who else are to pay the debt of gratitude for a healing? It is reasonable to suppose that Socrates' final request implicitly addresses a command to a plurality that expands out beyond Crito in specific ways. The mutual gratitude only begins with Crito, who understands so little of what Socrates stood for but loves his friend dearly; it reasonably extends to those whose gratitude to Socrates is all the greater as the depth with which they understand the healing brought by Socrates' philosophy increases. Beginning with Crito, the debts of gratitude owed to the god of healing at Socrates' death imply acknowledgment of mutual or reciprocal debts incurred on one side by Socrates for a healing that is in part dependent on others, and debts incurred to Socrates for healing acts he performed. Socrates and the small company present at his death form

a community of the gratefully indebted. The *you* who are to pay the debt
and not be careless encompass the different kinds of debt displayed in the
Phaedo as incurred by the different kinds of friendship with Socrates, with
each of the grateful caring in his own way for what remains of Socrates.

Phaedo and Socrates share the debt of an Iolaus and his Herakles, a debt
being paid by Iolaus in Phlia faithfully retelling the heroic tale, a debt Socrates can expect Phaedo to pay, given the steps he took to win his alliance
and devotion. But the debt owed by Phaedo is also a more general debt
owed by the others present, for if Phaedo alone tells the tale, the others
will all have their tales to tell and what their tales will have in common is
gratitude to Socrates for the fact that "he healed us" (89a) from the misology and misanthropy into which they would have fallen had Socrates not
acted. Socrates' generosity to them allows them to satisfy their deepest
wish, to believe in the immortality of their souls at the same time that
they believe their belief to be rational and themselves to be philosophers
because they trust reason. From Socrates' side, this debt to those he made
the friends of philosophy is a debt incurred for the devotion with which
they enjoy the tales of his heroic acts on behalf of philosophy. These followers preserve the logos in its edifying and ennobling function, its civiliz-
ing power. Socrates stands to these followers as a general to his army; they
are the soldiers of reason who help fight for reason's place in the world.

But a higher indebtedness and a deeper gratitude obtain between Socrates and the solitaries driven by a passion to know, as the unnamed manly
objector was. Such a person resembles him in his natural immunity to misology and misanthropy, blaming himself rather than the logos, knowing
himself to be always not yet whole, always in need of another argument.
Socrates is most indebted to an auditor like that: manly and remembering,
but restraining mere manliness, he hears Socrates' own ultimate objection
to his last argument with understanding and silence, imitating Socrates
in pursuing its implications alone without endangering those who have
no need to pursue yet another argument. If the unnamed manly objector
is named *Plato* Socrates would owe a debt to the one fit to compose the
tale that a Phaedo tells by rote, like a rhapsode reciting Homer. In the tale
Plato gave Phaedo to tell, Plato would continue to be present and absent —
present in the way Socrates can be heard conveying what is needed in exact
words and exact silences, *absent* for any palpable sensing as others completely fill his stage. Present as an author absenting himself, he would carry
Socrates' gift of healing forward through its full range from Crito upward, a
debtor himself who, as the last objector to Socrates' last argument, displays

himself as the grateful recipient of the greatest of all gifts. Plato pays his
debt and is not careless, for he ensures, as far as possible, the transmission
of the teaching that Socrates himself, in part at least, received from others,
from Homer through Parmenides. Plato pays his debt for the greatest of
Socrates' gifts with the greatest of all monuments, ensuring as far as possible that the death of Socrates will not be the death of philosophy.

What is the meaning of Socrates' final words then? Their finality is essential to them: he held them to the last possible moment as his last possible speech, the only fitting way for a Socrates to end his life of speaking:
gratitude and its expression in fitting words and deeds. As last words they
attest to Socrates' composure, his capacity to save for last what belongs
last, gratitude for a life of thought that comes to know itself in its knowledge of ignorance, its knowledge of knowing. The *Phaedo* itself does not
convey just what a philosopher's drive to know can come to know with
respect to the whole — the *Parmenides* and the *Symposium* are necessary for
a more complete understanding of Socrates' gratitude at his end. But it is
already clear that Socrates' gratitude is the gratitude of the thinker for the
world as it is, a world conducive to human knowing, limited though it be.
This knowing, as Leo Strauss expressed it, is awareness of "the dignity of
the mind . . . the true ground of the dignity of man and of the goodness of
the world."[128] Socrates' last words are the fitting words for a Greek philosopher to command as an act of Greek religion. As Nietzsche made prominent by contrasting Greek religion with Christian religion, the religion of
the Greeks is characterized by "the unrestrained fullness of gratitude that
streams out of it: it is a very noble kind of human being that stands before
nature and before life *this way*."[129]

But the Nietzsche who praises Greek religion for its gratitude is well
known for *condemning* Socrates for his last words. In "*The Dying Socrates*,"
he says, "I admire the courage and wisdom of Socrates in everything he
did, said — and did not say."[130] Socrates was "great in silence," Nietzsche
says, while adding, "I wish he had remained silent also in the last moments
of his life — perhaps he would then belong to a still higher order of minds.
Whether it was death or the poison or piety or malice — something loos-

128. Strauss, *Liberalism Ancient and Modern*, 8.

129. *Beyond Good and Evil*, §49. Nietzsche inserted this brief aphorism on Greek religion
into his chapter on religion between longer aphorisms dealing with our religion, which is
grateful only for deliverance from this life, a religion Plato's Socrates helped prepare with
his arguments for the immortality of the soul.

130. *Gay Science*, §340.

ened his tongue." And Nietzsche says that his "ridiculous and terrible 'last word' means, for those who have ears, 'O Crito, *life is a disease!*' Is it possible! ... Socrates, Socrates *suffered from life!*" Nietzsche adds the most condemning word in his vocabulary: "Did a Socrates really need *revenge*? ... O friends! We must overcome even the Greeks!" I would like to think that Nietzsche thought that it was not possible, that his 1881 denunciation of the "one turning point and vortex of so-called world history" is part of his effort to undermine and destroy the prevailing Platonism — one main fragment of *Nietzsche's* killing all 108 suitors in order to found a new spiritual order. But whether Nietzsche can be spared his condemnation of Socrates in that way or not, Socrates' last words share the feature of all his public words: they are Odyssean; with an exoteric ring of edifying piety, they convey the esoteric and deadly content of philosophy. Crito and the pious others express their gratitude to Asclepius in the fitting Greek way, Socrates does that too while implying gratitude for life as it is, life that peaks with philosophy's effort to understand life, always mortal life.

Socrates' arguments on his last day, all invalid, point to the soul being mortal, a conclusion Socrates reinforces by forcing his friends to watch him "turn into a corpse."[131] He chose not to die alone, as he could have in the private chambers provided by his Athenian cell; nor did he die before his wife and children — he was careful to spare *them* by sending them home (116b). But he chose to die in front of his friends, forcing them to watch as the cold caused by the poison advanced up his body from his feet to his heart. Socrates had begun his last day with his friends by rubbing his leg after the shackles were removed, and remarking on the wondrous relation between what human beings call pleasant and its seeming contrary, the painful (60b). Socrates ends his last day with his friends watching as the executioner gives his foot and thighs a hard pinch and asks Socrates "if he sensed it." "No," Socrates said: he sensed neither pleasure nor pain at the end. "And going upward in this way, [the executioner] showed us that he was growing cold and stiff" (117e). When the cold reached his heart, the executioner said, "He'd be gone." Socrates gave his friends the opportunity to conclude with their own eyes what their minds would suggest if they attended closely enough to his arguments: Socrates is mortal. What happens to him is what happens to fire and snow. When the unity that is soul and body ends its union, and soul no longer senses body, the human being is gone; everything that remains can be buried or burned or left to the dogs and birds, though Crito and the rest could not possibly let that happen.

131. Benardete, "On Plato's *Phaedo*," 279.

The last words of the dialogue are Phaedo's words bestowing the highest praise he knows: Socrates is as wise and good as Nestor, worthy of the praise bestowed on Nestor, the man popularly honored for his thoughtfulness and justice, qualities in him that stem from his loyalty to the gods. No. Plato, author of every word Phaedo spoke, knew higher praise, knew it from Homer, and he bestows it here in the fitting unspoken manner, bestows it Homerically, on Socrates, a man as wise as polytropic Odysseus.

* * *

Gratitude is what Socrates expresses in his last words. It is a passion and a word that ring throughout the history of philosophy, but never more gracefully nor with more deadly intent than in Descartes. In the last book he would get to write, *The Passions of the Soul*, Descartes ended by elevating gratitude as a "remedy for all the disorders of the passions."[132] The greatest disorder of the passions occurs in the "self-satisfaction" celebrated by "the great friends of God," satisfaction that allows them to believe that their passion is "righteous zeal" that grants permission to commit "the greatest crimes man can commit such as betraying cities, killing princes, and exterminating whole peoples because they do not accept their opinions." In the depths of the religious wars that tore Europe apart and threatened the Renaissance, Descartes, in his discussion of gratitude, dares to permit his reader to see that the righteous zeal of the millennial inheritor of Platonism, Christianity, must be opposed and opposed wisely. Taking his guidance from the history of philosophy and from his older contemporary, Francis Bacon, Descartes practices the quiet virtue of generosity at its highest reach in the philosopher, daring to become a turning point and vortex in so-called world history, advancing the scientific-technological view that came to rule Christendom, tempering its zeal and thereby benefiting humanity while unavoidably containing its own deep flaws, *its* need to be surmounted.

Gratitude. The passing on of philosophy from one great philosopher to another. With these themes I touch the theme that has been the overriding topic of all my books: they are installments in the new history of philosophy made possible by Friedrich Nietzsche. Each great historic philosopher of our tradition came to know his predecessors and to know the necessities

132. Descartes, *Passions of the Soul*, §156. Descartes sets out his view of the related passion, generosity, in the final sections of his book, §§193–212. I treat those great sections in *Nietzsche and Modern Times*, 265–71.

that drove them to say and do what they did. And each came to know the same necessities prevailing over him, historical necessities that ensure that every philosophy that comes to rule politically is mortal, but that the life of philosophy can be revived time and again with wise actions performed on behalf of philosophy itself. Philosophy, the passion to understand, owes to the world it partially understands its deep passion of gratitude.

CHAPTER 2

Parmenides

The Second Stage of Socrates' Philosophic Education

> Nature embedded the human in nothing but illusion. That is his genuine element.
> —Nietzsche, *Kritische Studienausgabe* 7:19 [179] (Summer 1872)

Prologue: A Socrates for the Philosophically Driven

In 1872, in his late twenties Nietzsche made a crucial discovery about the human way of knowing, an advance in skepticism and its proper grounds that he wrote out in an 1873 essay that he then decided not to publish. Thirteen years later, he made his most fundamental ontological discovery and published his most important book tracing Zarathustra's way into that discovery. Immediately after that, he decided that he had to review all his books and publish autobiographical forewords to each of them in order to enable his serious reader to follow the trajectory of his own philosophic education through its main stages. In the sentence he wrote that served as the foreword to *Schopenhauer as Educator*, he reported the title of his unpublished 1873 essay, "On Truth and Lie in the Extra-moral Sense," and told his reader that with that essay he attained "the moral skepticism and deconstruction, *that is to say, as much in the critique as in the deepening of all hitherto pessimism* — and already believed 'in nothing at all' as people say."[1] The "pessimism" he had attained was a pessimism about knowledge, an epistemological skepticism that is insurmountable because it is based in the human way

---

1. The italics are Nietzsche's. Nietzsche provided short "forewords" to all four of his *Untimely Meditations* in the Foreword to *Things Human All Too Human*, Part II, 1. On this great event in Nietzsche's philosophic education, see my *What a Philosopher Is*, 43–72.

of knowing that cannot be thrown off. What Plato shows Socrates gaining in the second stage of his philosophic education — what Parmenides guided Socrates to in his youth — was a similar skepticism about knowing, a skepticism he could discover only if he proved worthy of it, proved capable of solving the puzzles of the gymnastic exercises Parmenides assigned him. The *Parmenides*, that most puzzling of all Platonic dialogues, thus provides an extension to the Socratic turn beyond what Socrates himself reported on his last day. The young Socrates' passion to discover the causes of all things turns out to have taken a direction he did not report to Cebes, an insight into the character of all human knowing as itself causative of the structure, the form, of the known, an insight into an epistemological skepticism akin to the one Nietzsche gained as a young man.

   Among the three dialogues that report the stages of Socrates' philosophic education, the *Phaedo* and *Symposium* each have Socrates himself report the stage of his philosophic advance, framing it each time to fit their very different settings and audiences. The stage recorded in the *Parmenides*, however, the central stage, is not reported by Socrates: he is dead when the great event was recovered by nameless foreigners bent on hearing it — "men of Clazomenae" said to be "very much philosophers," residents of the Greek city in Asia Minor in which essential advances in natural philosophy had been made. And the whole of it is narrated not by one of those philosophers but by their countryman, Cephalus, who led them to the Athenian who they hoped might be able to remember what had been said when a young Socrates met old Parmenides and his associate Zeno some sixty years earlier.[2] Cephalus narrates it at a later unknown time to an unidentified audience: the *Parmenides* is unique as the only Platonic dialogue whose actual narration lacks a specified setting, date, and audience. And it is unique among the three dialogues that record the stages of Socrates' philosophic education in being the only one not reported by Socrates himself.

   Plato made it clear that the stage of Socrates' learning recovered by the nameless philosophical travelers in the *Parmenides* fell chronologically between the events of learning Socrates himself reported in the *Phaedo* and the *Symposium*. It was after Socrates' turn to the logoi and his invention of transcendent forms because he uses such forms to refute the view argued by Parmenides and Zeno. Their meeting occurred at the Great Panathenaia of 450, making Socrates about nineteen, years before his meetings with Diotima as he presents them in the *Symposium*. Socrates at nineteen

---

2. Christopher Planeaux (pers. comm.) sets the dramatic date of the frame of the *Parmenides* in 394/3 based on the political relations of Athens and Clazomenae and on the ages of the Athenian participants in the frame.

had therefore both devised his transcendent forms view and been shown by Parmenides that it was rationally indefensible. No wonder Socrates did not narrate this stage in his philosophic education: his later public use of the forms as edifying realities for young men like Glaucon and Adeimantus and Cebes and Simmias precluded it. As for the final stage, Socrates himself reports it in the *Symposium* as occurring sometime in his early maturity but still before he mounted the public stage at about thirty-five or around 434, the event Plato reported in his *Protagoras*.

In a late essay Seth Benardete called attention to this salient feature differentiating the *Parmenides* from the *Phaedo* and *Symposium*: "Only in the *Parmenides* do we catch Socrates before he became Socrates, without the framing Socrates himself gives to his younger self."[3] *Catch* is the fitting word for our learning about a transformative event that comes to us completely outside of Socrates' control. And Benardete's commentary on the *Parmenides* makes it possible to understand why *catch* is fitting in a deeper sense: his commentary unlocks the "gymnastic training" Parmenides offered the young Socrates in a way that is unparalleled in the existing tradition of commentary on Plato. In thus providing guidance to the guidance Parmenides gave to the young Socrates, Benardete reveals just how radical it was: it points to an "ontological psychology" that is Parmenides' true monism, a truth about the self as knower that makes all possible knowledge the result of human sorting and ordering, the epistemological skepticism endemic to philosophy as such. My commentary on the first main part of the *Parmenides* is my own; but my commentary on Parmenides' gymnastic is dependent on Benardete's because there and only there can one gain insight into what young Socrates could learn from Parmenides if he proved to have the philosophic aptitude and drive to rationally unlock the puzzles of the gymnastic.

1. First Words

When we came to Athens from our home in Clazomenae, we chanced upon both Adeimantus and Glaucon, and taking me by the hand Adeimantus said, "Welcome, Cephalus, and if you need anything here that's in our power, declare [it]."[4]

In this first sentence of his *Parmenides* Plato brings together a Cephalus, an Adeimantus, and a Glaucon, unmistakable names from the *Republic*. The

3. Benardete, "Plato's *Parmenides*: A Sketch," 230.
4. I use the translation of the *Parmenides* by Albert Keith Whitaker.

Cephalus, who narrates every word of the *Parmenides*, is a different person from the old Cephalus of the *Republic*, but Adeimantus and Glaucon are the same. As young men they were the chief interlocutors of Socrates that night in the Piraeus now many decades in their past. What is it about what is coming in the *Parmenides* that made Plato want every reader of it to be reminded first of the *Republic*? The dramatic dates he gave to the *Parmenides* and the *Republic* help answer this question. Chronologically, the *Parmenides* encloses within its two dramatic dates the events of the *Republic*, for Plato set the frame of the *Parmenides*, which opens with that meeting in the Athenian agora, some time after Socrates' death in 399, probably 394/3, and he set the event the men of Clazomenae sailed to Athens to learn about in 450.[5] As for the *Republic*, Plato set it in 429, two decades after the main events of the *Parmenides* and some four decades before the meeting in the marketplace.[6] Plato's reason for forcing his reader to think about the *Republic* in the first sentence of the *Parmenides* seems to have two elements. First, how does the Socrates that the men of Clazomenae learn about compare with the twenty-years-older Socrates of the *Republic*? When compared to the *Republic*, the *Parmenides* silently opens a gap between Socrates the young thinker and Socrates the older teacher, inviting the engaged reader to wonder about Socrates' becoming: What does the *Parmenides* show him to be in his youth, and what does the *Republic* show he became in his maturity? Second, what does the reappearance of Adeimantus and Glaucon in their late maturity in the frame of the *Parmenides* suggest about the effect their exposure to Socrates in their youth had upon them? The *Parmenides* will show that Socrates measured Adeimantus and Glaucon correctly in the *Republic*, for its frame will soon prove that they had no real interest in Socrates' philosophy proper, however engaged and persuaded the *Republic* shows them to be by his teachings on justice and the soul and the forms and the other matters of individual and political concern to them.

5. The dramatic date of the core conversation of the *Parmenides* is generally recognized to be the Great Panathenaia of 450.

6. The dramatic date of the *Republic* is disputed, but it is indisputable that Plato thought the date mattered; he secured it by putting it in his first sentence: it was the day after the night on which the Athenians took the unprecedented step of introducing a foreign goddess—and Plato made the date exact only later in the conversation by adding that the new goddess was Thracian Bendis. Every Athenian would know that date because of its religious and political significance, but it has become difficult to secure it now. Christopher Planeaux's argument that it is 429 is secured by his demonstration that Bendis was introduced in early June, 429; see Planeaux, "Date of Bendis' Entry into Attica"; and my *How Philosophy Became Socratic*, 405–11.

In the first sentence of the *Parmenides* Plato has chance and purpose align as the chance meeting of the philosophic men of Clazomenae with Adeimantus and Glaucon in the agora fulfills their purpose in sailing across the Aegean Sea. Cephalus's prior acquaintance with the Athenian brothers was the basis of their hope to meet a man whose name they didn't know but who, they had heard, might remember a conversation of extreme interest to them, a man who was the half brother of Adeimantus and Glaucon. Cephalus can't remember that brother's name because he had been just a boy during Cephalus's earlier stay in Athens, a long time ago now (126b); but Cephalus can recall the name of his father, Pyrilampes, scion of a noble Athenian family.[7] Adeimantus tells Cephalus that his name is Antiphon, but he expresses surprise: "Why in the world do you ask?" Cephalus did not ask for himself but for "these" men who accompanied him from Clazomenae: "These are fellow citizens of mine and very much philosophers and they" — *they*, he says, not *we*, are very much philosophers and for that reason they enlisted him as their means of realizing their hope, he who had spent a long time in Athens and had come to know the family of the man they were seeking. "They heard that this Antiphon happened to spend much of his time with a certain Pythodorus, a friend of Zeno, and that those speeches which Socrates and Zeno and Parmenides once made in conversation — that Antiphon heard them so many times from Pythodorus that he has them memorized" (126c).[8]

The rumor they heard is true, Adeimantus says, and Cephalus replies, "This is what we need — to hear [the speeches] through and through." A thrill must course through those philosophically driven travelers when Adeimantus says, "Oh, that's no difficulty, when he was a boy he practiced them quite well, thoroughly." Still, there may be a problem, because "nowadays . . . he spends much of his time on horsemanship" — on the paradigmatic idle pursuit of Athenian aristocracy, to which Plato's family belonged. Adeimantus reports that Antiphon had just been with them in the marketplace and left for his nearby home, and he leads them there (127a). When they reach Antiphon's home he is in fact engaged in what occupies him now: they see him "handing a bridle-bit or something to a

---

7. Pyrilampes was the second husband of Perictione, who was the mother of Adeimantus, Glaucon, and Plato by her first husband, Ariston. See the stemma of Plato's family in Nails, *People of Plato*, 244.

8. Pythodorus became an important Athenian general (Thucydides 3.115.2–5; 4.2.3; 6.105.2); he was banished in 424 for allegedly taking bribes to leave Sicily instead of subduing the cities there (4.65.3). Debra Nails determined that Pythodorus died before 414 (*People of Plato*, 259).

smith to fit"—Cephalus is evidently not himself a horseman. When Antiphon is told why they are there, he recognizes Cephalus from his earlier stay in Athens and greets him warmly. But when they ask him to go
through the speeches he had once memorized he balks, saying it is "a lot of
work"—as Parmenides will say later when Socrates asks him to go through
the training exercises Parmenides says he needs (136d). "But at last he led
us through them in full."

The driven travelers from Clazomenae have to persuade a reluctant Antiphon to tell the tale that he alone remembers but has not spoken for a
long time—and that necessity is a little revelation: Why haven't his brothers, Adeimantus and Glaucon, seen to the preservation of these speeches?
Saved at a late moment by the efforts of anonymous, philosophy-driven
foreigners, Antiphon's memorized tale would have died with him for all
that Adeimantus and Glaucon cared—these recipients of Socrates' teaching decades earlier did not even bother to ask their own brother to tell
them the story of a life-altering philosophic experience of the young Socrates, even though they often heard him practicing it. That fact may be
the ultimate reason for the prominent place Plato gave his two brothers
at the opening of the *Parmenides*: in their young manhood they had been
privileged to have Socrates abolish their fears that a decent life, a just and
pious life, was not worth living by grounding such a life for them in persuasive reasons that made the whole order of things and the gods themselves
guarantee the advantages of justice and piety. The *Republic* with its edifying
teaching was enough for them, they who deeply desired to be good citizens
but needed new reasons, given their exposure to the Greek enlightenment
with its skeptical assignment of base motives to political leaders and its
ridicule of the conflicting stories of their religious tradition. The prominent presence of the brothers at the opening of the *Parmenides* puts them
into dramatic contrast to the men of Clazomenae: the zeal for philosophy
of these anonymous travelers from afar makes the indifference of Adeimantus and Glaucon palpable. The *Parmenides*, this contrast suggests, is
intended only for those driven by philosophic passion. Adeimantus and
Glaucon get to listen, but they will not memorize its contents; they will
not join the chain of transmission preserving a philosophic conversation of
extreme importance for the philosophically driven: that's "hard work," and
they are not the kind to perform it. It is entirely fitting that the audience
edified or charmed by Socrates' teaching in the *Republic* not be inclined to
exert the hard work necessary to learn from the perplexities of the *Parmenides*: the *Republic* is enough for them, noble, honorable men on whom
the well-being of the city depends.

And how did the core of the *Parmenides*, preserved through its being narrated to those who are very much philosophers, get transmitted to us? By a Cephalus wholly unlike the Cephalus of the *Republic*, who left that conversation before it really began. Who might this Cephalus be, this *kephalē*, a talking head indeed who performed the hard work of memorizing it? He seems to be a stand-in for that other brother, Plato, who cared enough to learn what he could about Socrates young and old and to transmit his spoken words in written spoken words. Plato structured his *Parmenides* to be the last-minute preservation of an almost lost conversation critical to Socrates' becoming, and the way he offers it keeps its puzzles available for nameless future travelers from afar. For as A. E. Taylor says about Cephalus's narration of every word of the *Parmenides*, the "complete silence about the place and personnel is a thing unparalleled in the rest of Plato's dialogues. . . . That the immediate speaker in the *Parmenides* should be, as he is, quite uncharacterized, and should be speaking no one knows where and to no one knows whom, is quite against Plato's usual practice, and the departure from custom has, therefore, presumably a reason."[9] The uniqueness of the *content* of the *Parmenides* seems to be the reason, for the *Parmenides* is singular in its content: after Parmenides and Zeno discover just who this young Athenian is who dares to step up and refute them, it becomes a dialogue on philosophy. First, Zeno touches on the indispensable matter of what the intentions of a philosophic writing are. Then, Parmenides treats the fundamental matters of being and knowing for a nineteen-year-old just starting out but immensely gifted, Parmenides himself being a sixty-five-year-old rightfully celebrated philosopher capable of making followers of the brilliance of a Zeno, now near the end of his storied career yet still on the lookout for promising candidates for the transmission of what matters most. And Cephalus's narration, that placeless and timeless Platonic exception, itself exists for nameless future philosophic travelers from unknown Clazomenaes.

2. At Pythodorus's House during the Great Panathenaia

"Pythodorus used to say that both Zeno and Parmenides once came to the Great Panathenaea." Antiphon's first words reporting the long-ago events assign a date and setting to Socrates' meeting with Parmenides and Zeno: it was midsummer 450, at the height of the summer heat in late July or early August after the grain harvest. By giving it that date, Plato tacitly gives

9. Taylor, "Parmenides, Zeno, and Socrates," 30, 31.

the age of the "very young" Socrates (127c): he was about nineteen when this life-changing encounter occurred. Placing this event in his life next to the events he himself recounted of his beginnings in the *Phaedo* makes it evident that Socrates encountered Parmenides and Zeno after he had acquainted himself with the whole history of Greek natural philosophy on his primary question of the cause of all things, and after he had embarked on his second sailing, his turn to the logoi, which led him to posit transcendent forms as cause. What Parmenides did with Socrates that summer marked an epoch in his life because Parmenides refuted that view of which he was so proud, a view he thought could prove great Parmenides and his follower Zeno wrong about the one and the many — and the very view he is still retailing to Simmias and Cebes on the last day of his life.

Plato set this philosophic event during the Great Panathenaia, the most significant, most distinctive of all Athenian festivals. Held every four years as the grand version of the annual Panathenaia, it was the festival during which Athens' Panhellenic games were celebrated, drawing large numbers of contestants and spectators from all over Greece to a celebration of Athens and its founding. It was the festival that for Athenians marked "a new year and a like renewal of society."[10] Plato set other dialogues during specific festivals in the Athenian calendar, and each time the setting gave the dialogue a powerful symbolic focus for its interpretation.[11] Why did he set

10. Robertson, "Athena's Shrines and Festivals," 28. A detailed account of the Great Panathenaia is found in Connelly, *Parthenon Enigma*, 247–93. The new year came at the beginning of that month, Hecatombion, and the Panathenaia at its end. As Noel Robertson notes, that new year festival also brought "the birth of a marvelous child, Erichthonios, 'He-of-the-very-earth'" (28, 62), one of the autochthonous ancestors of all Athenians and the founding hero of the Panathenaea.

11. Plato set the *Republic* on the night of an unprecedented Athenian event: the introduction of a foreign god, Bendis, through a new festival in the Piraeus. On that night and in that place Socrates introduced his foreign teaching to young Athenians. In the *Timaeus* Plato set the pivotal tale of Atlantis on the third day of the Apaturia when Critias as a boy first heard the story of Athens' early greatness that he tells as an old man — on that day of the Apaturia Athenians celebrated a legendary Athenian act of deception that gave them the victory in a war (see Lampert and Planeaux, "Who's Who in Plato's *Timaeus-Critias* and Why," 97–98). Plato set the *Phaedo* during a festival to Apollo that celebrated Theseus as the founder of the city, thereby introducing the heroic element of Socrates' actions on his last day. Plato put historic events, as well as events in Homer, to the same metaphoric use; in the *Lesser Hippias*, for example, he set Socrates' praise of polytropic Odysseus against Hippias's praise of straight Achilles on the days of Alcibiades' polytropic deception of the Spartan ambassadors, thereby winning over Athenians for an alliance of Peloponnesian cities to defeat Sparta (see my "Socrates' Defense of Polytropic Odysseus," 234–35). For other examples of Plato's care in giving his dialogues religious, mythic, or historic settings, see my *How Philosophy Became Socratic*.

the *Parmenides* during the Great Panathenaia and give that setting prominence by making it the first thing Antiphon mentions about the visit of Parmenides and Zeno?

Antiphon is an exacting reporter of the details Pythodorus reported of the events he witnessed; he gives the ages of Parmenides (65) and Zeno (40) and describes the impressive appearance of each. And he reports that Zeno was said to have been the beloved of Parmenides when he was young—perhaps a popular way of stating that special love of an older philosopher for a philosophically gifted young man, a love that explains the admiring reaction Parmenides and Zeno will have for a young Socrates on attack against them (130a). Pythodorus also reports the detail that Parmenides and Zeno were staying with him at his house "outside the city wall in the Keramikos" (127c). Why *that* specificity? Perhaps because that location in northwest Athens was a special and very busy place early on the most important day of the Great Panathenaia: a massive crowd of Athenian celebrants had to assemble there, and with them the numerous horses that would be ridden by the young horsemen and pull the four-horse chariots in the procession, plus the hundred cattle and all the other sacrificial animals that would be driven or carried in parade in order to be killed on the great altar on the Acropolis at the end of the procession. Outside the city wall in the Keramikos was the assembly point for the most important event of the most symbolic festival of Athenian life, the procession that every four years began at the northwest city gate on its winding ceremonial way through the city, on up the Acropolis to the sacred altar of Athena just northeast of where the Parthenon would be built a few years hence.[12] Could that background of the most important civic event in Athenian life—supplied by Plato in seemingly extraneous details he has Cephalus pass on from Pythodorus and Antiphon—help explain some small curiosities he built into Pythodorus's report? Pythodorus says that "Socrates and many others with him went there, since they desired to hear Zeno's writings—after all, that was the first time they brought them there" (127c). How many desired to hear Zeno's writings? "Many others" turn out to be *two*, for the total number of those present for the whole exchange is later said to be seven (129d). "Many others" is not many at all: this historic meeting in Athens with world-famous Parmenides and Zeno and destined-to-

---

12. That procession is depicted on the celebrated frieze of the Parthenon, which had not yet been built in 450; Connelly, *Parthenon Enigma*, offers an interpretation of the procession depicted in the frieze different from the traditional one, but in her view too the procession of the Great Panathenaia remains the central event of the central Athenian festival.

be-famous Socrates is a small private meeting. And Pythodorus reports that for most of Zeno's reading of his treatise he himself was not present: the initial audience for Zeno's reading consisted of just three, Socrates and the nameless "many" who are in fact just two, for, as Pythodorus says, he and Parmenides came in from outside when Zeno was almost finished with his reading, and coming in with them was the final person of the seven, the youngest, Aristoteles.[13]

Why, in the detailed precision of Pythodorus's report, are *many* just two? And why were he and Parmenides and Aristoteles outside for most of Zeno's reading?[14] Plato is economical in what he wrote: every item has its purpose, and he was reputed to have especially polished his openings, adjusting them till the end of his life. These details at the opening of the *Parmenides* must serve a special purpose, for ahead lies the pivotal exchange in Plato's scattered story of how Socrates became Socrates. Is it possible then that he meant to have a contrast rise in the reader's mind? A small Athenian indoor event occurs in private where *many* shrink to *two* and only seven are present for an event worth memorizing while outside the beginning of the greatest of all Athenian ceremonial spectacles was being arranged, the beginnings of which three of the seven may have been observing until Zeno is almost finished with his reading. That private, inside event, an event in the life of Socrates, turned out to be a more consequential founding than even the historic founding of Athens celebrated outside by all Athenians: that private event humbled an arrogant young Athenian, driving him to further inquiries through which alone he could become what he was, the founder of genuine, Socratic philosophy — for Plato, the most consequential founding, Athenian but also trans-Athenian, even perhaps trans-Hellenic. And it was the private event that nameless men of

13. It must be Antiphon who reports that Aristoteles "became one of the Thirty," the tyrants who briefly ruled Athens almost fifty years later (129c-d), thus disgracing in the eyes of the democracy the one who serves as Parmenides' interlocutor for the largest part of the dialogue. On Aristoteles, see Xenophon, *Hellenica* 2.2.18; 2.3.2, 13, 46; he is mentioned in Thucydides 3.105.3.

14. It was not indifference to the writings Zeno had brought to Athens for the first time that kept Pythodorus outside: he says that "he had heard them before on his own from Zeno" (127d). According to Socrates in *Alcibiades I* (119a), Pythodorus paid Zeno a lot of money, 100 minae, in order to have Zeno make him "both wise and distinguished." Thucydides reports that Pythodorus was active during the war with Sparta: he became an Athenian general in command of the fleet in Sicily in 426 (3.115) but was exiled for not conquering Sicily when he might have (4.65); he was one of the Athenians who took the oath for the Peace of Nicias (5.19.24) but was one of the three generals who violated that peace (6.105).

Clazomenae traveled to Athens to hear more than half a century later, saving it for a possibly longer future than even that of imperial Athens.

In the *Parmenides*, as Plato chose to introduce it, driven philosophic travelers come to Athens from the eastern geographic extremity of Greek philosophy, from the home of Anaxagoras, who had brought philosophy to Athens during his thirty-year stay before being tried for impiety and forced to leave. They come in the hope of hearing about an event in which the greatest representatives of the western geographic extremity of Greek philosophy speak with the young Athenian who evoked their intense interest. Philosophic east and philosophic west meet in Athens in the retelling of a private philosophic event through which the Athenian Socrates learned lessons that would transform him and prepare a new future for philosophy with Athens the center of philosophic wisdom to which philosophically driven foreigners would stream.

3. Socrates and Zeno: How to Read a Philosophic Writing

The words of young Socrates' first speech to Zeno in the *Parmenides* are chronologically the first words Plato has Socrates speak in his writings. In the *Phaedo* Plato has the oldest possible Socrates describe who that young speaker is: a driven inquirer deeply engaged in the question of the causes of all things (96a), aware of the conclusions of his predecessors and of the difficulties they entail (96b–98b), difficulties that led him to embark on a "second sailing," resorting to the logoi in order to "look in them for the truth of beings" (99d-e). He "launched himself," old Socrates says, by positing hypotheses, or "more plainly," by busying himself with what "I've never stopped talking about," transcendent forms (100a-b). The young Socrates of the *Parmenides* had ostensibly come to Pythodorus's house to hear Zeno read his treatise, but he soon shows that he actually came armed and eager to refute and correct both Zeno and Parmenides with the transcendent forms he had already devised.

Socrates listened as Zeno read for him and the two others; when Zeno finished reading, Socrates spoke up to ask him, as Pythodorus phrases it, to "reread the first hypothesis of the first logos" (127d7). After Zeno reread it, Socrates said in his first quoted words, "Zeno, what are you *saying* (*legeis*) with this?" (127e1) — Socrates' first words use the verbal form of *logos*, which he repeats in his question at the end of his first short speech: "Is that what you're *saying*?" (127e5). Plato has the young Socrates do literally in his *Parmenides* what Plato had him say he did in his *Phaedo* to launch himself on his second sailing. In the *Phaedo* Socrates' examples were logoi on the topics of the beautiful, the good, and the big; but there Socrates emphasized that his new way is the "safe" way to understand cause, while the way of the investigators of nature is confounding and dangerous — and he encouraged Simmias and Cebes to abandon the investigation of nature, implying that *he* abandoned his early investigations into nature with his discovery of the forms. But in the *Parmenides* Socrates' first words suggest that his way of forms *continued* on the way he first began; his "turn" to the logoi included the logoi of the investigators of nature that he had been reading from the start. The *Phaedo* shows that Socrates had good reason to advise Simmias and Cebes to abandon the investigation of nature: misology threatened them. But the *Parmenides* shows that Socrates himself had no need to abandon the investigation of nature: what he needed was a proper understanding of how to pursue that investigation. Socrates' intention in the *Phaedo* required him to misrepresent his initial purpose in devising his transcendent forms.

Socrates interprets the first hypothesis of the first logos of Zeno's writing as saying, "If the things that are are many . . . then they must be both like and unlike," which is "clearly impossible" (127e). And because *that* is impossible, "it is also impossible for there to be many things." Socrates generalizes from the first logos, asking if that is what all Zeno's logoi seek, "to battle against everything that is commonly said by maintaining that there is no many?" He can even add an ironic little twist by asking Zeno if "each of his logoi" proves that, and therefore "the supposed proofs that 'There is no many' are as many as the logoi you have written?" "You have beautifully grasped what the whole writing seeks," Zeno answers, *beautiful* perhaps pointing to Socrates' indication of the nice little contradiction implicit in Zeno's *many* logoi.

Hearing Zeno's confirmation and praise, Socrates turns away from him to address Parmenides: I'm coming to understand, he says, "that Zeno here not only wants to have become your own by the rest of his friendship with you but also by his written composition."[15] A hidden intention drove Zeno's writing, Socrates charges, an erotic intention to impress Parmenides and win his friendship. That charge leads him to his main point: the pair united in friendship also *say* the same thing, "For he has written, in a certain way, the very same thing as you but by changing it around he tries to trick us into thinking that he is saying some other thing" (128a). Young Socrates can praise each of the two older philosophers for their respective proofs that "all is one" and "is not many" (128b) while uniting them in trickery: "One

---

15. Trans. Benardete, "Plato's *Parmenides*," 232.

says 'the one' and one says 'not many' and so each speaks so as to seem to
say nothing the same while you are saying nearly the same thing." He ends
what is surely a well-planned little speech on what he intends to be a criticism: "And that's why what the two of you say appears to be beyond the
rest of us." Together, Parmenides and Zeno trick their readers with effective proofs of what amounts to the same view leaving them dumbfounded.
Young Socrates' attacking speech — demeaning Zeno's intention, charging
both with trickery for a shared view, and accusing both for making their
writings seem to be beyond us — turns out to be tactical preparation for
what he seems to have come to Pythodorus's house to flaunt: that what
they wrote was not beyond *him*, for he devised a view of being that solves
the mere perplexities these famous philosophers left their readers with.
Socrates' first speeches in the *Parmenides* display a young thinker deeply
involved in the key issues of philosophy, being and knowing, and already
adept at exploiting a dialogical situation to gain a rhetorical advantage: he
indicts the master's best pupil, then the master himself, and then presents
his own solution to the problem they failed to solve.

Socrates had addressed Parmenides, but Zeno responds: "Yes, Socrates," he says, stopping him and turning his attention back to Zeno. "But
you have not entirely perceived the truth of my writing" (128b). He can
still praise Socrates — "You chase and hunt down what I said like a Laco-
nian hound" — but "this much has escaped you from the first" (128c). Young
Socrates' pursuit of the argument was exemplary, but he failed as a reader
or listener by attributing false intentions to Zeno: "In no way whatsoever
is the writing so pretentious as to have been written with the intention you
offer, to conceal from people that it's furthering some great accomplish-
ment for myself; what you mentioned is just an incidental consequence."
Zeno did not intend to trick people into thinking he was saying something
different from his teacher, nor was the erotic intention Socrates mentioned what his writing meant to conceal. "The truth" Socrates had not
perceived is that Zeno intended his writing "as a sort of aid to Parmenides'
logos against those who attack him by joking that if the one is, then he
and his logos suffer many laughable and contradictory results." Zeno had
a philosophic intention: refute those who assert "the many and [pay] back
the same and more" by showing that what they assert "would suffer even
more laughable results than that of the one's being" (128d). By showing
the insurmountable logical puzzles of perception, Zeno's paradoxes aimed
to encourage a reconsideration of Parmenides' one as the unitary ground
of human experience — as Parmenides' exercises for the young Socrates
will reveal.

Zeno's explanation of his intention does not stop there, for he adds two arresting comments about his writing, and both concern intentions that are more hidden. "I wrote it, in fact, when I was young because of a love of victory (*philonikian*), a love to fight"—when Zeno was young, he was moved to write by what young Socrates is showing moves *him*, the spiritedness he displays in picking a fight with his elders, the most respected philosophers, imagining that he can win a victory and show his superiority, a self-aggrandizing intention that Zeno alleges he shared when *he* was young, even while his main intention was to serve Parmenides or serve philosophy. Zeno adds a second comment, isolated and seemingly incidental: "Someone stole a copy, so I wasn't allowed to decide whether it should be brought to light or not" (128e). *Would* Zeno have published his writing if someone hadn't stolen it and published it? Young Zeno seems to have recognized a need for caution with respect to making philosophic reasoning public, a need to weigh the advisability of publishing such reasonings at all. Socrates imputed to Zeno a common erotic intention familiar to him—plus trickery. Zeno's correction shows his overriding intention to have been philosophic, an aid to Parmenides, and to have included a feature that young Socrates should attend to, philosophy's reasonable caution, its concealing from the non-philosophic the radical implications it entails. Properly reading or hearing a philosophic writing involves understanding both what it says and what it intends—young Socrates' flippant attribution of erotic intention, self-aggrandizement, and mere trickery points to his failure to understand that philosophy must be cautious, practicing an exotericism that shelters views that could do damage; as befits the topic even Zeno's indication of this need for caution is indirect or oblique. What Zeno suggests to young Socrates in the *Parmenides* resembles and supplements Socrates' own disclosure about his youthful reading of Anaxagoras in the *Phaedo*: he had not yet learned how to read the philosophers because he misread their intentions.

Zeno ends his speech on what escaped young Socrates as a reader or listener by saying, "You didn't think it was written because of a young man's love of victory but because of an older man's love of honor." Socrates, he says in effect, take time to reflect on the possibility that my book was written by someone like you, a young lover of victory—but one who even then was aware of the need for caution. By favoring Socrates with these remarks, Zeno does what Parmenides will do in an extended way: both of them favor young Socrates with guidance for learning what only a philosopher needs to know. Socrates had charged that Parmenides' and Zeno's writings were "beyond the rest of us" (128b). After Zeno's response, Socrates' charge can be appreciated as almost right: Parmenides and Zeno *intended* their writings to be beyond the rest of us, but they published them so that a reader like Socrates, some unknown philosophically driven reader somewhere or other, could read them and find himself challenged to prove that they weren't beyond *him* — as Socrates aimed to prove with his transcendent forms .

Socrates' direct response to Zeno's lessons in reading and writing is more than curt; he simply dismisses Zeno's points as if they hardly concerned him: "I accept that and believe it is as you say. But tell me this . . ." Socrates is eager to get on with what he had prepared before Zeno broke in, so he rushes on to say to Zeno what he had been about to say to Parmenides before Zeno interrupted. Plato's dialogues demonstrate that Socrates came to recognize the truth and importance of what Zeno implied about the written and spoken words of a philosopher: for good reasons a philosopher masks his intentions or purposes, and if one is to adequately understand what he has written, those intentions and the reasons behind them must be understood. By its very nature this is a topic that precludes being stated openly, even in private. Zeno honors the imperatives of exoteric discretion — that is to say, the author of his every word, Plato, honors those imperatives here as everywhere. Zeno's lesson in reading for young Socrates serves as the proper preparation for Parmenides' lessons on being and knowing: they too are conveyed in deference to the imperatives of discretion. The things that need to be learned cannot be taught — but they can be learned.

4. Socrates' Solution to What Parmenides and Zeno Made to Seem beyond Us

Socrates' speech (128e–130a), delayed by Zeno's intervention, sets out his solution to the problem raised by the first hypothesis of Zeno's first logos, the problem of the many, a solution that at the same time solves the problem of the one. He addresses three questions to Zeno that set out his view of transcendent forms with notable economy. First:

> Don't you think that there exists, in itself, some form (*eidos*) of likeness to which is opposed a different one which is unlike, and that both you and I and the different things which we do in fact call "many" come to partake of these two things that are? (128e–129a)

Socrates' question states the two basic aspects of his solution, forms transcendent to particular things and participation in them by things. His second question effectively elaborates the consequence of viewing things as having the qualities they have of both likeness and unlikeness because they participate in the forms likeness and unlikeness:

> And that the things that come to partake of likeness become like in both the manner and extent that they partake, but those of unlikeness unlike, and those of both, both?

The incessant becoming of particular things is explained by their participations in unchanging forms. Socrates' final question simply expands transcendence and participation to "all things" before ending on a point that he reiterates throughout his response to Zeno:

> And even if all things come to partake of both these opposing things and are, by partaking in both, both like and unlike in themselves — why wonder?

The view that young Socrates has set out is, as Reginald Allen says, "substantially that of the *Phaedo* and the *Republic*"[16] — and precisely that is the chronological puzzle that modern Platonic scholarship has failed to solve, because it fails to take seriously the chronological order that Plato took pains to assign to his dialogues. The mature Socrates, from the *Republic* through to the *Phaedo*, employs the very view that the young Socrates devised in order to solve the basic problems of the one and the many posed by Parmenides and Zeno — only to have famous and honored Parmenides refute it as irrational. The drama of Plato's dialogues as a whole affords the problem he engineered an elegant solution based on exegesis alone.

Young Socrates ended his first statement of his transcendent forms solution with a question he will reiterate throughout his response to Zeno: "Why wonder?" He structures his whole speech on this question, which rises from his criticism that Zeno and Parmenides leave their readers in wonder, believing that these things are beyond them.[17] They're not beyond *me*, he says in effect. Refusing mere wonderment, he worked out a solution. And exactly this turns out to have been Zeno's intention, for he and Parmenides exchange glances and smiles throughout Socrates' speech — this is what they intended their writings to be, sorting devices

---

16. Allen, *Plato's "Parmenides,"* 90.

17. Socrates uses the word "wonder" (*thauma*) at 129b1; c1, 4, 5; d5; e3; he also uses near synonyms: "marvel" (*anomoia*), 129b2; "out of place" (*atopon*), 129b4.

that leave most readers in wonder while spurring some unknown reader in some unknown place to do what young Socrates just did. Socrates took the challenge of their writings to be a fight he could win; they view them as rational competency tests that they've just won.

To continue with his demonstration that his view of the forms eliminates the wonder in which Parmenides and Zeno leave their readers, young Socrates, despite his inexperience, employs a fine rhetorical device, introducing a "someone" to set out a condition that would justify Socrates feeling that the problem was beyond him:

> For if someone were to show that the like things themselves become unlike and the unlike like, I would think that a marvel (*anomia*). (129b)

That someone, moving to the basic pair, one and many, then sets out the conditions under which things would not be beyond him:

> But if he shows that whatever partakes of both of these has experienced both, then Zeno, it does not appear to me out of place (*atopon*); no, not even if he were to show that all things are one by partaking of the one and that these same things are many, in turn, by partaking of multitude. (129b)

The someone ends by restating the condition under which Socrates *would* be justified to wonder:

> But if he demonstrates that whatever one is, this very thing, is many, and that the many in turn are one, of course, I'll wonder at that. Likewise for all the different things, if he should reveal that both the kinds (*genē*) and forms (*eidē*) themselves experience these opposites in themselves, it's right to wonder. (129c)

The thinking of the young Socrates on likeness and unlikeness, one and many, spurred by Parmenides' and Zeno's writings, began in wonder at something that he refused to take as beyond him. Instead, he devised a view their made their writings radically deficient even though their authors were celebrated for them. He has thought his way through to the proper solution—all the glory should belong to him. The young Socrates of the *Parmenides* exemplifies what the old Socrates of the *Theaetetus* said is the beginning of philosophy, wonder as stimulant, not as a steady state (*Theaetetus* 155d), but his youthful, self-aggrandizing motive is suspect, and experienced Parmenides will aim to remedy his motive while demolishing his solution.

Socrates' speech then moves to particular instances of one and many, the fundamental topic of Parmenides' and Zeno's books (129c). If someone were to prove that *he* was one and many, "why wonder?" because that someone could easily show that he has a right side and a left side, a back and a front, an upper and lower, "for I do, I believe, partake of multitude." As for his being one, someone could refer to "the seven of us who are here" to say that Socrates is one of seven, thus showing that it is simply true and not worthy of wonder that he is both one and many (129d). Similarly for things like stones and sticks: they too can be said to be one and many without "anything worthy of wonder" being said. Socrates then nicely summarizes his argument for transcendent forms and his criticism of Parmenides and Zeno for leaving their audience with a sense that the whole issue of one and many is beyond them: if someone were to distinguish the forms as separate, "such as likeness and unlikeness, and many and one, and rest and motion . . . and then show that *these* things can be mixed together and separated, I'd admire that with wonder, Zeno" (129e).

Young Socrates ends with a condescending judgment on Zeno and expressly withholds his admiration: "Now I do believe that you've worked over these things quite bravely; but as I've said, I would admire this much more, if someone could demonstrate that even in the forms themselves, in the things grasped by reasoning (*logismos*), there is everywhere tangled up the same impasse (*aporia*) which you proved is present in the things we see" (130a). Thus believing that his solution can show that the world is open to rational analysis through the positing of transcendent forms, young Socrates believes that he has saved philosophy from the absurdities into which Parmenides and Zeno plunged it. He ends his speech secure in his conviction that he has won his fight against his famous elders who tried hard but failed to show that the world is irrational. Admire me, he says in effect, I succeeded where you failed. And Pythodorus reports that Parmenides and Zeno did in fact admire him. But what Parmenides will go on to show him is that the very things he claims to have grasped by reason, his forms, are themselves tangled up in the impasse that Socrates said would move him to wonder. In fact, he will show him that *each* of the things that he has said would move him to wonder applies to the forms themselves, leaving Socrates in the state of wonder that his forms were meant to overcome. But Parmenides will not stop there; he will offer the encouragement that there is in fact a way ahead that Socrates might be able to follow, and he will offer the necessary guidance to that way, guidance that will be an exercise in wonder, directed wonder at a set of seemingly contradictory hypotheses. And he will not fail to suggest that Socrates should grow up, grow out of the need for *thumos*-driven self-aggrandizement that still rules him "because of his age" (130e).

Having reported Socrates' speech, Pythodorus, for the only time in Antiphon's long report, told Antiphon his own reaction: "Pythodorus said, that while Socrates was speaking, he himself thought that at each word both Parmenides and Zeno were going to get angry"—*anger* seems to Pythodorus the proper response to the insulting manner in which his swaggering young countryman argued against his famous guests. Pythodorus must have looked often at Parmenides and Zeno to see how they were reacting to this outrage, for he says that "they kept their mind on Socrates and, with frequent glances to one another, they smiled as if admiring him. Which is, in fact, what Parmenides told him once he was done" (130b). The pleasure Parmenides and Zeno share at Socrates comes from keeping their minds on what Socrates' mind displays about him. Admire me, Socrates implies, and Parmenides and Zeno do admire him. Not angry, they respond as philosophers to a young fighter giving evidence of an admirable mind and high spiritedness: he might be one of those for whom they wrote their wonder-inducing books. Pythodorus's expectation that they would be angry is entirely natural, but so is the very different reaction of the two philosophers. For Socrates is right, they did make their writings seem beyond the rest of us. But Socrates did not know that they *intended* to give that impression: leave these crazy-sounding things alone, there's nothing of importance in them. But these writings of thinkers from far-off Elea also intended what they stimulated in him: fervent engagement in thinking about the nature of things by someone like this young person in Athens. They smile; they admire him. Here in Athens at the Great Panathenaia of 450 they learn that their writings have had the effect they intended on a young Athenian unknown to them when they wrote, a youngster who parades himself before them as their rational vanquisher. As Leo Strauss said of the books of the philosophers, they "owe their existence to the love of the mature philosopher for the puppies of his race, by whom he wants to be loved in turn: all exoteric books are 'written speeches caused by love.'"[18]

It is Parmenides who, with his first words in the dialogue, reports the shared reaction of the two of them to Socrates' speech to Zeno: "Socrates, how worthy you are to be admired for zeal for logoi!" (130b). Parmenides' first words, like Socrates' first words (127d-e), refer to the very thing Soc-

---

18. Strauss, *Persecution and the Art of Writing*, 36.

rates said he turned to in the *Phaedo*, the logoi, here the logoi of the philosophers, which he never stopped considering. In the *Phaedo* Socrates made
his turn to the logoi culminate in transcendent forms, which apparently
brought his autobiography of his development to a successful end. But
the movement he described in the *Phaedo*, from the passion to know the
causes of all things to a turn to the logoi and to putting down as hypothesis
whatever logos he judged mightiest, and then to transcendent forms as the
exclusive cause — all that can now be seen to have been only a first stage,
even though he treated it there as complete. In the actual next stage of
Socrates' philosophic becoming, saved from oblivion by nameless philosophers from Clazomenae, he was guided first by Zeno to read philosophic
texts with a view to their intention and then guided by Parmenides himself
on the fundamental question of form as cause. Delighted at Socrates' attempt to refute him, Parmenides will offer the young fighter the necessary
guidance to keep pushing toward the only adequate solution to the problem of form.

What the efforts of the men of Clazomenae preserve turns out to be a
model for the transmission of philosophy's deepest insights, the wise way
of speaking and writing the truth about nature and human nature. While
all of Athens participates in the spectacle of the greatest of all Athenian
festivals, the private event inside Pythodorus's house turns out to be the
truly historic event, the meeting of the young Socrates with Zeno and
Parmenides. What the men of Clazomenae witness and pass on through
Cephalus is the passing on of philosophic wisdom. And when the wisdom
of Parmenides passes to a Socrates, who can tell what the future of philosophy might be? In fact it turned out to be the changing of an age, a
founding event by the philosopher Socrates. Schooled early by Zeno and
Parmenides, he matured into the thinker who came to recognize that he
was witnessing the twilight of the Homeric gods. What passed from Parmenides to Socrates would require a new form of shelter different from
what Parmenides' goddess provided for him.

5. Parmenides the Guide

The first question Parmenides asks Socrates is the natural one: "Tell me,
did you yourself come up with this division that you speak of between
these forms, separate unto themselves, and, separated from them, the
things that partake of them?" (130b). It matters to authors whose writings
are philosophic recruitment tools whether Socrates himself is the inventive reasoner who thought up this solution, and although he gives Socrates

no opportunity to say, Yes, I came up with it myself, it becomes evident that he is the author of his view of transcendent forms. Parmenides asks a second question, extending his restatement of Socrates' view: "And does it seem to you that likeness itself is separate from the likeness that we possess, and so on with one and many and everything that you heard of just now from Zeno?" When Socrates answers with a vehement "It certainly does," Parmenides initiates a sequence of problems with the view he clearly summarized, increasing in difficulty and importance right up to his final one, "the greatest" impasse this solution introduces. The structured coherence of Parmenides' sequence of difficulties suggests that he had already thought through the possibility of transcendent forms; the wonder evoked by his writings coupled with Zeno's seems to lead naturally — for a philosophic problem-solver raised with Homer's many gods — to a solution like Socrates' that turns out to be no solution at all.[19]

Parmenides' first set of questions asks about the range of the forms in three stages of ascending improbability for them. After hearing Socrates strongly assent to separate forms for matters just dealt with from Zeno's book, Parmenides asks about forms for categorically different matters: Does Socrates hold that there are forms of "justice in itself, and of beauty [*kalos* — also fine, noble] and of good and all such as these?" Socrates answers with a simple yes, but how remarkable Parmenides' question is. It asks about those three matters for which such forms would be most useful or desirable, transcendent standards of measure for justice, beauty, and goodness, the three domains of human evaluation where disputes are keenest and most divisive, most in need of objective arbitration: what is right, what is beautiful or noble, and what is good. Parmenides knows exactly which transcendent forms would be of the greatest practical importance — and it is especially to forms of this sort that the mature Socrates will appeal in the *Republic* and the *Phaedo*. Parmenides' next question on the range of forms exposes serious difficulties for Socrates in defending his view. Is there "a form of human separate from us and all those like us, some form itself of human, or of fire or water?" (130c). There are immediate difficulties with a form of the human: Is it male or female? Does it age? Does it speak, go to war, eat? As for fire and water, they are the two elements whose very nature it is to alter and flow. "I've been at a loss many times,

19. Reginald Allen gives an apt characterization of the careful structure of Parmenides' series of criticisms: "The internal structure of this scheme of argument is neat to the point of elegance. Perhaps no theory in the history of philosophy has been exposed to a more tight-knit and subtle series of objections" (*Plato's "Parmenides,"* 104).

Parmenides, over these," Socrates admits, "whether it is necessary to speak much the same about them or differently"; in answering the experienced Parmenides, Socrates readily acknowledges being a beginner. But he is a beginner with the virtue of openly admitting that he does not know how to answer Parmenides' perfect questions while knowing they need an answer.

Parmenides' final question on the range of the forms asks about what he calls "things that would seem to be laughable, such as hair, mud, and dirt or any different thing that's very worthless and lowly." He asks, "Are you at a loss over whether it is or is not necessary to say that there is a separate form of each of these?" (130c-d). Socrates is *not* at a loss about forms for hair, mud, and dirt: "No, not at all!" He categorically refuses to extend the logic of his argument to such things, and his reason for not doing so betrays a gap in his logical consistency and unsophisticated convictions about being and knowing: "These things are as we see them right here." But why wouldn't they too lead to the logical difficulties of Zeno's arguments about like and unlike and one and many? Moreover, Socrates' answer shows that he believes that perception gives simple, direct access to the things as they are, only some of which merit the dignity of a form. This part of his refusal expresses the merely aesthetic basis of his criterion: it would be "grossly out of place" to posit forms of such things. The particulars Parmenides asked about — hair, mud, dirt — point toward unlaughable particulars he avoided asking about: If there are forms of both like and unlike or one and many, why aren't there forms of justice *and injustice*, beauty *and ugliness*, good *and evil*? Socrates is admirably candid about his lack of consistency in applying his forms solution, readily admitting that he is "troubled" by his inconsistency and that he "runs away" from the possibility of such forms in fear of falling and perishing in an abyss of foolishness. Refusing to face up to the logical difficulty, he simply returns to things like those they have been talking about and busies himself with cases where his solution does not offend his taste. Young Socrates' willing acknowledgment of his inadequate rigor is met by encouragement from Parmenides that is itself a kind of praise, an inducement to persevere: "You're still young, Socrates, and philosophy has not yet taken hold of you as it will, in my opinion" (130e). Parmenides has witnessed enough to predict that philosophy will take full hold of Socrates and when it does, "you will dishonor none of these things" — you will apply reason indifferently to all fields of inquiry and settle all questions on the basis of reasoning alone. But "because of your age you look to the opinions of human beings." Young Socrates is still subject to the common opinions, allowing them to infect his rational practice and limit his inquiry into being and knowing.

Turning from the range of forms to the participation of things in forms,
Parmenides starts with forms already discussed, likeness, beauty, and justice, but substitutes largeness for good. Doesn't the participation in a
form by a multiplicity of particulars imply a fragmentation of the form,
a breakup of its wholeness into a multiplicity of parts? Socrates is ready
for this with a likeness that he thinks eliminates the problem: "Not if [the
form] is like a day (131b)" — a day remains whole while being spread through
each item in the day. For Seth Benardete this likeness bristles with implication, displaying both the nature and the limits of Socrates' youthful thinking about the forms. Taking day and daylight seriously as the image of the
form's relation to the particulars that participate in it implies that Socrates
holds that the form causes the particulars "to be and be known."[20] Benardete measures this view of the young Socrates from the perspective of his
subsequent Platonic career: Socrates "has not yet seen that though to be
and to be intelligible go together, it does not follow that the beings disclose
themselves" — they do not disclose themselves to human awareness as Socrates imagined they did when he said that hair, mud, and dirt "are as we see
them right here." Because the beings do not disclose themselves, standing
before us in the light of day as they are, "Socrates' recourse to speeches,"
that turn of the *Phaedo*, will "have to be refined." That refinement is what
Parmenides aims to effect and it requires something unexpected, as Benardete says: Socrates' "attention" will have to be "turned away from opinions"
because it is not the case that "he could . . . read off from [opinions] the
way the beings are." A turn away from opinions could afford insight into
what opinion *is* — it could bring the ground of opinion to light. *Refined* is
the necessary word: the *Parmenides* shows where Socrates must change the
focus of his turn to the logoi as reported in the *Phaedo*: Parmenides shows
Socrates his path after that turn. That "opinions stand in the way of what
the beings are" is suggested by the image with which Parmenides counters
Socrates' image of day: "a sail covering many people" as "one whole over
many": a sail darkens what day lights up, obscuring access to what beings
are. As Benardete says, "The single day of Socrates becomes the single
night of day in which nothing can be known." Parmenides' sail image for
forms countering Socrates' day image leads to the general question of how
to conceive of the participation of parts in wholes and wholes in parts. His
examples show Socrates that he lacks a way to conceive of such participation that does not entail the breakup of wholes into parts (131c-e).

20. Benardete, "Plato's *Parmenides*," 236. Benardete's account of the *Parmenides* is singular and groundbreaking; I make extensive use of it from this point on.

Parmenides' next question also concerns the participation of things in the form, but it focuses on the reasoning by which Socrates moves from a shared quality spread among many particulars to the one that they participate in. The many *large* things share that quality, Socrates argued, because they participate in the singular form large (132a-b).[21] But that very move from the large things to the form large must logically be repeated with respect to the largeness shared by the large things and the form large: "A different form of large will be revealed . . . so each of your forms will no longer be one but will be boundless in multitude." Socrates' immediate way out of this problem is a suggestion about the character of forms: Couldn't "each of the forms be a thought and properly come to be nowhere but in our souls?" But doesn't that imply of the things that participate in that thought that "either each *thing* consists of thoughts and everything thinks or, although thoughts, they are thoughtless?" (132c).

Socrates immediately surrenders the view that the forms might be thoughts, and suggests a view that seems to be as far as his thinking about the forms has led him so far: "Here's how it really appears to me to be: these forms stand in nature like patterns (*paradeigmata*) . . . so the different things' participation in the forms turns out to be nothing else than to be made in their likeness" (132d). But on this conception too, the likeness shared by the form in nature and the things made in its pattern necessitates a further form to account for *that* likeness so that "there will never be an end to the genesis of new forms" (133a). Parmenides ends this first set of problems with transcendent forms by saying, "It is not by likeness, then, that the different things come to partake of forms. Instead, it's necessary to seek a different way of partaking." Does Parmenides know that different way of partaking? He never says he does, nor does he ever explicitly show Socrates what it might be. Instead, when he is finished with his immediate lessons for this young would-be philosopher, his refutations, he will prescribe a set of intellectual exercises for him, a *gymnastic*, within which that different way of partaking will be secreted. Only by mastering that gymnastic will Socrates learn the proper way of partaking: he has to earn it or even in a way discover it himself. "Do you see then, Socrates, how great an impasse" — an *aporia* — "lies before anyone who tries to determine that there are forms in themselves?" Socrates confirms his openness to learning by answering, "Very much so!"

In an insight that will prove fundamental for his interpretation of the

---

21. At 132a8 Parmenides introduces the word *idea* as a synonym of *eidos*; he will use it this way six more times (132c; 133c; 134c; 135a, c; 157d). Socrates never uses the word.

Parmenides, Benardete says that Socrates' last two quickly offered options —
forms are thoughts in the soul, forms are patterns in nature — harbor "an
inchoate psychology" and "an inchoate ontology"[22] with no way of bringing the two together. For Benardete, these two un-thought-through options and Parmenides' arguments against them prefigure his gymnastic,
that strenuous exercise of thinking that he will offer the young Socrates.
And the gymnastic will intimate, Benardete shows, the possibility of an
articulated psychology and then even an ontology that follows from that:
Parmenides' guidance will lead to a proper account of the beings that
passes through a proper understanding of human being and its way of
knowing. Socrates' last two suggestions will turn out to be moves in the
right direction.

Having dealt with problems entailed by participation, Parmenides
turns to problems entailed by the very positing of transcendent forms because so far they have "not even touched upon how great an impasse there
is if you try to posit each form as one, somehow distinguishing them from
the beings" (133b). There are many reasons for the impasse in separating
forms from the beings, Parmenides says, but he treats only "the greatest"
reason, the knowability of such forms: "If someone should argue that the
forms themselves — should they be as we say they must be — cannot properly speaking be known, no one could prove to the person who argues
this that he is mistaken, unless that person happened to be experienced
in many things and not ungifted." Such a denier "would have to be willing
to follow the one working over the proof through many cases and over a
long distance, otherwise he who forces them to be unknowable would be
persuasive" (133c). Parmenides will end the argument he is now beginning
by bringing back this capable denier to say that either the forms are not,
or if they are, they are unknowable to human beings. "And while he says
these things he will even be said to be talking sense and as we said before
will be wondrously hard to convince" (135a). Parmenides thus frames his
final argument concerning transcendent forms with a capable denier of
their knowability.

When Parmenides at the start of his argument spoke of the capable
denier as seeming to be persuasive, Socrates asked, "Why's that?" To show
him why, Parmenides no longer includes himself as one who holds that
there are separate forms (cf. 133b7) but speaks instead of "you and anyone
else who posits such forms" — you would agree first that none of the forms
exist among us (133c). But then the *relations* among them are not among us

22. Benardete, "Plato's *Parmenides*," 236.

either but are confined to relations among forms. Similarly, the relations of the things among us are confined and do not extend to the forms (133d). "What are you saying?" Socrates asks, but it is clear that Parmenides is saying that there is an insurmountable separation between the two domains, the forms and the things among us. To fully explain what he's saying, Parmenides chooses to give an example, master and slave, that proves to be part of his preparation for the radical conclusions that are coming. A slave is not slave to the form master nor a master master to the form slave; instead, because the domains are entirely separate, the form mastership is master to slavehood, and the form slavehood slavery to mastership. Parmenides then adds a word well chosen for its coming effect: "The things among us have no *power* (*dynamis*) in relation to those things nor they to us" (133e). Emphasizing the separation of realms, he explicitly asks Socrates, "Or do you not understand what I mean?" (134a). Socrates seems in fact to be recognizing the devastating drift of Parmenides' argument: "Oh, I understand well" (134a1–2). Parmenides then moves to a second telling example: *knowledge* is a relation, and therefore the form knowledge is of truth itself while knowledge among us is of truth among us (134a). Parmenides' generalized conclusion will be deeply sobering to Socrates: "None of the forms then is known by us since we don't partake of knowledge itself" (134b). Therefore, "what the beautiful itself is and the good and all the things that we suppose to be ideas are unknown to us." Socrates is compelled to say about this demolition of his forms as standards of measure, "I'm afraid so" (134c).

It's bad enough that what Parmenides has so far argued is fatal to young Socrates' view of transcendent forms, but now he states that there is an implication "still more terrible than this" — and introduces the gods. Securing Socrates' confirmation that he holds that there are forms of knowledge and of beauty, he focuses on knowledge, asking if the god possesses "this most precise knowledge." "Necessarily," Socrates replies. But when Parmenides asks if "the god will be able to know the things among us, since he possesses knowledge itself," Socrates resists: "Why not?" he asks (134d), seemingly reluctant to yield this limit on the *gods'* knowledge even though the arguments already made show the separation of domains to be complete. Parmenides' argument about the gods is not the center of Socrates' philosophic education, for as Plato presents that education it is a tale of continuous ascent through its three stages; nevertheless, this is a decisive item in that ascent, for with this argument authoritative Parmenides deprives the young Socrates he has closely observed not only of his forms but also of his piety. Parmenides dares to draw out the obvious but terrible conclusions from their arguments about mastership, powers, and knowledge. Reminding Socrates first about their agreement regarding powers, he again states that the gods possess the form mastery, but specifically adds the necessary limitation that they "could never master us, nor could their knowledge know us or anything else of the things among us." The reverse is also true: "We do not rule over them by the authority among us, nor, by our knowledge, do we know anything of the divine" (134e). Parmenides is relentless; he repeats himself: "According to this logos, they are not our masters nor do they know anything of human affairs — *because* they are gods."

"But what an altogether wondrous logos," Socrates replies, "if it strips the god of knowing!" He thereby singles out one aspect of the devastating conclusion, not mentioning what Parmenides had just stated: the argument also strips *us* of any knowledge of the gods. When Socrates first stated his forms solution, he repeatedly referred to what would be worthy of his wonder and what would not (129a–130a). Parmenides has just caused wonder to arise in him on the most terrible matter, wonder that challenges, through reasoning based on his own premises, the residual piety befitting a youngster like him. Socrates had also said that when implications of his forms theory led to troublesome conclusions, he ran off in fear to work on less threatening aspects of his theory (130d). Don't run off from this, Parmenides implies by making his arguments about mastery, powers, and knowledge apply to the gods as the culminating conclusions of his refutation of transcendent forms: don't remain subject to "the opinions of human beings" on matters of piety.

While outside Pythodorus's house the Athenians celebrate their supreme festival to their protecting goddess Athena, inside the foreign philosopher Parmenides points the young Athenian Socrates toward a complete separation from the gods. Speaking with the young Pythagoreans Simmias and Cebes on the last day of his life, Socrates not only assumed their youthful piety, he made it a part of his arguments and even gave them irrational forms as the rational-looking means of keeping their piety safe from skeptical philosophy. Old Parmenides, however, speaking with the nineteen-year-old Socrates, whose measure he had taken, definitively refuted his view of the participation of things in separate transcendent forms, and in this second part of his argument, concerning transcendent forms themselves, chose to extend his argument to conclude that the gods are not our masters and are completely separated from us. Parmenides does not teach atheism in his "altogether wondrous logos" but his proofs of the limits on the gods' power, rule, and knowledge cause them to drift off into irrelevance, unknowing of us, unknowable by us.

cf. Christendom / imperial Christianity

In commenting on Parmenides' arguments about the forms and the gods, Benardete states one of their unspoken upshots: Parmenides "draws the conclusion that the gods are not our masters. Parmenides declares that man is free."[23] Benardete goes on to state a corollary that Socrates could not even have begun to think about: "Insofar as [man] has knowledge of human things in accordance with his nature he is their master." In this way, "Parmenides calls Socrates' attention to the arts," for the arts accord with human nature in its effort to gain mastery in its own domain. Benardete then looks again to the only place where one could find out what young Socrates learned from Parmenides' effort to guide his attention to mastery in the arts: "If we look ahead to Socrates' subsequent Platonic career, the political things are obviously the [arts] that Parmenides offers Socrates."[24] Looking ahead to the *Republic* and *Statesman*, he draws a conclusion that separates philosophy's ultimate question from the question of the human and the political: "The complete understanding of the political does not depend on a comprehensive account of the whole"—the necessary skepticism about knowing the whole that will be conveyed by Parmenides' gymnastic does not imply a skepticism about knowing the human and political. This is one way in which Benardete makes good on his early promise: "Parmenides, then, who appears to be the most high-falutin of the philosophers, is the one who brings Socrates down to earth."[25] Parmenides of all people guided Socrates toward what Plato's *Republic* showed he achieved: knowledge of the soul and the city, knowledge that made it possible for him to establish philosophic or spiritual rule over the minds of political men like young Glaucon and Adeimantus—a foreshadowing of Plato's actual historic achievement. What Benardete shows about Parmenides bringing Socrates down to earth, especially through his gymnastic, compels reflection on something unexpected: the philosopher Parmenides had already come down to earth and understood the human through the logoi. Plato's account of Parmenides' lessons for the young Socrates requires that the "Socratic turn" be reexamined in order to determine what is truly unique to Socrates.[26]

Parmenides has brought Socrates to a point of wonder about transcendent forms, and he ends his questioning by stating that "many more" problems exist with forms as Socrates defined them (135a). Having completed

23. Benardete, "Plato's *Parmenides*," 236–37.
24. Benardete, 237.
25. Benardete, 230.
26. See below, section 9 in this chapter, "The Socratic Turn."

his two arguments, first against Socrates' view of participation and then against his transcendent forms, Parmenides reintroduces the *someone* from the beginning of the second argument (133b): "The result is that whoever hears this hits a dead end and argues that these things *are* not; and if, at most, they should *be*, well, then, great necessity keeps them unknown to human nature." The one who says this "will even seem to be talking sense and, as we said before, he will be wondrously hard to convince." Parmenides had spoken of this someone as "not ungifted" (*mē aphuēs*, 133b10), and now he says that "only a naturally gifted (*euphuous*) person could learn that there is a certain kind and beinghood in itself for each thing" (135a). The argument framed by that gifted person proves that if transcendent forms exist they are unknowable, and their absolute separation implies that the gods are unknowing of us and unknowable to us. But Parmenides' arguments about participation had shown that transcendent forms cannot possibly exist because they entail logical contradiction. Could that proven impossibility of transcendent forms be employed to allow space for the gods then, allow them back into a world without transcendent forms as knowing of us and known by us? On the contrary, Parmenides seems to count on Socrates' evident drive to inquire being more powerful than any need on his part to believe: the two prongs of his argument serially deprive Socrates of the two premises of his theory. Parmenides frees young Socrates from transcendent forms and from gods.

Is Socrates a naturally gifted person who "could learn that there is a certain kind and beinghood in itself for each thing"? He has already proven himself gifted in inventing a solution to problems that the writings of Parmenides and Zeno pose and he has proven himself capable of setting aside that proudly held view in the face of rational objections. Parmenides then introduces a still higher state that such a person might aspire to: "Only a still more wondrous person will discover all these things and have the power to teach someone else who has examined all these difficulties for himself" (135b). Parmenides knows himself; he was Zeno's guide and he seems to be offering himself as Socrates' guide and offering him an understanding of the highest state to which a person aspiring to knowledge can ascend. Deprived of the view that backed his swagger, Socrates assents to Parmenides' order of rank among persons: he puts himself in the hands of the most wondrous person for guidance.

Parmenides returns to the person who denies "that there are forms of the beings and does not distinguish a certain form of each single thing; wherever he turns he'll understand nothing" (135b). But just how *are* forms to be understood if Socrates' initial way is indefensible? At the least one must allow "that there is an ever-same idea for each of the beings." Without suggesting how that might be understood, Parmenides emphasizes the disastrous consequence of denying forms: one who does not allow that there is an idea for each of the beings "will utterly destroy the power of dialogue (*dialegesthai*)," of thought and discourse, of rationality itself (135c). Parmenides has already drawn his conclusion about Socrates: "But you seem to me only too aware of this." "You speak the truth," Socrates replies. Parmenides then puts the essential challenge to a Socrates he has forced to face that truth: "What will you yourself do with philosophy? Where will you turn if all this is unknown?" Socrates answers the two questions by admitting that "at present, at least, I can't seem to see." Parmenides knows exactly why he can't: he is "trying too soon" to solve immense problems of understanding, *too soon* because of a precise lack; he has not been properly "trained" (*gymnasthēnai*), he has not submitted himself to the rational discipline that can make his mind fit to subdue such problems. And Parmenides identifies the problem Socrates is not yet trained to solve: he tried too soon "to define some beautiful and just and good and each one of the forms" (135c). Socrates cannot yet define what a form as such is, and therefore cannot define the beautiful, just, and good that Parmenides had already noted were the most obvious candidates for Socrates' view of forms (130b).[27] These three are the core matters of human judgment that determine both private and social life, and each of them marks a domain of controversy dividing human beings. These are the matters that most stand in need of a clear understanding that could arbitrate the controversies and give security to human private and social life — and these matters Socrates is not yet trained to confront.

Parmenides now makes a small remark that helps explain why he ran the risk of destroying Socrates' view of forms and potentially of his piety: he had been forming his judgment about the capacity of this young Athenian even before the events narrated by Pythodorus; he had observed Socrates "the day before yesterday" when he overheard him conversing with Aristoteles (135d). Socrates had therefore already gone at least once to Pythodorus's house to seek out the famous philosophic visitors, and he had already caught their attention. Parmenides "noticed already then" that Socrates needed to be trained before defining the beautiful, just, and good. Still, he had been powerfully impressed: "Beautiful and divine — know this

---

27. In this second listing of the three, Parmenides changed the order of beautiful and just. The three also appeared in pairs at 131a (beauty and justice), and 134b (beautiful and good).

well!—is that zeal which drives you toward the logoi." From what he had already observed Parmenides knew that Socrates was driven by a powerful philosophic urge, driven toward the logoi that he reported in the *Phaedo* was his first step on his own toward the kind of inquiry that could satisfy the beautiful and divine urge within him. Having taken young Socrates' measure, old Parmenides can dare to do with him the opposite of what old Socrates did with young Simmias and Cebes: Parmenides can lead this philosophically driven exception to face up to the problem of skepticism that will inevitably follow doubt about the forms. Parmenides seems to have judged that a young man as driven by philosophy as Socrates would not long be content with running away from the problems inherent in his rationally deficient solution. Let him confront those problems with a guide who can point the way forward.

Having satisfied himself that Socrates possessed the philosophic urge, the drive to understand things rationally, and knowing the danger of skepticism awaiting the inevitable failures that that urge faces, and having gained the standing of a guide with him, Parmenides can command him: "Drag yourself back and train yourself more in what seems to be useless and is called idle talk by the many, do it while you're still young; if you don't, truth will escape you." He challenges the Socrates who still looked "to the opinions of human beings" (130e) to undergo strenuous training in what is judged useless by the many and scorned by them: to understand what concerns everyone he will have to work at what interests almost no one. Favored with praise and a warning and a challenge, the Socrates bereft of his forms is eager: "What is this way, Parmenides, this gymnastic?" No wonder Plato had Socrates reflect very late in his life on what Parmenides meant to him, recalling with profound gratitude what meeting Parmenides when he was young meant to him: "He appeared to me to have some altogether great and noble depth."[28]

And no wonder then that Plato paired the *Republic* and the *Parmenides* by giving Adeimantus and Glaucon prominent presence in the frame of the *Parmenides*. The *Republic* shows that Adeimantus and Glaucon were exposed in their young manhood to a Socrates who was the teacher of transcendent forms, the teaching that provided them with a new foundation for their shaken faith in justice. But the *Parmenides* shows them in their old age hearing something unsettling when they stay and listen to the tale the men of Clazomenae sailed across the sea to hear. The young Socrates they hear about from their half brother Antiphon was, at first, the articu-

28. *Theaetetus* 183e–184a; see also 152d–153a, and *Sophist* 217d.

late advocate of the transcendent forms to which he had introduced them when they were young. But then they hear Parmenides refute that view, and they learn that the young Socrates immediately recognized the validity of the refutation and abandoned the view he taught them years later. The *Parmenides* says nothing about their reaction to that refutation—they seem to stand as silent models for all other hearers of the *Parmenides* made believers in transcendent forms by Plato's Socrates. The puzzle presented to them by their half brother's report is a puzzle for the reader of all the dialogues: What did the doctrine of transcendent forms really mean for the mature Socrates, given that he can teach it decades after he himself accepted the demonstration of its irresolvable contradictions? The chronological indicators that Plato was so careful to arrange for his dialogues offer the engaged reader of all of them a solution to *that* puzzle in the most puzzling of all his dialogues. These now quite old Athenian gentlemen can be left, like their younger horseman half brother, with a harmless puzzlement while those genuinely driven by philosophic wonder will work to resolve it.

6. What Is This Gymnastic?

Parmenides and Zeno could smile at Socrates despite his annoying manner because they saw the brilliance of his mind and the spiritedness of his temper. Now Parmenides sees a Socrates chastened by the demolition of his vaunted theory, a Socrates who honors Parmenides' evident rational authority and asks to be led: these qualities too deserve admiration. Parmenides tells Socrates that the gymnastic he must practice is what he "heard just now from Zeno." Except this" (135d)—except Socrates had already taken, on his own, the appropriate step beyond Zeno's puzzles: "I really admired it of you, what you said to him that you would not allow inquiry to wander among the things we see nor even concern them but rather concern those things that one should grasp by logoi and believe to be forms" (135e). Zeno's puzzles are themselves exercises, a gymnastic aimed at moving the puzzled beyond the things we see, and Socrates is already beyond *those* exercises: what Parmenides especially admires is his having already made the turn to the speeches and the forms.

This aspect of Parmenides' praise is especially instructive: he admires the young Socrates for the very step that the old Socrates described in the *Phaedo* as his first step on his second sailing, his turn to the logoi (*Phaedo* 99e) and to the forms of the "beautiful itself by itself and a good and a big and all the others" (100b). Plato shows Parmenides catching Socrates at nineteen after he had already taken the necessary step toward a still more demanding gymnastic that he doesn't know exists but that is indispensable for an adequate understanding of the logoi and forms. What Plato has Parmenides say of the way forward employs other wording from the *Phaedo*, for Socrates responds to Parmenides' praise by telling him why his turn to the logoi and the forms seemed necessary: "This way, there seems to me no difficulty in showing what the beings are like and unlike and experience anything else." "Beautiful," Parmenides says in response to this claim to a defensible account of the beings, even though he has just shown that by itself this step toward the being of beings — positing transcendent forms — entails insurmountable rational difficulties. Parmenides' way therefore uses but moves beyond Socrates' first way of avoiding Zeno's puzzles: "But, in addition, you must do this: do not only investigate the results of a hypothesis if each hypothesized thing is." This wording suggests that what Parmenides overheard Socrates saying to Aristoteles the day before yesterday was a version of what Socrates described to Cebes fifty years later in the *Phaedo* as his next step in his method of isolating forms: after "putting down as hypothesis that there's some beautiful itself by itself and a good and a big . . . and from them show the cause" (*Phaedo* 100b). Old Socrates confined what he told Cebes to this safe way alone: "In fright . . . holding tightly to this safe hypothesis . . . consider the things that spring forth from that hypothesis — that is, whether . . . those things are consonant or disconsonant with one another" (101d). And if an account of the hypothesis itself needs to be given, he tells Cebes, "Give it in just the same way, by hypothesizing in turn another hypothesis, whichever of the higher ones appeared best, until you come to something sufficient." That's "the way to discover something about the beings" (101e). Is it? Parmenides gave young Socrates a different way, one that entailed an entirely different kind of step as a test of adequacy for a hypothesis: instead of hypothesizing that a form is and then moving to a higher hypothesis of what is, instead of staying safe, Parmenides told Socrates that he "must . . . also hypothesize that this same thing is not. Do that if you want to get more gymnastic training" (*Parmenides* 136a). Hypothesizing that a thing is not — *that* is absent from what Socrates tells Cebes of his early steps; but hypothesizing is not is necessary for the way Parmenides guided Socrates to take — and it is hypothesizing is not that leads to true understanding as well as to the most radical, unsafe conclusions. Socrates, having exhibited to Parmenides traits that merit it — a powerful impulse to inquiry, an inventive bent toward solutions, an openness to being wrong, a receptivity to rational guidance — received from his honored guide a demanding gymnastic training in a rational approach to understanding beings. Cebes, having exhibited to Socrates a powerful need to believe his soul immortal, receives from his honored guide simple exercises in the safe way, a rationally deficient way but one that fits Cebes' needs.

Socrates is eager to learn the new gymnastic. And Parmenides presents a compact summary of what he will soon be compelled to set out in full. The gymnastic is an exercise with a basic pattern that Parmenides first gives for the fundamental pair, *is* and *is not*. Begin with "the hypothesis that Zeno hypothesized," he says, that "many is," the hypothesis that experience presents as necessarily true, the hypothesis that is the positive way of expressing "one is not." Then examine that hypothesis in a very particular way: "If many is, what must result both for the many themselves in relation to themselves and in relation to the one, and for the one in relation to itself and in relation to the many?" And then do the same with what Parmenides hypothesized, that one is, formulating it too in its negative form: "Then, in turn, if many is not you must inquire what will result both for the one and the many both in relation to themselves and in relation to each other" (136a). Having set out that basic pair and the proper way of inquiring into them, Parmenides moves to the category Zeno had read as the first logos of his writing, likeness, and performs the same operations with it: "If likeness is or is not, what in the case of each hypothesis will be the result both for the very things hypothesized and for the different things both in relation to themselves and in relation to each other?" (136b). The same logos, he says, is to be performed for "unlikeness and motion and rest and generation and corruption and even being or not being." The pattern of hypothesizing is the same "whatever you hypothesize about." Parmenides repeats himself in making emphatic to Socrates that whatever he hypothesizes he "must always investigate the results in relation to itself and in relation to each one of the different things." He must do that if his intention, "after being completely trained, [is] to attain a lordly view of the true" (136c); *lordly*, like a lord or master; the master Parmenides has gained the right to say such things.

No wonder Socrates has a double response to this first setting out of the gymnastic: "It's quite an impossible task that you're talking about, Parmenides, and I don't really understand it." But he's not willing to give up: "Why don't you hypothesize something and go through it for me, so that I can understand better?" Just as Antiphon did earlier in the dialogue, Parmenides balks, saying that's "a lot of work" (136d; cf. 127a), adding that his age makes it more difficult. With the last words he will speak in the dialogue, Socrates asks, "Well then, you, Zeno, why don't you go through it for us?" It's all the same to Socrates whether Parmenides or Zeno shows him the way, what matters is that he be shown: Socrates' last words are a testament to his eagerness; he will memorize the gymnastic and work at examples of it until it opens the way to the truth for him too.

Zeno responds to Socrates' request by laughing and deferring to the master, saying that they should ask Parmenides because the matter is so important. Repeating that it demands "much work," Zeno returns to the issue he raised when he last spoke, whether such matters should be made public (128d-e). He can ask Parmenides to perform the gymnastic only because they are a small group, for it is inappropriate to discuss such matters before the many, "especially for someone of his age" (136d), meaning perhaps not simply that it's hard but that a thinker with the built-in authority of age must be very careful about whom he invites to his gymnastic. The many do not know that "without this digressing and wandering through all things it is impossible to possess a mind that has hit upon the true" (136e) — the many believe they already know what's true and regard such exercises as idle talk. Truth is what the gymnastic aims at: Parmenides and Zeno have said that three times (135d, 136c, e). Only the few know that gaining the truth entails "digressing," for if "wandering among the visible things" is merely perplexing (135e), "wandering" — structured, purposeful wandering — "through *all things*" is necessary: the truth Parmenides aims at through the gymnastic is comprehensive, ontological truth. With that reinforcement for Socrates about the appropriateness of a small audience for the most important of inquiries into the truth, Zeno turns to Parmenides to say that he "joins Socrates in asking, that I too may listen after all this time" — a grateful and successful recipient of Parmenides' great gift, having himself become an authority, wants to hear again from the master what once changed his life. Cephalus reports Antiphon's report that Pythodorus said that he and every other member of the group joined Zeno in asking: *three* others, Aristoteles, and the two Socrates brought. So the old and singular philosopher of being and non-being in the Greek tradition of wisdom sets out to guide a young inquirer who has exhibited the gifts of mind and spirit that may qualify him for the philosophic life. Parmenides' gymnastic will open the way to a true epistemology and ontology, replacing Socrates' forms; it is an inquiry into the beings that is attentive to the being of the inquirer: know thyself proves to be the only route to a knowledge of nature.

As he approaches the hard work of the gymnastic for Socrates, Parmenides introduces a likeness from a poem by Ibycus to describe his condition: he is like an old racehorse experienced in winning but trembling now before a chariot race because he knows the exertion it demands (137a). But he may have a deeper reason for introducing just that poem here, the reason why Ibycus likened himself to the racehorse. Though old and unwilling, necessity forced him to fall in love. Parmenides returns to just how demanding the exercise is — "I remember what sort of speeches and how great a multitude they are that I must swim through." Still, like Ibycus, he too seems to have fallen in love again, he whose love for the young Zeno has already been noted (127b). *Eros,* the first word of Ibycus's poem,[29] seems to be Parmenides' impetus in overcoming his reluctance: the gymnastic is a speech caused by the love of a mature philosopher for a youngster of his own kind by whom he wants to be loved in turn.

7. Guiding Socrates

I have chosen an unusual way to treat Parmenides' gymnastic:[30] my discussion will consist mainly of an exposition of Seth Benardete's exegesis of the gymnastic in his essay "Plato's *Parmenides*: A Sketch." I have two reasons for doing this: first, Benardete's account is entirely unique among modern approaches and in that singularity provides access to just what Parmenides' gymnastic guided young Socrates to discover; second, his account makes an essential contribution to the theme of my book, Socrates' becoming, showing that the second stage of Socrates' philosophic education is the refutation of transcendent forms *plus* a profound positive gain, insight into the nature of human experience, which points the way to the third stage.

Benardete began his "Sketch" of Plato's *Parmenides* by distinguishing the first part of the dialogue from the second: "The first is narrated, the second is not."[31] The second part, the gymnastic, of course falls within the narration by Cephalus, who narrates every word of the *Parmenides* and narrates Antiphon's narration of the narration by Pythodorus on the historic meeting itself: everything in the *Parmenides* is in that sense narrated, most of it triply narrated. But the narration by Pythodorus began in indirect speech with constant "he said"s and then, after a final "he said" to open Parmenides' exchange with Aristoteles (137c4), he shifted to direct speech for the whole of the gymnastic; the result is that the exchange be-

---

29. The full text of Ibycus's poem is given in Whitaker's translation of the *Parmenides*.

30. A version of this section was published as "Reading Benardete: A New *Parmenides*," in *Interpretation* 44, no. 3 (2018): 403–23.

31. Benardete, "Plato's *Parmenides*: A Sketch," 229. The "sketch" of the subtitle of Benardete's article fits especially his account of the gymnastic — and Parmenides' gymnastic itself: both consist of a series of strokes that must be filled in, painted in, to be understood; the full portrait of "is" and "is not" can come into view only by completing the sketch and securing the implications of the linked series of gymnastic exercises.

tween Parmenides and Aristoteles is, as Benardete says, "performed" for
Socrates. Benardete took leave of the first part by calling attention to the
importance of the second: "If the first part of the *Parmenides* foreshadows
Socrates' later development [as he had shown it did] the second part seems
all the more superfluous. It is not."[32] The second part is indispensable to
the young thinker for whom it was performed, the Socrates who demonstrated that he possessed the qualities of the intended reader of the books
of Zeno and Parmenides. And the second part, as part of Plato's dialogue,
is performed for every reader of the dialogue in order to guide those few
whom Plato can address in a particularly exacting fashion on the way into
Socratic philosophy, his own singled-out reader.

   Benardete indicated the significance of the gymnastic early in his essay.
He calls Parmenides the "philosopher who first thought through the question of being. . . . Socrates was the second, as far as we know, to take over
the question and make it his own in the form of 'What is?' . . . The very
form of [Socrates'] question indicates that we are to replace the dogmatic
Socrates who has an art with the skeptical Socrates who embodies *eros*."[33]
So a "Who is?" lies embedded in Socrates' "What is?" question as Benardete framed it: Who is Socrates? And Benardete just says that we find out
by *replacing* the Socrates so evident in the dialogues, the practitioner of
the maieutic art, with what Socrates really is, the skeptical embodiment of
the *eros* he reported himself learning in the *Symposium*, the thinker whose
fundamental question is "What is?"—ultimately an ontological question
about being and beings. Inquiry into just who Socrates is replaces the more
public Socrates with a less accessible one—and the *Parmenides* has already
shown that Socrates was taught in his youth by both Parmenides and Zeno
that it is necessary for a philosopher to guard his public speech as their
writings did, that he embed what a philosopher is as a skeptical, radical inquirer into nature and human nature in a salutary shelter that filters access
to basic truths unsettling to the social order.

   Early in his essay Benardete looked ahead to the ultimate stage of Socrates' becoming and said that Parmenides "prepare[d] the ground for Diotima's instruction." But he added that Parmenides' gymnastic is not simply "preparatory to the *Symposium*"; it is more: what "I propose to show it
is," he declares, is "the setting forth of the task of Socrates' philosophic
life and the challenge to enter into his thing." "Setting forth" exaggerates
the openness of Parmenides' depiction for Socrates of the task of his phil-

32. Benardete, "Plato's *Parmenides*," 238.
33. Benardete, 229–30.

osophic life; but in expending the effort required to decipher Parmenides' guidance, the young Socrates, already arrested and sobered by being deprived of transcendent forms, learns his genuine task and experiences the challenge to enter what is his own, the way that could lead him beyond even Parmenides to the third stage of his philosophic education in the *Symposium*. One additional feature of Benardete's four and a half pages on the performed gymnastic is that they sustain the focus present in the earlier part of his essay; here too, frequent reference to Socrates' "subsequent Platonic career" can help show what he learned from Parmenides' special guidance.

Paragraph 16.[34] In discussing the gymnastic, Benardete spends no time whatever testing the validity of any of Parmenides' arguments, the natural preoccupation of virtually all other modern commentators on the *Parmenides*. He focuses instead on the implications of their conclusions and of the relations among their conclusions: he focuses on the action of the argument. He finds the first two of the eight hypotheses definitive in "forcing Socrates to face the either/or of his ideas." These hypotheses are two of the four that hypothesize that one is, the two that examine the results of that hypothesis for the one itself. The first finds negative results for the one and concludes that *neither* of the contraries forming the ten categories that Parmenides examines (neither part nor whole, neither beginning nor end, etc.) holds for any single idea; the second finds positive results for the one, concluding that *both* of the contraries hold for any single idea. "The first declares that nothing can be thought or said about an idea"; the second declares "that whatever holds for visible things . . . equally holds for any idea." Benardete concludes: "Hypothesis I and II divide between them incommunicable separation and indistinguishable communion." The either/or that Socrates must confront at the start is that the forms as he conceived them either totally transcend any thinkability or are totally obliterated in the flow of particulars. Socrates is to infer from the results of the first and second hypotheses that rational examination of the forms as he conceived them uncovers paired impossibilities: a transcendence that cannot be thought and a participation that dissolves form into flow. These paired eliminations of form provide the impetus pointing the gymnast, the thinker engaged in the exercises, to a step that is sheltered among the eight basic hypotheses in its own fitting place but that turns out also to be a key to the rest, a step that teaches that *it* is truly first.

Paragraph 17. Benardete's second paragraph on the gymnastic focuses on

---

34. For greater precision in referring to Benardete's account of the gymnastic, I treat it paragraph by paragraph and refer only to paragraph number, not page number.

"Parmenides' way." While presenting itself as "didactic," as starting from principles, his way is in fact "latently zetetic" because it "indicates that one is to go to the principles and not start from them." This "doubleness of the way"—present in Parmenides' poem as in the gymnastic of Plato's *Parmenides*—reduces in the actual procedure followed "to only one way, the way of inquiry." Showing then how the actual procedure of the gymnastic "infers" or "goes to" the categories it employs, Benardete isolates "an hypothesis behind the hypotheses"—namely, "to be is to be measurable." He confirms that this is the unstated fundamental hypothesis of reason by analyzing Parmenides' procedure in the first two hypotheses: Parmenides seems to assume that anything that is like or unlike is thereby either equal or unequal, and that does not follow "unless it is further assumed that likeness necessarily is a matter of measurable degree." Parmenides' one, fully demythologized, stripped of all features but its most basic hypothesis, thus becomes the hypothesis that to be is to be measurable, the hypothesis of the rationality of the whole. Benardete concludes his paragraph by noting that in the positive hypotheses generally, this homogeneity of measurable degree "operates . . . in the form of its scientific counterparts, arithmetic and geometry." The way of inquiry is therefore a process that aims to test a reasoned hypothesis: Can the posited rationality of the whole be confirmed?

Paragraph 18. After drawing his conclusions about the first two positive hypotheses, *positive* in that they hypothesize that one is, Benardete moves to one of the negative hypotheses because it contains within itself a feature that makes it singular. That is, the next move in Benardete's account presumes an already exacting investigation of all the hypotheses out of which alone such a recognition of uniqueness could arise, a possibly fruitful uniqueness latent within one of the hypotheses, which, when examined, reveals itself as key. In the negative hypotheses generally Parmenides does what he earlier told Socrates he had to do in addition to hypothesizing that an idea is, "hypothesize that this same thing is not" (135e). Benardete's interruption of a serial account of the eight hypotheses to turn to one of the negative hypotheses is prefaced by his saying that "it is accordingly not surprising that when the being of one is canceled in the negative hypotheses, the soul and its experiences come to light."[35] This is not surprising to the inquirer who, in thinking through all the hypotheses of the gymnastic, realized that in our experience ones are *inexorably* present, present even while hypothesizing that one is not—the inquirer is thereby forced to

---

35. The four negative hypotheses examine the results of "one is not" for the one itself and for the different things.

wonder how that is possible. The answer is found in the crucial difference quietly present in one of the negative hypotheses, "the only hypothesis that is not an hypothesis . . . the seventh." The seventh hypothesis treats the results for the different things if one is not where the results are all positive as exhibited in the way we speak of them: the different things are, are different from one another, have mass and number, are odd and even, and so on through all the categories. The reason that it can be said that the seventh hypothesis is *not* a hypothesis is that there "Parmenides gives two examples—dreaming and shadow-painting—and thus grants that one may be or not, but there is still dreaming and shadow-painting where one is not"—*grants*, that is, recognizes that is and is not, being and non-being, are not determinative for beings as humans experience them. Benardete states the conclusion that can therefore be drawn about the extent and character of dreaming and shadow-painting: "Neither the absence nor the presence of the one alters appearance and illusion." The seventh hypothesis states, if indirectly, that human experience as such is experience of appearance and illusion, two descriptive words for Parmenides' words, with the second word qualifying and intensifying the first. Human experience is indetectably active and constructive—*that* is the comprehensive conclusion about the soul and its experiences that can be gained by recognizing the uniqueness of the seventh hypothesis in not being a hypothesis, a uniqueness reinforced by there being "no examples anywhere else in the gymnastic."[36] The seventh hypothesis is an assertion whose merit will have to be tested in reference to all the hypotheses.

Because the seventh hypothesis implies that comprehensive conclusion about the soul and its experiences, Benardete can say that "everything . . . turns on the seventh hypothesis." He explains what "turns on" means with a metaphor that is typically effective and at first confounding: the seventh hypothesis "is the enfolding of the unfolding of all the other hypotheses." This states exactly what is to be done from this point on; having found out what Parmenides folded into the unique seventh hypothesis, one is to use that as the key with which to unfold what Parmenides folded into all

36. Benardete, "'Night and Day, . . .': Parmenides," in *Archaeology of the Soul*, 202. In this essay on Parmenides' poem, originally published a few years earlier (1998) than "Plato's *Parmenides*: A Sketch," and in many ways a companion to the latter, Benardete gave a similar account of the seventh hypothesis, but at that time he called it the "eighth," probably because he treated what Parmenides labeled the "third" as a separate, additional hypothesis. The brief description of the seventh hypothesis that he gave there is a useful supplement to the one he gives here.

the others: to see the uniqueness of the seventh hypothesis is to see the proper way forward; the uniformly applicable key unlocks all the others. This insight into the gymnastic as the activity of folding and unfolding grounds the enduring importance of Benardete's essay for understanding Plato's *Parmenides*: what Benardete discovers in the seventh hypothesis is what Parmenides intended the young Socrates to discover if he was able; it is what Cephalus's narration makes it possible for every future auditor of it to discover if he is able. Parmenides constructed his gymnastic to have a key whose natural or systemic place falls just after the impasse created by the first two hypotheses and provides the only possible entry into an understanding of those two and of all the others—presuming again the practiced familiarity with all of the hypotheses that allowed the singularity of the seventh to come to mind. This discovery reveals a certain misleading quality to naming the whole set of operations a *gymnastic*: it is not simply a set of exercises that hone the mind into fitness for dealing with the most sophisticated issues of reasoning; it is a set of exercises that itself conveys the essential instruction on how to approach *all* issues of reasoning, or how to understand understanding itself.

So what did Parmenides enfold into the seventh? The inexorable power of human experience to mask the whole while making the whole seem to lie before us unmasked, the whole that is only dreamt and shadow-painted while certifying itself as demonstrably, securely true: "I refute it thus," said Samuel Johnson of Berkeley's view of ideas and kicked a large stone. All the other hypotheses "assume their proper proportions once they are traced back to the indisputable character of appearance and opinion"—once human experience is understood to be the dreaming and shadow-painting of the soul in all its perceiving and conceiving, the other hypotheses submit to being unfolded and measured in light of that fundamental insight. Only here, only now can one appreciate the full appropriateness of Socrates' early image of the form's presence in the thing as being like *day* illuminating each separate thing and Parmenides' counterimage of its presence actually being like a *sail* covering it.[37]

After stating what the seventh hypothesis indicates about dreaming and shadow-painting, Benardete says, "Socrates is told that this is where he must start." Socrates is *told* nothing at all in the gymnastic in any literal way. Nor does Parmenides "arm" Socrates as Benardete says he does in paragraph 20, or "suggest" to him (20), or "ask" (21) or "tell" (23) him anything.

37. See above, section 5, "Parmenides the Guide," on 131b-c.

Socrates sits silent through the whole of Parmenides' gymnastic with Aristoteles. But eager to learn from the one who stripped him of his forms, Socrates will memorize the exchange as an exercise of the mind addressed directly to him; by testing it, interrogating it, following its foldings, he will be granting his guide the authority due him. And his guide will tell him and arm him and ask him as the pathway unfolds. By treating the gymnastic dialectically Socrates will make it the guide to the fitting way of solving the problems of being and knowing. And he will find that the gymnastic tells him where he must start — the seventh hypothesis tells him that he must start with a turn that recognizes human experience to be immersion in inescapable dreaming and shadow-painting. Socrates had started with forms as knowable transcendent realities, an advance in the sense that it did not stay confined to the puzzles of perception, but an impossible way out of those puzzles because it viewed perception naively as a window on being and cognition as acquaintance with external fixity.

A "simple consideration," Benardete says, shows that Socrates had not started properly, and for that consideration he looks to Socrates' final proposal about the forms in Parmenides' refutation of them, his proposal that forms are "paradigms in nature" while what participates in them "are their images that look like them, and are their likenesses" (132d). Benardete takes Parmenides' shadow-painting example to be a response to Socrates' claim of likeness: his example implies that Socrates did not distinguish, as Parmenides does, between the "art of geometry" that deals with likenesses or images of things and "the phantastic art of shadow-painting" that deals with the products of the necessary structuring by human fancy. Because Socrates failed to make that distinction, Parmenides implies, he "did not put to himself the question whether speeches" — the logoi — "were necessarily phantastic," always articulations of human-based fancy, never likenesses of what is. Plato again makes it clear that Parmenides caught Socrates just after his initial step as he reported it in the *Phaedo* on the last day of his life: he began correctly by turning to the logoi, but his examination of them mistook them for likenesses representing the true; he did not ask himself if the speeches could necessarily be only *mis*representations of what is, only fantasy presentations despite their stability and regularity. By making it possible for Socrates to see his misstep, Parmenides makes it possible for him to correct it — and it is this possibility that Socrates refrains from passing on to Cebes and Simmias: he measures his audience as Parmenides measured him.

What would Socrates have to have already done to ensure himself that it is true that the soul's experiences are necessarily fantastic? "He would have had to have mastered an ontological psychology were he to be sure that whatever showed up in speech had not first shown up in soul" (para. 18). In *speech*—Socrates' turn to the logoi could have led him to ask: Are the logoi what they are because the soul is what it is? Parmenides turns Socrates toward an ontological psychology; he tells Socrates, "Know thyself," and in knowing yourself come to know that the soul, the seat of human experience, necessarily generates the form of all experience and so of all speech and thus blocks any means of accessing being directly. An ontological psychology begins by gaining knowledge of the self as knowledge of the human way of "knowing"; it thereby provides the necessary prolegomenon to any future understanding of being that could claim to be rational. Without a genuine ontological psychology there is no way to be sure if there is any escape from experience-based fantasy. An ontological psychology would also have to pursue a psychology in the more customary sense, the attempt to understand the drives and goals of the soul and—looking far ahead—*this* understanding could, perhaps, lead to a rationally defensible inference about beings as a whole on the basis of knowledge of the knowing being. In the *Symposium* Socrates will credit Diotima with guiding him to an ontological psychology in that sense, and to what could ultimately be ascertained by that inquiry: the third stage of Socrates' philosophic education, understanding the being of the soul as eros offers a way into an inferential understanding of beings as such via a rational parsimony of principles.

Early in paragraph 18 Benardete referred to the "imperialistic impulse" of the one, its drive to absorb and rule everything, to rule out "many." That imperialism "is stopped dead in its tracks," he says, by the recognition of dreaming and shadow-painting: "Neither the absence nor the presence of the one alters appearance and illusion." But speech recognized as fantastic can itself exercise imperial rule: at the end of paragraph 18, having unfolded what Parmenides folded into the seventh hypothesis, Benardete pictures a "latent art of phantastic speech [that] threatens to be as imperialistic as the Parmenidean one." If that latent art became "successful in absorbing everything into itself, it would be a psychology without an ontology." Our actual absorption into the unbreakable sway of the generative fantasies of human experience could give rise to a theory of the soul's ways that denied any possible route to an understanding of the beings. That art of fantastic speech gone imperial is the art of Protagoras, the sophistic art that accompanies the inquiry into the logoi as an always threatening possibility; it is an epistemological skepticism that is a counterfeit of genuine philosophy.[38] Plato had his own way of emphasizing the perennial danger of this counterfeit of philosophy: his chronological arrangement of the dialogues put *Protagoras* first with Socrates mounting the public stage around 434 in order to counter Protagoras and the whole sophistic movement he generated. Then, in the *Theaetetus*, whose frame makes it chronologically the last of Plato's dialogues, Socrates called Protagoras up from the dead in order to refute him in the presence of his followers, who could not argue for his view as well as Protagoras could. Parmenides alerted young Socrates to a conflict between genuine philosophy and sophism that will never end: philosophy's necessary epistemological skepticism will be taken as terminal by all but a few thinkers for whom it can be a stage on the way to the fundamental insight.

Benardete's account of the seventh hypothesis makes it clearer why Parmenides gave the label *gymnastic training* to what young Socrates had to do in hypothesizing is and is not. The training entails gaining complete familiarity with all eight hypotheses and constant exercise comparing them and treating them dialectically, interrogating them for their mutual implications. Only such rigorous exercise could lead to the insight that the seventh hypothesis differs from the rest and in that difference illuminates all the others, demanding that each be interrogated again to see what the inescapability of dreaming and shadow-painting might imply for it. The silent presence of significance throughout the gymnastic yields its content only to the unfolding that the seventh hypothesis makes possible; and the galvanizing effect of the unfoldings confirms that *this* is the way, *the* way. The inquirer thus gains a confident stance toward the whole of Parmenides' exercise: each hypothesis bristles with significance because each can now be viewed as an aspect of the soul's experiences. What Benardete shows about the gymnastic of Plato's *Parmenides* gives a different formulation to what he had already said in his earlier essay on Parmenides' poem itself: both lead "to an understanding of the true perplexity, knowledge of ignorance. This is to be on the way of the man who knows."[39] Knowledge of ignorance is knowledge of the soul in its way of "knowing." By consistently speaking of his knowledge of his ignorance, the mature Socrates

---

38. Parmenides had earlier warned the young Socrates about Protagorean skepticism by describing someone who denies "that there are forms of the beings" and does not "distinguish a certain form of each single thing": he will "understand nothing" and "entirely destroy the power of dialectic" (135b).

39. Benardete, "'Night and Day, . . .'" 227.

seemed to modestly deny that he knew anything. But knowledge of ignorance is not ignorance; it is a negative way of claiming knowledge of a special and wide-ranging sort: knowledge of knowledge. Socrates came to know, thanks to Parmenides' guidance, that human knowing is an active ordering of the world that cannot be thrown off. Socrates' characteristic claim is an exercise in politic philosophy: while affording him near innocence in the face of charges that he knew forbidden things, it staked a masked claim to knowledge of these things.

Benardete's paragraph 18 shows without explicitly saying so that a "Kantian" form of skepticism about the accessibility of being to knowing has a long history that reaches back through Socrates at least to Parmenides and that comes to light as an indispensable feature of genuine philosophy: an epistemological turn that impels the driven inquirer to a prolegomenon to any future account of nature. This insight into the seventh hypothesis as the essential step of Parmenides' gymnastic is an especially important event for a Nietzschean history of philosophy because — as the epigraph to this chapter indicates — the young Nietzsche took precisely that step without the guidance of Parmenides or Plato but with a heavy debt to Kant and Schopenhauer.[40] When he was twenty-eight he wrote but never published "On Truth and Lie in the Extra-moral Sense," his essay in epistemological ontology that set out the grounds of human experience through an analysis of language — the result of Nietzsche's own turn to the logoi. In his typically dramatic wording, human experience as such is an in-part knowable structure of "lies" that systematically and inescapably distort what the truth of beings might be — "illusion" is the word Benardete used. Nietzsche was fully aware that this early unpublished essay marked the decisive event in his own becoming a philosopher; he reported in an autobiographical foreword to one of his books thirteen years later that the interested reader could confirm that the profound epistemological skepticism everywhere present in his mature books had been his view since he arrived at it in that essay. He reported its title for the only time in his published writings yet still refrained from publishing it, leaving no access to the evidence for the consistency of his thinking from that early point on.[41]

---

40. And a greater debt to an almost unknown and now wholly forgotten philosopher of language, Gustav Gerber, whose 1871 book, *Die Sprache als Kunst*, Nietzsche simply mined without acknowledgment for his chief points and his vocabulary on this form of epistemological skepticism. See my *What a Philosopher Is*, 54–55.

41. Nietzsche, Foreword to *Things Human All Too Human*, Part II; Nietzsche, "On Truth and Lie in the Extra-moral Sense," in *Writings from the Early Notebooks*, 253–64. See my *What a Philosopher Is*, 43–72.

Kinship with Socrates in this early insight into epistemological skepticism prepared in Nietzsche subsequent insights of comparable importance that result from it. Just as Socrates recognized philosophy's perennial conflict with sophism, Nietzsche recognized that philosophy's conflict with skepticism was the central problem of contemporary philosophy: he placed his most beautiful treatment of that problem at the center of the chapter of *Beyond Good and Evil* called "The Free Mind"; addressing modern epistemological skeptics, he encouraged doubt about simply stopping at skepticism. What he put next for these skeptics marks his most profound kinship with Plato's Socrates: he invited modern skeptics to consider an argument whose conclusion was a comprehensive ontology, an ontology of will to power closely akin to what Plato showed Socrates gaining in the third stage of his philosophic education, his ontology of eros.[42] The trajectory of Nietzsche's thinking life is therefore remarkably similar to Socrates' as Plato presents it: sharing this second stage of Socrates' philosophic education, he too went on to the third stage as Plato presents it, rational inference about beings as a whole based on knowledge of the soul. As Nietzsche put it in the book constructed to chart his own way to the most basic gain, "Psychology is once again the path to the fundamental problems."[43] *Once again* — as it once was for Socrates.

Paragraph 19. Benardete's way through the hypotheses — Socrates' way, *the* way through the hypotheses — moves from the revelatory seventh back to the positive hypotheses, to an unfolding of the second that will in turn touch the first. "If there is at least a partial phantastics" — a non-imperial construal of the soul's constructs of experience — "the second hypothesis is an eikastic fragment of it, for everything that seems to hold if there is one does hold in the realm of appearance."[44] An eikastics of a partial, non-imperial fantastics is of the highest significance: it would discern the stable likenesses that structure fancy-generated appearance; it would study the

---

42. *Beyond Good and Evil*, §§4–37; see my *Nietzsche's Task*, 84–91. Such epistemological skepticism seems characteristic of the great philosophers; Descartes, for instance, shared it while retailing the view in his *Discourse on the Method* that "there is nothing so far distant that one cannot finally reach, nor so hidden that one cannot discover." See my *Nietzsche and Modern Times*, 222–23.

43. *Beyond Good and Evil*, §23.

44. "Eikastics" is based on *eikastikos*, a word found only in Plato's *Sophist* (235d ff.) and defined by LSJ as "able to represent or conjecture." In order to identify for Theaetetus what a sophist is, the Stranger in the *Sophist* divides the art of image-making (mimetics) into its two kinds, eikastics and phantastics. The art of eikastics aims at images of resemblance, whereas phantastics produces an apparition, a non-resemblance (236b-c). See Benardete's commentary on the *Sophist*, *Being of the Beautiful*, II.109–12.

logoi and the whole of appearance as a science of appearance on the model of arithmetic and geometry; as a genuine science of the stable structures of appearance, it would be a knowing of "knowing." And it would recognize its limitation to appearances, while not peremptorily, imperially closing off the possibility of a rational move to what is blocked by appearance, the beings as they are; it would be an ontological psychology open to ontology simply, a comprehensive account of the character of the always-mediated beings that could defend itself as true. And it would yield the only proper way to understand *form*: as the non-voluntary structures built into the human way of experiencing, giving it its characteristic orderliness.

Benardete calls attention to Parmenides' introduction of "the sudden" at the end of the long examination of the second hypothesis (156d). Parmenides introduced this "in order to gain a between that sets out of time the transition of all becomings and passings-away that are in time." The timeless "between" avoids the logical contradiction entailed in becoming, the transition from being at rest to being in motion or vice versa — one of Zeno's puzzles. The posited "between" is not in time but between times, enabling all change from one state to another state (157a-b). The function of the sudden, Benardete says, is to put together the mutually contradictory first and second hypotheses: the sudden is "the utopia where the separated idea of the first can be." *Utopia*, noplace/perfect place, is Benardete's variant for Parmenides' actual word: "Parmenides calls the sudden *atopon*, strange and placeless." Benardete can then state more explicitly just what this operation with these two positive hypotheses is: "the first two hypotheses, then, with their *specious* reconciliation in the third" (emphasis added). The third hypothesis examines the results for the different things of hypothesizing "one is," and its arguments conclude that all the categories are true for the different things. The reconciliation is specious, but the conclusion is not: for the different things of experience all the categories always hold. The non-specious way to the conclusion is achieved through the key operation: all three hypotheses "are to be enfolded into VII. All of them are really out of place." Putting the first three hypotheses into their proper place following the seventh means that they "assume their proper proportions once they are traced back to the indisputable character of appearance and opinion" that the unique seventh hypothesis makes visible. Placing the first three hypotheses properly within dreaming and shadow-painting unfolds them: Parmenides enfolded them into the seventh as he did all the others, enabling their proper unfolding. Parmenides' way leads to a genuine science of experience that can account for its always evident fixities; it nevertheless relativizes experience, makes it human, while remaining open to the whole. Driven to understand the whole, the philosopher can partially succeed while continuing to seek a way through the actually knowable to the ever unknowable.

In his next two paragraphs Benardete shows how the double-focus characteristic of Socrates' actual practice — eidetic analysis and investigation of the arts — can be understood as a consequence of Parmenides' argument; the action of Parmenides' argument includes an invitation to Socrates to investigate the nature of human experience via two distinct means.

Paragraph 20. Benardete signals a special importance for paragraph 20 by two unusual interventions: he uncharacteristically inserts himself and uncharacteristically moves from what Parmenides offered Socrates to what *Plato* found important in it. In addition, Benardete gives dramatic force to Parmenides' act of guidance here by his description of what Parmenides does: he "arms Socrates," equips him with a "defense" against a possibility bound to arise for him as he pursues Parmenides' way from the seventh hypothesis back through the rest. Arming Socrates is not only a defensive measure, for in this step, the unfolding of the third hypothesis with the key of the seventh, Parmenides prepares Socrates for what will eventually become the most important of all philosophic gains in the third stage of Socrates' philosophic education.

The seventh hypothesis is non-hypothetical because its claim of dreaming and shadow-painting implicitly proves that the soul "resists the homogenization of being," absorption into an all-encompassing one. But it is still a hypothesis, and as such it opens the way to the opposite extreme: "It threatens to cancel homogeneity altogether in favor of infinite heterogeneity or individuality." Is the whole an infinite flux of manynesses in which every seeming one dissolves into a many? It is against this version of the irrationality of the whole that Parmenides arms Socrates, the version argued by Protagoras and the sophists he generated; Socrates, or philosophy as such, must arm itself for never-ending battle against this natural upshot of the rational investigation of experience. Benardete sets out the two ways in which Parmenides arms Socrates, "the first way is the third hypothesis." Benardete's sequential march through the hypotheses after locating the key that unfolds them thus continues. With the third hypothesis, "for the first and only time Parmenides offers a version of what a whole is that is not reducible to a sum."[45] A whole that is not reducible to a sum points to

---

45. The third hypothesis examines the results for the different things if "one is"; its arguments result in positive conclusions about the existence of each of Parmenides' categories.

a non-mathematical understanding of wholes that would allow a *partial* fantastics or a limit on heterogeneity. Parmenides "calls a whole an *idea*" (157d9), a word Socrates will take over as a name for wholes — in setting out his own, now-refuted view, young Socrates had consistently used *eidos*. In his examination of the third hypothesis Parmenides speaks of *pieces* generally and isolates that piece that is "not a piece of the many nor of all things, but of one certain idea, a certain one which we call whole" (157d7–e1) — *this* is what survives of Socrates' forms in Parmenides' gymnastic or what takes their place. As Benardete says, Parmenides uses *idea* in "accordance with his usual practice, he uncovers wholes with their proper parts (*moria*) before he reveals the unlimited behind them."[46] Out of the unlimited, Parmenides isolates ideas in a sense that is immune to the kind of attacks he marshaled against Socrates' transcendent forms. Ideas in Parmenides' sense must therefore do what he told Socrates he could learn that ideas do: capture "the certain kind (*genos*) and beinghood (*ousia*), in itself," that things have (135a). Parmenides is showing himself to be a "naturally gifted man" who discovered these things *and* that "still more wondrous person" able to "teach someone else" (135b) — he teaches Socrates, guides him to discover through his own working out of the gymnastic how to conceive of wholes or kinds or forms in the proper way without calling in his irrational transcendent forms. While "uncover[ing] wholes" or ideas out of the unlimited, Parmenides uncovers too "their proper parts," the two-word translation of *moria* that Benardete consistently uses in his description of the proper use of *idea* in understanding appearance.

Benardete inserts himself into a sentence that says how Parmenides arms Socrates: "He thus suggests to Socrates that the first defense against either homogeneity or heterogeneity is what I call eidetic analysis."[47] He then gives a three-sentence definition of eidetic analysis using a principle and an "example" that is more than an example: "Eidetic analysis always begins with the one of the unlimited, what Parmenides calls 'the other nature of the *eidos*' [158c], the stream of articulate sound, for example, prior to the discovery of vowels, consonants, and semi-vowels." "The stream of

---

46. Benardete's footnote to Parmenides' use of *ideas* at 157d7–e2 refers to *Theaetetus* 203e2–5 and 184d1–5. Benardete translates *idea* in the *Theaetetus* passages as the "single look" a single species of things has, while at 203e he translates *eidos* as "species"; he uses the same translations of these two basic words elsewhere, e.g., *Tragedy and Comedy*, 117, 122–23.

47. What Benardete called eidetic analysis he set out in *Socrates' Second Sailing*, 4–5, 100, 137; *Tragedy and Comedy*, 227–29, 236–42. In "On the *Timaeus*," he distinguished "eidetic analysis" from "genetic analysis" as present in both the *Timaeus* and the *Republic* (*Argument of the Action*, 379–80).

articulate sound" is an expression for the logoi, a differentiable part of the undifferentiated whole. Eidetic analysis begins with that stream and isolates "kinds," the fitting limited sortings within articulate sound, aiming to isolate the elements of speech, down through words and syllables to the letters of syllables that sort themselves into the most elemental classes: vowels, consonants, and semivowels.[48] "These kinds establish a number between one and many [a finitude within the two opposite and imperial infinitudes of homogeneity and heterogeneity] and do not betray [do not do an injustice to] the simultaneous copresence of one and many that Socrates found in himself"—as he said when first arguing for his own notion of forms (129c-d). "There is now . . ."—in this last sentence of his definition Benardete seems quite pointedly to use one of the poles of the is/is not hypotheses in order to attach a temporal modifier to it. There *is — now —* what there had not been before the eidetic analysis, "a stable number of proper parts whose whole consists of a single grammatical art," an art of the logoi whose proper parts expand out into numerous kinds and kinds of kinds from the simple parts of sound that are vowels, consonants, and semivowels. Benardete's definition of eidetic analysis, beginning with the "example" that is a turn to the logoi, ends on the word "art." The art or science of human language seems to be the indispensable tool whereby a human being can begin a proper study of the experiences of the soul aiming ultimately at a psychology, a knowledge of human being, that could perhaps open onto insights into beings as such, ontology. Starting here with the "single grammatical art," Benardete will show in the next paragraph that Parmenides makes the arts a necessary study for a philosopher, for Socrates, *arts* being fundamental to the human way of being in the world, an active and reactive way of constructing or making. Analysis of the arts is therefore the other way—eidetic analysis being "the first way"—that Parmenides arms Socrates to resist the attraction of infinite heterogeneity. "On Method" would be a fitting title for paragraph 20, but then "On Method" would be a fitting title for the whole of the gymnastic.

Benardete moves from his own term for Parmenides' guidance in the third hypothesis to Plato himself: "One cannot stress too much the importance of this for Plato: he discerned among its proper parts a kind that constitutes sound but can never be sounded by itself." "This" and "its" seem to refer to the "single grammatical art" of "eidetic analysis" that begins with the stream of articulate sound, the logoi humans use to structure

---

48. Benardete's commentary on the *Theaetetus* passage to which he here refers— 203e2–5—falls in the subsection entitled "XV. Letters" (*Being of the Beautiful*, I.169–75).

the non-linguistic stream in which we are immersed. And the *kind* "that constitutes sound but can never be sounded by itself"? — that seems to be, judging from Benardete's analysis of the *Theaetetus* passage to which he referred (see note 46 above), the consonants and semiconsonants that constitute sound but can never be sounded by themselves without being joined together with vowels to form syllables. The next sentence, the end of the paragraph, generalizes from this kind: "The idea, one might say, always shows itself as other than it is." Ideas show themselves only in the stream of articulate sound but show themselves as if they could be sounded apart from the stream. The ideas are, through eidetic analysis, the inlet into the nature of appearance in whose stream kinds are embedded. What Plato shows Parmenides doing for the young Socrates is how to succeed in what he aimed at by turning to the logoi: subject the logoi to eidetic analysis, which begins with language and its way of structuring the whole and grounds a rational science of experience through the isolation of kinds that are always only a feature of particulars and not some reifiable thing as young Socrates had imagined. Eidetic analysis is one of the active ingredients in an ontological psychology, analyzing the experiences of the soul with a view to understanding the being of beings; the other, an investigation of the arts, Benardete takes up next.

Paragraph 21. From the third hypothesis, which he now makes simply "the outline of eidetic analysis," Benardete moves to the fourth, the last of the hypotheses that posit "one is."[49] Here again he establishes the genuine action of the argument by putting the fourth hypothesis into its proper place by unfolding it in the light of the seventh. With the fourth hypothesis "Socrates is asked to reflect on the arts if number were to withdraw from them," the arts that rely simply on experience.[50] Benardete's footnote on the arts apart from number refers to Plato's *Philebus*, where Socrates describes the arts of experience as "a kind of knack, using the powers of guesswork."[51] What Parmenides asked Socrates to do, Benardete says, is "to consider the worthless things, what blacksmiths and shoemakers deal with." "Worthless" repeats Socrates' intentionally misleading judgment on these arts in the *Philebus*: "virtually worthless," which Protarchus strengthened to "really worthless" (55e). As Benardete notes, what blacksmiths and shoe-

49. The fourth hypothesis also examines the results for the different things if one is, but its arguments draw negative conclusions for all of Parmenides' categories.

50. The withdrawal of number therefore seems to be Benardete's interpretation of the negative conclusions for all the categories as exhibited in the arguments of the fourth hypothesis.

51. *Philebus* 55e1–56a2; trans. Benardete, *Tragedy and Comedy*.

makers deal with is also judged worthless by Alcibiades in the *Symposium*; he believes wrongly that they are only "the laughable exterior of Socratic speeches."[52] With the third and fourth hypotheses, "Parmenides rehearses in the small the tension between heterogeneity and homogeneity"—the many and the one—"and how they can be discerned and understood in the human things." Benardete almost repeats his earlier statement of "the specious reconciliation" of the first two hypotheses in the third in a statement of what the argument has made possible: "The spurious collapse of the first two hypotheses into the third and their genuine reattachment to the seventh hypothesis opens the way for eidetic analysis and its necessary adjunct, the exemplary character of the arts." Socrates did what Parmenides asked: he "always starts" with "the exemplary character of the arts whether it be on the track of justice or persuasion."

Justice and persuasion are not just two among many possible tracks; they are the basic two. The first leads to understanding morality, to knowledge of good and evil; and the second leads to understanding language as the human means not only of organizing experience but also, ultimately, of rule. Had Socrates not done what Parmenides asked, had he not "taken his bearings by the arts in their infinite divisibility, on the one hand, and the wholeness of the soul, on the other," that many and this one, he could not have followed the track of the arts to understand "the nonreducibility of the dyadic nature of justice"—that dyadic nature seems to be what Benardete called "a precise and an ordinary sense" of justice, where the ordinary is the citizen's justice and the precise is the philosopher's.[53] Nor could he have understood that persuasion or "rhetoric is the flattering disguise of the desire to punish and looks like the unintended justice of inducing perplexity." So the two basic tracks of understanding through the arts are intimately entwined: understanding rhetoric or the ordinary human way of speaking about good and evil leads one to the actual core of citizen's justice, the desire to punish.[54] The other and irreducible form of justice,

---

52. *Symposium* 221e; Alcibiades gives four examples of the arts Socrates considered: "pack-asses, blacksmiths, shoemakers, and tanners." Socrates' own examples in the *Philebus* are flute playing first, then all of music, and medicine, farming, piloting, and generalship (56a-b); he contrasts such arts with those in which what Benardete calls "the application of number to knowledge" is basic; Socrates' model for these arts is carpentry.

53. Benardete, *Socrates' Second Sailing*, 83, 88–89.

54. As Benardete's analysis of Socrates' story of Leontius in the *Republic* shows (*Socrates' Second Sailing*, 100–102). In his essay "'Night and Day, . . .'" (221–22), Benardete shows that Parmenides himself, in his poem, argued that this view of justice is built into the human way of experiencing existence: existence is deserved punishment. To arrive at this conclusion about Parmenides' view, Benardete judged that six lines of the longest surviving fragment

the "unintended justice" of the philosopher, is a rhetoric that does good to friends who are good without harming anyone,[55] in particular not harming citizen's justice but speaking in a way that does not overtly call it into question. And "unintended"? Benardete's word points to the genuine ground of a philosopher's doing good to friends who are good: it is not justice, morality, for it is beyond good and evil and is moved by the fundamental drive, eros. The Parmenidean way combining eidetic analysis with an understanding of the arts ultimately makes *philosophy* possible: "Socrates' use of the arts [serves] the purpose of discovering kinds and their proper and improper parts." An improper part here seems to be the sophist, an improper part of the kind *philosopher* because the sophist's analysis of language stops at an imperialism of infinite heterogeneity, and, equally important but on a practical level, the sophist's use of language is less careful about exposing the roots of justice.

Paragraph 22. Continuing his sequential move through the eight hypotheses, unfolding them through their key, their being enfolded into the seventh, Benardete turns to the four that hypothesize one is not. The conclusions he draws are as radical and as illuminating as those he drew about the four that hypothesize one is. He first draws a general conclusion about all four negative hypotheses based on the disappearance in them of words for fixity:[56] that absence signals the obliteration of the present, what *is*, but leaves intact *was* and *will be*. This opens the way to Timaeus's cosmology, Benardete claims, a cosmology that "makes it possible to get rid of being

---

of Parmenides' poem (frag. 8, lines 13–18) are "superfluous" to the argument into which they are inserted, the goddess's argument for the impossibility that being comes from non-being. Those six lines put being on trial with Justice presiding; the judgment of Justice is that "being is a punishment for a crime that being must commit. Its fate is to be guilty." The apparent absurdity of this disappears, Benardete says, "if the goddess first presents being as mortals primarily experience it, and not as it is in itself." When the goddess later presents what being is in itself, "Necessity replaces Right." In *The Bow and the Lyre*, Benardete shows that this key insight into the distinction between nature and morality is among the lessons Odysseus learns on his way to philosophy: "the great strain the will is under to reinterpret necessity as right" (75). *The Bow and the Lyre* is perhaps the most valuable and certainly the most far-reaching of Benardete's investigations of Greek philosophy before Socrates: Homeric poetry, the *Odyssey*, contains the paradigmatic odyssey to philosophy and political philosophy. See my essay "Extending the History of Philosophy back to Homer," in *Enduring Importance of Leo Strauss*, 156–85.

55. This is the definition implied but not spoken by Socrates in his refutation of the view of justice offered by Polemarchus in the *Republic*, that justice is doing good to friends and harm to enemies.

56. Benardete lists seven such words for fixity: "time, place, figure, nature, kind, whole, and proper part."

in becoming," a cosmology of flux where "is not" is literally true because of
the sovereignty of becoming; Plato's Parmenides embraces the universality
of flux but as a process in which "ones" or kinds of relative permanence are
generated and extinguished.[57]

Moving to the individual hypotheses of "is not," Benardete sees a reversal in the expected order of the first two, the fifth and sixth hypotheses, a reversal that serves to indicate that the fourth and fifth hypotheses
"belong together."[58] The fifth "looks at opinion and . . . establishes that
its premise is that to be is to be possible and nothing is necessary." The
premise of opinion that nothing is necessary is illuminated by a conclusion that Benardete drew earlier, from Parmenides' final argument against
Socrates' view of the forms.[59] There, Parmenides' coordination of knowledge and rule implied that "whatever we do not rule by our knowledge
looks to us [humans] like chance and our opinion [human opinion] assigns the mastery of chance to the gods." Opinion therefore holds that
the whole is ruled by the gods' will. But the hypothesis that lies behind the
eight hypotheses, "that to be is to be measurable" (para. 17), depends upon
unbreakable necessity, and that carries an implication for the gods that
Benardete will state in his next paragraph. Here, he draws a conclusion
based on the reversed order: putting the fifth hypothesis "up against" the
fourth brings out "the second component that Socrates will need for his
analysis of the city." The first component needed was the theme of the
fourth hypothesis: "The true city is the city of arts, in which everyone
who enters it comes equipped with some part of knowledge." In the *Republic* Socrates had to supplant that "true city" of arts and knowledge at
Glaucon's insistence: he judged it a "city of pigs" (372d), he demanded the
amenities to which he is accustomed. The true city is therefore supplanted
by "the city whose spurious unity is grounded in the education in opinion
of its warrior-defenders." By bringing the fifth hypothesis up against the
fourth, Parmenides set Socrates on the way to a proper, twofold analysis of the city or the political: understanding the arts as parts of knowledge must be supplemented by the second component, understanding the
city's opinions as stamped-in education; the city's always spurious unity is

57. Benardete notes here that the fragments of Parmenides' poem that survive do not
permit a definitive judgment on whether "the goddess's speech on opinion" already indicated this "get[ting] rid of being in becoming" that Plato's *Parmenides* indicates.

58. The fifth hypothesis examines the results of "is not" for the different things, whereas
the expected order would have examined first the results for "the nonbeing of one in relation to itself," the topic of the sixth.

59. Benardete, "Plato's *Parmenides*," 237, para. 15.

grounded in that education in exceptionalism. Such education is always vulnerable to exposé by ambitious rhetoricians like Thrasymachus while also being susceptible to alteration and reform by a ruler who knows the art of rule as Socrates will come to know it. Parmenides' gymnastic thus pointed Socrates toward an understanding of the city that would also show him why the true understanding of the city and of nature would have to remain a private possession whose communication must be as guarded as the gymnastic is or as Parmenides' poem was: philosophy itself depends upon maintaining the spurious unity of the city and its grounding education in the rule of the gods.

Paragraph 23. The sixth hypothesis "discusses the nonbeing of one in relation to itself." Benardete observes that Aristoteles asks no questions as Parmenides' arguments serially conclude that one is not, and he states that Aristoteles' "silence" makes him "the boy of Parmenides' poem who listens in silence to the goddess's speech and does not question his own nonbeing"—the boy fails to question even where a question is obviously called for. Aristoteles' silence is the device, Benardete says, by which "Parmenides tells Socrates" why he failed to understand his poem—which can be true only if Parmenides so controlled the conversation that *he* caused Aristoteles' silence. What Parmenides "tells" Socrates here is "that he failed to understand his poem because he was unaware that he too practiced an ontological psychology"—Parmenides taught in a way that demands that its *way* be recognized: Socrates "took straight a teaching that was essentially dialectical." Parmenides' teaching depends on interrogating its claims and discovering answers that he left implicit to questions that he left implicit; its giving depends on an active taking that is a constant questioning. As with Parmenides' poem, so with Parmenides' gymnastic: don't be a boy listening silently to some god—*question* what is said and discover what is intended. That the particular lesson of the sixth hypothesis occurs this late suggests the necessity of delay in facing up to the answer to the "crucial question" now posed about the non-being of the one. Benardete poses the question twice and answers with assertions twice. His questions ask "is not?" His assertions state "is not." He too proceeds in a dialectical manner.

Benardete's first formulation of the crucial question runs: "Is there not a difference between the conclusion that something is not and the way to that conclusion?" His second rewords it with terms from the gymnastic: "Is there not a difference between the examination of opinions that the fifth hypothesis proposes and the discovery implied in the sixth?" This second asking restores the proper order of the two elements, "the way" and "the conclusion," that his first asking had reversed: the restoration shows that Parmenides' reversal of the fifth and sixth hypotheses was itself proper when viewed dialectically; it impelled the right questions. The *way* puts the fifth first as philosophy's examination of opinions that arrives at understanding them as constructs of the human way of being, and that conclusion, philosophy's conclusion, is the indispensable way to the conclusion of the sixth or rather to the discovery implied in the sixth, an ontological discovery about the non-being of one in relation to itself, a discovery Parmenides did not voice because it states the ontological atheism that is not to be spoken if the spurious unity of the city is to be maintained. Benardete speaks it, if only in a question and only about an antique highest being, the discovery "that 'Zeus not even is.'"[60]

Benardete's first sentence following his two questions contains two assertions of "is not," each answering one of the questions. The first assertion runs: "The temporal order of discovery is not the same as the order of the parts." The temporal order makes discoveries through an ontological psychology that uncovers an order of parts among the beings as a hierarchy in which opinion's highest being is not the actual highest being because he not even is. The second assertion runs: "just as the enfolding of the hypotheses as a whole is not the same as their enfolding into the seventh." Parmenides' way is an order of enfolded hypotheses whose temporal unfolding requires that the questioner first discover the difference of the seventh, its not being a hypothesis at all. The truth discoverable in that difference — the enfolded truth that human opinion is inescapable dreaming and shadow-painting that structures all of human experience — can unfold the other hypotheses as a proper ordering of parts in a teaching on the truth about the beings: begin with human being and its way of being and move to the other beings as they appear to the human, ending with the truth about opinion's highest being. Benardete's second sentence, the final sentence of the paragraph, applies what he just said about Parmenides' way to Plato's *Parmenides*: "It was just such a difference that dictated the narration of the first part of the *Parmenides* and the atemporal pattern of the second."[61] Plato's way in his *Parmenides* makes the first part a narration in

60. Benardete's way of wording the conclusion mirrors the is/is not hypotheses of the *Parmenides* but putting it in quotation marks when it is not a quotation from Plato's *Parmenides* or Parmenides' poem may suggest Aristophanes' wording when he had his Pheidippides speak the unspeakable to his father, Strepsiades: Pheidippides asks whether Zeus is; Strepsiades answers, "Is"; Pheidippides responds, "Is not" (*Clouds* 1465–70).

61. This observation nine lines from the end of the essay was first made in the second line of the essay.

which the young Socrates undergoes a temporal process of discovering his
need to learn, and makes the second part Parmenides' performance of an
atemporal gymnastic that Socrates is to learn. Plato learned from Socrates
who learned from Parmenides. To learn from Plato is to see the difference
between the way and what it is the way to.[62]

Paragraph 24. Benardete's final paragraph treats the final, eighth hypothesis in just three sentences. It begins by bringing the eighth hypothesis
into connection with the sixth. "The eighth hypothesis, seems as empty
as the sixth, but it supposes that everything else than the one that is not is
not among the nonbeings of the *phenomena*." In the sixth, the one is not—
that is its "empty"-ness: Zeus not even is. The eighth hypothesis hypothesizes that the many are not, which Benardete takes to mean are nothing
apart from what humans experience: the eighth hypothesis "thus puts the
question whether there would be nothing if there were not soul and its
experiences." His final sentence makes the answer to this question accessible. It begins, "This question is one of the deepest questions of Platonic
metaphysics . . ."—of *Platonic metaphysics*, that is to say, of *Platonism* as the
final sentence goes on to make clear—". . . whether the idea of the good,
if it is to be the single cause of the being of the beings and of the beings
being known . . ." Benardete invokes the peak of Platonic metaphysics in
the *Republic*, the peak of Socrates' persuasion of Glaucon that there is a
permanent cosmic foundation of justice. The idea of the good could be
said to be the shape Zeus takes in Platonic metaphysics as the form of
forms, beyond being in dignity and power and the sole cause of the being
and rationality of the beings. The deep question of Platonic metaphysics
that Benardete puts is whether that idea of the good "does not entail for
all time if not for all times that some rational animal be." The symmetry
of the sixth and the eighth hypotheses would then consist in the eighth
being as empty in its way as the sixth was in its: the eternity of the rational
animal, the being for all time of the human, not even is. But the eighth
is not in fact empty: the answer to the deep question it puts is that there

---

62. In light of Benardete's view that the Parmenides of Plato's *Parmenides* teaches a skepticism that knows the limits of skepticism and the route to knowledge, it is illuminating to
study the second paragraph of "'Night and Day, . . .'." It begins with three things Benardete
finds surprising for their absence and a fourth he finds surprising for its presence: "The
goddess never ascribes eternity (*aiei*) to being, or falsehood (*pseudos*) to nonbeing; nonbeing
disappears as soon as the goddess turns to Opinion, even though 'to be not' is as much a
mortal name as 'to be' (8.40)," and fourth, "The goddess promises that Parmenides will
know (*eisēi eidēseis* [10.1,5]) and learn (*mathēseai* [8.31]) mortal opinions, but she herself never
uses such verbs about Truth" (200–201).

would not be nothing if the human did not exist. The upshot of the sixth and eighth hypotheses is that a highest being does not exist, the human is not eternal, there is a universe apart from the non-being of Zeus and apart from its being perceived and ordered by human beings.

With his analysis of the gymnastic of the *Parmenides* Seth Benardete performed a powerful service for a Nietzschean history of philosophy: he showed the way into an understanding of the essential step in Plato's presentation of Socrates' becoming. Plato's account of the second stage of Socrates' becoming, intended only for the philosophically driven, put Parmenides' refutation of Socrates' initial view of the forms in the first part of the dialogue and made it easily understandable. And for its intended audience it is relatively easy to sort out chronologically just what that refuted view means when it reappears later as Socrates' teaching in the *Republic* and in the *Phaedo*. But Plato chose to make the positive gain of the second stage, the results of the gymnastic, extremely hard to enter even for its intended audience. Its lesson in the necessary epistemological skepticism would require even in one of those philosophically driven men of Clazomenae a certain rare genius schooled in the art of veiled speech practiced by the Greek wise since Homer and attentive to the small indicators through which alone the gymnastic yields its genuine guidance. Benardete's achievement makes available to contemporary Plato scholarship Socrates' step into an intentionally almost closed world of radical philosophic insight into human nature and human knowing—and brings Plato that much closer to Nietzsche.

8. Last Words

The last words Plato gave to Parmenides bring the gymnastic to a fitting end, for they summarize its results as a whole: "Whether one is or is not, both it and the different things, both in relation to themselves and in relation to each other, all, in all ways, both are and are not, and both appear and do not appear" (166c). "This majestic finalé"[63] states with great brevity what can be understood only by thinking each of its declarations — "both are and are not," "both appear and do not appear" — in the sense that the gymnastic makes accessible after the singular character of the seventh hypothesis is secured and the implications of its non-hypothetical claim are applied to all eight hypotheses. Aristoteles' last words seal Parmenides' last words with the fitting judgment: "Most true." The fact that Aristoteles

---

63. As Whitaker calls it; see *Parmenides*, trans. Whitaker, 89n23.

had applied that superlative to five other conclusions by Parmenides[64] may suggest that he has not understood the singularity of this summary judgment. But how could he have? It is the last statement of a gymnastic whose truths, whose hidden treasures, disclose themselves only after long, cumulative work that only a few could or would work through.

Back in his second paragraph Benardete had touched on an obvious puzzle Plato built into the first half of his *Parmenides*: "In the *Phaedo* . . . Socrates reverts to an apparently identical view of the ideas that Parmenides had disposed of fifty years before." The puzzle yields to the chronological solution that Benardete touched on in his essay "On Plato's *Symposium*": Plato presented Socrates' becoming as a three-stage event of intellectual maturing that he spread across the *Phaedo*, *Parmenides*, and *Symposium*.[65] In order to solve the direct contradiction between the *Parmenides* and the *Phaedo* on forms, the chronological solution requires a further conclusion that Benardete chose not to emphasize but that the young Nietzsche recognized: he called Plato's forms "decorative" while holding decoration to be foundational to culture that can flourish only within fictions, decorations, revered as truths.[66] What Plato suggests by the contradiction between the *Parmenides* and the *Phaedo* is that the mature Socrates carried on his Parmenides-guided inquiry into the being of beings and of human beings behind the protective security of the edifying decoration that he came to see his failed theory of forms could be. Transcendent forms of the beautiful, just, and good — or bigness and littleness — while fictions, serve as safe stopping points for those exposed to philosophy, for a Cebes and Simmias, for a school of erstwhile Pythagoreans turned into Socrates admirers — and for spirited young Athenian citizen-warriors like Glaucon and Adeimantus, yearning to live a decent and just life but turned suspicious about its worth by the skepticism of the sophistic enlightenment and the obvious contradictions of the poetic tradition. And the puzzling *Parmenides* itself? That sole report on Socrates' past not controlled by Socrates himself could serve as an invitation to who knows who? — some philosophically driven unknown auditor in some unknown Clazomenae — to enter the epistemological skepticism that genuine philosophy comes to know as necessary.

64. Aristoteles had used this word at 141b, 160b, 162b, and 165b, e. Socrates had used it once to express his agreement with Parmenides' argument that his view of forms implied an unstoppable infinity of forms (133a).

65. Benardete, "On Plato's *Symposium*," 79.

66. Nietzsche, *KSA* 7:29 [171] (Summer–Fall 1873); 8:30 [14] (Summer 1875).

9. The Socratic Turn

Plato's *Parmenides* shows that the "Socratic turn," the novelty that Socrates is credited with introducing into philosophy, cannot be understood as his turn to the logoi in order to understand cause, nor his turn to the human, nor his turn to the city: Plato's *Parmenides* makes those tasks of understanding already integral to Parmenides' thinking; and perhaps they were part of the thinking of others before him.[67] Moreover, these elements of a philosophic turn were also made by philosophers after Socrates who were not directly influenced by Plato on this matter. Such a turn therefore seems to belong not to a person but to philosophy as such. Driven to understand the world rationally, the philosopher naturally comes to wonder about the role of human understanding itself as a possible source of the way the world presents itself in human experience as formed — and eventually to conclude that it is a world dreamt and shadow-painted.

What is it then that is unique to Socrates in the Socratic turn? The fragmentary character of the writings of the philosophers prior to Plato makes it difficult to answer that question by studying Socrates' predecessors, but the writings of later philosophers help make up for that difficulty by the novelties they expressly attribute to Socrates. Writing around 45 BCE, Cicero, a philosopher who studied philosophy in Athens shortly after the destruction of the Academy, indicated what was novel with Socrates or what he was the first philosopher to do.[68] Looking briefly at the history of philosophy, Cicero spoke of Socrates after touching on Pythagoras and his historic effect on philosophy. He praised Pythagoras for enlarging the range of subjects embraced by philosophy and for his success in establishing philosophy in Italy, where he founded "the most excellent institutions

---

67. Is Plato's Parmenides the historical Parmenides in these great enterprises of turning to the logoi, the human, and the city? There seems to be no reason for Plato to deviate with Parmenides from his customary practice with historical figures and invent a non-historical Parmenides — he did not do that with Zeno, for example, or with Protagoras or Hippias, or Alcibiades or Critias, and so on. And there is a powerful reason for him not to: he is presenting a formative event in the life of Socrates, and he ties it to a major predecessor whose poem was available to all, a poem that could be studied as a source for the very matters Parmenides guided Socrates to understand according to Plato — an invented Parmenides would have discredited his presentation of a decisive event of learning on Socrates' part. Inventing Diotima is not a counterargument: deviating from his customary practice in order to invent her, a figure with no historical anchor, is another matter entirely; she is a fictional character of *Socrates'* invention and serves a salient purpose in his guidance of Agathon.

68. See also what Plutarch attributed to the Platonic Socrates about a century and a half after Cicero (above, chapter 1, section 5, final pages).

and arts both in private and in public."[69] But then, Cicero says, from the time of Pythagoras down to the time of Socrates, philosophy became a matter of treating "numbers and motions and the beginning and end of everything," with its students inquiring into "magnitudes, distances and courses of the stars and everything concerning the heavens." Saying of Socrates that he had "heard the lectures of Archelaus, a disciple of Anaxagoras," Cicero then says that "Socrates first called philosophy down from heaven, and gave it a place in cities and introduced it even into people's homes, and forced it to inquire into life and morals and things good and evil"—but Cicero says "first" with respect to Socrates only after he had just said that the philosopher Pythagoras had established excellent institutions and arts in private and in public, as in fact Pythagoras had done, establishing philosophic rule in some Greek cities in southern Italy and establishing private philosophic schools there. After stating what was studied in the Pythagorean schools in order to provide the setting into which Socrates called philosophy down from the heavens, Cicero looks to philosophy after Socrates in order to describe Socrates' historic effect: "His many-sided method of discussion, the variety of his subjects, and the greatness of his genius—made memorable in the writings of Plato—gave rise to many schools of philosophers differing from one another." As for himself, Cicero says that he too followed Socrates, attaching himself primarily "to the method which I think Socrates pursued, concealing my own opinion, relieving others of their errors, and on every question seeking to ascertain what is most probable." Cicero was a Socratic who took seriously the necessity that philosophy endeavor to rule in the city for the well-being of philosophy, for he lived a philosophic life at the highest reaches of rule in the Roman republic.[70]

69. Cicero, *Tusculan Disputations* 5.10.

70. Leo Strauss used this passage from Cicero plus a parallel passage from his *Brutus* (§31) to suggest, in the first paragraph of *The City and Man* (after the introduction), that what in fact originated with Socrates was a particular necessity for philosophy. Philosophy, Strauss intimates following Cicero, is the natural propulsion to investigate nature, which includes investigating human nature, particularly through a study of the good and bad things as humans experience them, thereby gaining a knowledge of good and evil, of morality. But Plato has Socrates say at the very center of the *Republic* (439c-d) that the philosopher must go down to the human things in order to rule them. That going down is unlike the natural ascension of the philosopher to understanding in that it must be compelled (519c-d), because the profound pleasures of the investigation of nature would otherwise keep the philosopher in that study exclusively. The first word of the *Republic* is Socrates' word, *Katebēn*, "Down I went": the compulsion to make philosophy defensible in the city by ruling the city for the well-being of philosophy, by bringing a new good and bad, drove Socrates to compel

As with Plutarch, what Cicero praised Nietzsche blamed. His primary
blame of the Platonic Socrates — simply Plato for him — was that he introduced into Greek philosophy something non-Homeric, non-Hellenic,
which Nietzsche regarded as an eruption of "Asia" into the Greek tradition. That the teachings of the Platonic Socrates are non-Homeric was
more than known to Plato: he announced their non-Homeric character
when he introduced them in the *Republic*, which almost ends on Socrates'
devastating indictment and dismissal of Homer measured by criteria he
had himself introduced; earlier that night Socrates had introduced non-
Homeric moral gods, a non-Homeric understanding of the virtues with
reason ruling over Homeric *thumos*, non-Homeric permanent transcendent forms governed by a monotheistic form of forms, and, at the very
end, a non-Homeric Hades as the place of punishment or reward for the
way one had lived one's life. Plato gave the *Republic* with its novel teachings a most significant chronological placement within his dialogues: its
first sentence says that the dialogue happened on the very night and in the
very place where the Athenians introduced a foreign goddess into their
city, Thracian Bendis. Because of its unprecedented character in the religious history of Athens, that date would have been easily known to his
early readers: early June 429 a desperate moment in Athens' war with
Sparta, made worse by the renewed outbreak of the devastating plague
that summer. That chronological placement of the *Republic* gains singular importance because of the date Plato assigned his *Charmides*. *Its* first
sentence also makes its date clear: it was the day after Socrates returned
from Potidaea, where he had been for two and a half or three years with
the Athenian army besieging the city. And his early readers could easily
know just when that return happened because of its significance in the
great war with Sparta: Socrates was returning with other stragglers from
the defeated army, which had just lost the battle that ended its long siege of
Potidaea in late May 429. Plato placed the *Charmides* a week or two earlier
than the *Republic* and gave prominence to each date by putting it in the
first sentence of each dialogue. That chronological pairing takes on high
significance because of what Plato has Socrates say in the *Charmides*: that
he came back different, having learned while he was away a new manner
of healing from a doctor of Zalmoxis, a Thracian god, a monotheistic god
whose power over his believers had been set out and admired by Herodo-

himself to go down. Political philosophy in that sense seems to be what Socrates founded.
And Pythagoras? His founding gains seem lost in the secrecy practiced even within the
schools he founded, schools of "so-called Pythagoreans," as Aristotle said.

tus. The cure he brought back, Socrates says, consists of a certain leaf plus incantations that can be the means of healing young Charmides' sickness, a disorder of the head. The leaf disappears in Socrates' conversation with Charmides, leaving only his promised healing incantations—which he never describes in the *Charmides*. The chronological relatedness that Plato assigned to his *Charmides* and *Republic* with Socrates' announcing that he came back different, bringing a new healing teaching, serves as Plato's indirect way of informing his reader that the non-Homeric novelties of the *Republic* are the incantations Socrates brought back from Potidaea.[71]

What is the Socratic turn then, given that it cannot be what Plato's *Parmenides* showed Parmenides having already achieved before him? Plato's dialogues suggest that it is the revolutionary, non-Hellenic teaching Socrates brought back in the *Charmides* and introduced in the *Republic*, introduced in the Piraeus on the very night the Athenians themselves introduced a foreign god there. Socrates advocated that public teaching from the time of the *Republic* through to his dying day. It is the teaching by which the Platonic Socrates saved Greek philosophy from the superstitious, as Plutarch said, the teaching that gave philosophy a place in the cities and in the very homes of human beings, as Cicero said. In the centuries after Cicero and Plutarch, popular Platonism would prove to be part of the means by which the Platonism for the people that is Christianity could rise to a position of tyrannical power in the Roman Empire and place its stamp on Western civilization for two millennia.

71. The arresting details of this pairing of the *Republic* and the *Charmides* and their consequences for Socrates' teaching are set out in my *How Philosophy Became Socratic*. The definitive arguments for setting the *Charmides* and the *Republic* together in early summer 429 are found in three important articles by Christopher Planeaux: "Socrates, Alcibiades, and Plato's *ta poteideatika*," "Date of Bendis' Entry into Attica," and "Socrates, Bendis, and Cephalus: Does Plato's *Republic* Have an Historical Setting?"

CHAPTER 3

The *Symposium*

The Final Stage of Socrates' Philosophic Education

I know you and your secret, I know your kind! You and I, we are of the
same kind! You and I, we have one secret.
  — Nietzsche, *The Gay Science*, §310, "Wille und Welle"

Prologue: Socrates' Ontological Psychology

Nietzsche made the greatest philosophic gains of his life in his midthirties,
in the summer of 1881, the fundamental gain being insight into a genuine
ontology, an inference that could be drawn about the character of all beings
based on self-knowledge, a philosopher's knowledge of what drives him
most deeply as an inquirer. In the book that first reported that discovery
Nietzsche presented it in a subtle, enticing, metaphoric way, addressing
the waves of the Mediterranean crashing into the cliffs, driving themselves
into the most hidden crevices, and falling back white with excitement: "I
know you and your secret, I know your kind!" he says to them. Nietzsche
is the late modern philosopher who rediscovered the difference between
exoteric and esoteric known to all philosophers prior to the modern Enlightenment, and he chose to present his most important discovery in a
way calculated to lure in and to keep out, the way followed by all philosophers who knew and respected that difference. Just so did Plato present
the third and final stage of Socrates' philosophic education, his gaining
an ontological psychology akin to Nietzsche's insight into what he came
to call will to power. Plato chose to present the fundamental ontological
truth as Socrates' contribution to a series of speeches on the god Eros in
his *Symposium*; in that speech Socrates too spoke in a way that is calculated

to lure in and to keep out, a choice governed by his recognition that "the truth about Eros is terrifying."[1]

The *Symposium* is the third of the three dialogues narrated by a person other than Socrates, each of which reports a stage in Socrates' philosophic education; it is narrated by Apollodorus, a particularly foolish devotee of Socrates. In his *Symposium*, as in his *Phaedo*, though not in his *Parmenides*, Plato has Socrates himself frame the report on his advance: Socrates determines the setting for reporting both the first stage and the final stage of his philosophic education, whereas anonymous philosophers from afar are alone responsible for the preservation of the central stage, which Socrates himself never speaks of directly in Plato's writings. In the *Symposium* Socrates presents his ultimate advance as a series of lessons he learned from a wise woman when he was a young man, years before Plato shows him mounting the public stage for the first time in the *Protagoras*, set in 434.[2] In the *Symposium* Socrates gives his ultimate learning a dialogic setting in his own past that carries forward the dialogue he had been conducting with Agathon, a gifted young tragedian about thirty years old, one of a series of private speeches given by a small circle of enlightened intellectuals. In this setting of long speeches, Socrates insisted on a dialogic exchange with Agathon, unwelcome though it was, for he threatened not to speak at all if he was not granted the right to examine Agathon. As in his *Phaedo*, Plato does not have Socrates himself report to a wider public this advance in philosophic understanding that he reported to a small private audience. Instead, the ultimate philosophic gains that he was willing to expose to that intellectual circle "leak out," as Leo Strauss observed,[3] in two stages, first through one disciple to a later disciple, then through a still later disciple to two wider audiences, both expressly shown not to be interested in philosophy but highly interested in what Socrates might have said to Alcibiades about eros. Plato portrays both disciple-reporters of the *Symposium* as laughably literalistic in their devotion to Socrates. But the issue of Socrates' disciples is made much more serious by the initial prominence and late appearance of an alleged disciple, Alcibiades, who is not at all laughable — and not a disciple, for he himself reports that Socrates had rejected him.

1. Benardete, "On Plato's *Symposium*," in Plato, *Symposium*, trans. Benardete, 190. I use Seth Benardete's translation of the *Symposium*, plus some changes he made in translating the *Symposium* for Strauss, *On Plato's "Symposium."*

2. Christopher Planeaux and Marty Sulek argue for this date in "The Dramatic Date of Plato's *Protagoras*" (unpublished manuscript).

3. Strauss, *On Plato's "Symposium,"* 21.

The *Symposium* is unusually complex in its chronological structure. The frame conversations suggest by their content that they took place just before Socrates' trial in 399.[4] From that frame, the *Symposium* moves back to its core, which is clearly set in 416, the year in which Alcibiades moved the whole city to what Thucydides called an eros for the naval expedition against Sicily, which ended in disaster.[5] Sixteen months after the Lenaia festival, during which the symposium took place, and shortly before the fleet was to set sail for Sicily in late spring 415 a shocking religious crime was committed: the stone herms throughout Athens were systematically desecrated one night by what must have been a large group of conspirators who intended their crime as a public shock and warning against the Sicily invasion. The investigation into that crime brought to light an even more shocking crime, the most serious of all possible religious crimes in Athens, committed in secret and frequently in the recent past, back even to the time in 416 when the core of the *Symposium* occurred: the crime of profaning the Eleusinian mysteries, the heart of Athenian religion, by speaking them and ridiculing them in the presence of the non-initiated. The private gathering at Agathon's house is expressly a night for revealing mysteries, those of the god Eros, but with the spectacular late arrival of Alcibiades, it seems to become a night of profaning the mystery of Eleusis, for Alcibiades arrives as the drunken, shouting leader of a Dionysian procession like the one that led the initiates from Athens to Eleusis — and Alcibiades had been accused and then convicted in absentia of being one of the leaders of the crime of profaning the mysteries.[6] What the frame audiences get to hear — and Plato provided two of them, similar in character — is a report that is far more deeply revealing than they could ever have imagined of what most explicitly concerned them about Agathon's party: "Socrates, Alcibiades and . . . the erotic speeches" (172b). When two audiences in 399 get taken back unexpectedly to a private party in 416 in which Socrates and Alcibiades and others make speeches on eros, and when their reporter for that event is a devotee of Socrates well known to be a blabbermouth lacking restraint, those audiences can expect that they are getting the real dirt about Socrates from the time in which Athens' worst religious crimes were committed — crimes for which Alcibiades was among those con-

---

4. For arguments in favor of 399 as the date of the frame, see below, section 1, "First Words"; and "Note on the Dramatic Date of the Frame of the *Symposium*" at the end of this chapter.

5. Thucydides 6.24.3.

6. Thucydides 6.50–52, 61.

victed. And an audience in 399 would have been well prepared for new revelations about those crimes because of a trial that had transfixed Athens a few months earlier, the trial of Andocides. Andocides himself had been accused in the profanations of 416–415, and he was the one whose report back then led to the trial and conviction of all the others, sixty-five in all, who either fled or were executed, except for Andocides and an associate, who were pardoned.[7] Andocides was put on trial again in late 400 for a different crime, and in his defense speech he reviewed the crimes of 416–415 in precise detail, naming names and making the shock vivid again for the whole Athenian population. Both the frame and the core of the *Symposium* are drenched in the religious crime of profanation: Were Socrates' disciples, beginning with Alcibiades, guilty? Was *Socrates* guilty?

Having taken the reader back from 399 to 416, the chronological structure of the *Symposium*, takes them further back to two significant events in the life of Socrates. He himself reports the earlier event in his philosophic life as his initiation into the mysteries of eros by a certain wise woman named Diotima (God's Honor). And late-arriving, drunken Alcibiades takes the company in 416 back to the second event, one that happened shortly before both Socrates and Alcibiades were sent with one of the two Athenian expeditionary forces in 432 that eventually settled in for the two-year siege of rebel Potidaea. Alcibiades' report would be heard with special attention by the two audiences Plato supplied for Apollodorus's narration, audiences whose interests are explicitly said to be non-philosophical and one of which explicitly called attention to Alcibiades' presence at the party.

As Leo Strauss noted, the *Symposium* and the *Protagoras* "very much belong together," most obviously because everyone at the symposium except Aristophanes had been at Callias's house for the *Protagoras* about eighteen years earlier, before the war broke out. Strauss also listed a series of small items that link the two dialogues, such as the door to the gathering in the *Protagoras* being locked and guarded, whereas the door to the gathering in the *Symposium* is open to someone simply wandering in, and Socrates arrived late in each dialogue after the others had assembled.[8] A main matter shared by the two dialogues is the presence in private of young men who became members of the Athenian intellectual and political and cultural

7. See the list of the sixty-five accused and the crimes they were tried on in Planeaux, Appendix A: "Socrates, Alcibiades, and Plato's *ta poteideatika*," in "Apollodoros and Alkibiades."

8. Strauss, *On Plato's "Symposium,"* 25. On the shared features of the *Protagoras* and the *Symposium*, see also my *How Philosophy Became Socratic*, 134–38.

elite. In the *Protagoras*, leading figures of the sophistic enlightenment, including its founder, Protagoras, were themselves present as the teachers of these young men; in the *Symposium* those gifted Athenian students of the sophists gather as men in their thirties already making their mark on the intellectual life of Athens.[9] Socrates is the older exception at about fifty-three. Four of those in the *Symposium*, two sets of lover and beloved, were associated with particular sophists in the *Protagoras*: Eryximachus and Phaedrus attended Hippias's lecture, while Pausanias and Agathon listened to Prodicus. In both dialogues Socrates is first paired with a relatively unknown young man but then closely associated with Alcibiades.[10] No one guards the door at the *Symposium*, but it is still a private gathering, and what is said there is intended for the small audience of those present. Plato thus chose to present the final stage of Socrates' philosophic education in a dialogical exchange that Socrates engineered with a brilliant, victorious young tragedian in a private gathering with the cream of enlightened young Athenians listening — and with Alcibiades himself arriving only after the speeches, late, drunk, and immediately their leader. And a devotee of Socrates, shown to be foolish and eager to talk about his master, years later blabs the whole thing to any audience that cared to listen.

The *Symposium* takes a long time to start. Two different scenes have to be set, different casts of characters sketched, and two very different times established for the settings. The relation between those two times is made prominent by the need to correct the ignorance of the first auditor on just when the symposium occurred, far earlier than he had imagined, at a fraught time that would no doubt make the report all the more interesting to him, given his stated interests. In the following account I pay close attention to these opening events; then, once the speeches start, I omit all of them in the interest of following Socrates' role in the *Symposium*: wherever he appears I look closely at the action and the speeches.[11]

---

9. Following the dates given in Nails, *People of Plato*, Phaedrus is about twenty-nine, Agathon about thirty, Eryximachus thirty-two, Aristophanes thirty-four, Alcibiades thirty-five, Pausanias less than forty.

10. In the *Protagoras* Socrates arrived with Hippocrates, son of Apollodorus; the Apollodorus who narrates the *Symposium* may be the son of Hippocrates, given the custom of fathers naming a son after their own father.

11. The most important omitted speech by far is Aristophanes'. Plato gave the famous destroyer of Socrates' reputation the most memorable and engrossing of all the speeches. What could be called its anthropology and theology present a profoundly pessimistic yet comic account of the human condition, a tragedy lived distractedly by all but the keenest investigators of the human condition. Socrates explicitly countered only Aristophanes, and when he finished Aristophanes tried to object but was thwarted by the noisy arrival

1. First Words

Dokō moi — "In my opinion" — are the first words of the *Symposium*, giving opinion great prominence at the start, Apollodorus's opinion and the opinion of those questioning him, for those two different sets of opinion become a major topic of the frame discussion, as Socrates, or the life lived by Socrates, becomes the focus of those opinions. Apollodorus's opinion about Socrates' way of life is extreme adulation for it, but the opinion of his questioners is what rises in importance: What should *their* opinion about Socrates be and on what grounds? The report Apollodorus gives in the main part of the dialogue is certified as not merely his opinion but rather a report as exact as a devoted disciple can make it.[12] If his questioners base their opinion about Socrates, their *judgment* on Socrates and his way of life, on that report then they too could admire him, or at least not be suspicious of him.

In Apollodorus's opinion he is "not unprepared for what you ask about for just the day before yesterday as I was on my way up to the city center from my home in Phaleron" — one of three ports of Athens enclosed within the high walls of the city — "and one of my acquaintances spotted me a long way off from behind and called, playing with his call: 'Phalerian,' he said. 'You there, Apollodorus, aren't you going to wait?'" The *play* in his call seems to be his employing legal language used in court to summon a witness to testify.[13] When the acquaintance caught up he said, "I was just recently looking for you; I wanted to question you closely about Agathon's party" — his close questioning will in fact be systematic and precise, like a prosecutor's inquisition of a witness. He wants to question Apollodorus about the party "at which Socrates, Alcibiades and the others were then present at dinner together — to question you about the erotic speeches. What were they?" (172b). He thus singles out Socrates and Alcibiades and knows that the speeches at Agathon's party were about eros: Socrates, Alcibiades, and eros — a topic of historic importance for Athens about which rumors had been swirling for decades because of Socrates' early association with the young Alcibiades and because of Alcibiades' rise to preeminence in Athenian life, a suspicious preeminence that led to his crime of

---

of Alcibiades: the intellectual/spiritual debate between the Athenian philosopher and the Athenian writer of comedy gets supplanted by the more overtly political issue of Socrates and Alcibiades.

12. Plato notes inexactitudes and omissions: 178a, 180c, 223d.

13. See Rosen, *Plato's Symposium* 12n30; Bury, *Symposium*, ad loc., sets out some other options.

defection to the Spartans and to the deadly counsel that he gave them, critically damaging the Athenian war effort. Suspicions about Socrates and Alcibiades seem to have arisen again, at the time of the frame of the *Symposium*, even though Alcibiades had been murdered some years ago. What had the erotic relationship between their famous philosopher and that notorious, gifted, criminal leader of the last generation actually been?

The questioner had heard about the party from "someone else who had heard about [it] from Phoenix the son of Philippus . . . and he told me that you too knew." That someone else had not been able to tell him anything with certainty, and certainty was what he wanted in going down to Phaleron just to seek out Apollodorus: "So *you* tell me, for it is most just that you report the speeches of your comrade" — justice is the standard he appeals to in order to get Apollodorus to give a report that may help him get to the bottom of the rumors. His first question asked what the speeches were; his second concerns the authority of his witness: "Tell me, were you yourself present at this party or not?" This question reveals a lot about the questioner and his informant: "It really does seem that there was nothing certain in what your informant told you," Apollodorus says, "if you believe that this party you are asking about occurred so recently that I too was present" (172c). Apollodorus reveals the questioner's ignorance of well-known events in the cultural life of Athens: "Glaucon, don't you know that it has been many years since Agathon resided here"; he doesn't even know that a famous Athenian tragedian left Athens sometime before 405 for the court of Macedon, probably as early as 408, and tragedy was at the core of cultural life in Athens.[14] And don't you know "that it is scarcely three years now that I have been spending my time with Socrates" — Glaucon is also uninformed about Socrates' circle. As for Apollodorus, he is a Socrates fanatic: "I have made it my concern on each and every day to know whatever he says and does"; Glaucon didn't know where he could have found Apollodorus every day, but he has at least now found the proper person to report on Socrates.

Poor Apollodorus, he can't help himself: he has to congratulate himself and insult his questioner for not being like him: "Before that, I used to run round and round aimlessly, and though I believed I was doing something of importance, I was more miserable than anyone in the world, no less than you are at this moment, for I believed that everything was prefer-

---

14. The Glaucon who questions Apollodorus cannot be the Glaucon of the *Republic* and *Parmenides*, Plato's brother, who is much older: as Apollodorus later says, he and this Glaucon, his questioner, were both "still boys" at the time of Agathon's party in 416.

able to philosophy" (173a). Glaucon does not allow himself to be deflected into a quarrel, ignoring the insults to ask a third question: "Tell me when this party did occur." It was "at the time of Agathon's victory with his first tragedy," Apollodorus says, a time Glaucon is uncertain about, for he says, "A very long time ago, it seems." Still, his interest is not diminished by learning that it happened much earlier than he thought, and he poses his fourth question: "But who told you? Was it Socrates himself?" — Did you get it from the horse's mouth? Apollodorus is emphatic: "No, by Zeus," it was "the same one who told Phoenix. . . . A certain Aristodemus" from [the deme of] Kydathenaia, "little and always unshod." *He* was an eye- and ear-witness: "He had been present at the party and, in my opinion, was the one most in love with Socrates at the time" — with a slavishly imitative love, it turns out, extending to not wearing shoes, devotion made ironic later on as a usually unshod Socrates turned up wearing fancy shoes to the party. The line of transmission thus passed from an eye- and earwitness who, more discrete perhaps, told another disciple, and from there the story spread, with Apollodorus knowing no restraint. Apollodorus attests to his own concern about getting an exact report: "Not, however, that I have not asked Socrates too about some points that I had heard from Aristodemus; and Socrates agreed to just what Aristodemus narrated." Apollodorus's inquisitor can be satisfied that his witness has done everything he could to get an exact report on Socrates and Alcibiades and the erotic speeches. He presses Apollodorus: "Why, then," Glaucon said, "don't you tell me? The way up to the city center, in any case, is as suitable for speaking, while we walk, as it is for listening." The report Apollodorus gave the day before yesterday was given to a persistent inquisitor with little interest in philosophy or cultural matters generally but a keen interest in what Socrates and Alcibiades and the others said in private about eros, even though it was many years ago. He had gone down to Phalerum with the sole purpose of seeking out Apollodorus, who gave his report as they ascended to the high city topped by the magnificent temples on the Acropolis: in Plato's *Symposium* a believable report about Socrates speaking in private is carried up into the city for an inquisitor wanting to hear right now about things that normally didn't interest him.

Apollodorus then speaks directly to today's inquirers, repeating that he is not unprepared to answer their request. But first he has to talk about himself and his questioners: "As for me, whenever I make any speeches on my own about philosophy or listen to others — apart from my belief that I am benefited — how I enjoy it! But whenever the speeches are of another sort, particularly the speeches of the rich and of the moneymakers — your kind of talk—then just as I am distressed, so do I pity your comrades, be-cause you believe that you are doing something of importance, but in fact it's all pointless" (173c). This audience too has no interest in philosophy and is as subject to Apollodorus's insults as Glaucon was: "And perhaps you, in turn, believe that I am a wretch; and I believe you truly believe it. I, on the other hand, do not believe it about you, I know it" (173d). Apol-lodorus has learned the basic philosophic distinction between belief and knowledge, but he employs it simply for the purpose of elevating himself and insulting others. This audience knows who he is: "You are always of a piece, Apollodorus, for you are always slandering yourself and others; and in my opinion you simply believe that—starting with yourself—everyone is miserable except Socrates. And how you got the nickname 'Softy,' I don't know, for you are always like this in your speeches, savage against yourself and others except Socrates." Foolish Apollodorus is not entirely wrong to imagine that no one is happy but Socrates, for Socrates knows that he en-joys the highest happiness possible for a human being, the happiness of knowledge. As for Apollodorus, he seems to love exchanges of insult: "My dearest friend, so it is plain as it can be, is it, that in thinking this about myself as well as you I am a raving lunatic?" (173e). His comrade has had enough: "It is not worthwhile, Apollodorus, to argue about this now; just do what we were begging you to do; tell what the speeches were." Like Glaucon the day before yesterday, today's non-philosophic audience puts up with Apollodorus's insults in order to hear a Socrates devotee report on a private event involving his master. Apollodorus ends the frame discus-sion, saying, "I shall try to tell it to you from the beginning as Aristodemus told it." The frame audience of the *Symposium* will not interrupt his narra-tion, which begins here and carries through to the end.

The frame of the *Symposium* sets the core discussion in a context of urgency: two different audiences need to learn immediately about the same event in Socrates' past, an event involving Alcibiades and eros about which rumors are circulating. Just the day before yesterday, a well-known undisciplined devotee of Socrates had been tracked down to tell the story about Agathon's party that those asking today also want to learn about. Neither Glaucon nor those asking today have any interest in philosophy. So why the urgency? One event alone rises in answer: the trial of Socrates for which five hundred citizen judges will be chosen to arrive at a life-deciding opinion about him. And here was a rumored event that might give a responsible judge a trustworthy opinion about what the famous man on trial said in private to the singularly important, traitorous political leader, Alcibiades, and on eros no less. Heightened interest in Socrates on the part of the non-philosophical points to a dramatic date of the frame of the *Symposium* as the spring of 399, during the thirty-day gap between the day the king-archon set the trial date and the actual trial, the day on which the five hundred jurors would be selected[15]

2. Socrates Beautifies Himself for Agathon

The first sentence of Aristodemus's report announces a different-looking Socrates, one who is "freshly bathed and wearing fancy slippers which was not Socrates' usual way" (174a). Aristodemus, barefoot in literal discipleship to Socrates, asked him where he was going "now that he had become so beautiful," and Socrates' beautification becomes the drawn-out first theme of their opening exchange: "To dinner at Agathon's," he says, explaining that he stayed away from the first day's victory celebration, "but I did agree to come today. It is for this that I have got myself up so beautifully — that beautiful I may go to a beauty." This is a Socrates who prepared himself, *beautified* himself for Agathon, a Socrates on the hunt.

Socrates' first action can be seen as itself part of his preparation, for he invites Aristodemus, asking him how he felt "about going uninvited to dinner" (174b). Aristodemus confirms his disciple nature: "I shall do whatever you say." So a record exists of the meeting between the beautified Socrates and Agathon, a report by a literal-minded devotee. Telling him to "follow," Socrates gives a reason: "so that we may change and ruin the proverb, 'the good go to Agathon's [literally, Good's] feasts on their own." And he brings in Homer: "Homer, after all, risked not only ruining it, it seems, but committed an outrage (*hybris*) on this proverb."[16] Homer's hubristic use of the proverb was to make "Agamemnon an exceptionally good man in martial matters and Menelaus a 'soft spearman,' yet when Agamemnon was making a sacrifice and a feast, he had Menelaus come to the dinner uninvited, an inferior to his better's" (174c).[17] That dinner in the *Iliad* is itself a pri-

15. Christopher Planeaux argues for this date in Appendix F: Sokrates' Trial, Imprisonment, and Execution, in "Apollodorus and Alkibiades," 30–31. In "Note on the Dramatic Date of the Frame of the *Symposium*," below, I summarize the evidence for setting the frame in the thirty-day time period just before Socrates' trial.

16. Socrates' claim is itself hubristic: the proverb did not exist in Homer's time; Bury, *Symposium*, ad loc.

17. In the *Iliad* Apollo used "soft spearman" (17.587) to taunt Hector in order to incite him back into battle.

vate feast, called by Agamemnon on the day that set the human action of the *Iliad* in motion after nine years at Troy.[18] He invited six leaders to his feast, including Odysseus. "Of his own accord came Menelaus, good at the war cry" (2.408). After feasting, they gather the army "to stir more quickly the fierce war god" (440). Odysseus had performed the indispensable action just before the feast, striking down Thersites, leader of a revolt of the common warriors, and winning their loyalty to fight for Agamemnon. Aristodemus responds fittingly to Socrates' Homer reference: "Perhaps I too shall run a risk, Socrates—perhaps it is not as you say, but as Homer says, an undistinguished man going uninvited to a wise man's dinner"—wisdom, not martial prowess, becomes the standard. But Aristodemus denies *he* runs a risk: "Consider what your defense might be in inviting me, for I shall not agree that I have come uninvited but shall say that it was at your invitation" (174d). He's an invited guest; *Socrates* invited him, so Socrates would have to make the defense if Aristodemus's presence is challenged.

Socrates makes no direct response to Aristodemus but says, "With the two of us going on the way together, we shall deliberate on what we shall say"—again quoting Homer, again about a meeting of the leading Greeks, this time on the desperate night before what they all feared would be the final Trojan push that could result in burning their ships and death for them all. They concoct a plan to send a spy into the enemy camp, hoping to learn something that might help save them. Diomedes volunteers and chooses a companion to accompany him, for "when two go together one discerns before the other how profit may be had."[19] He chooses Odysseus, "wise above all of us in discernment" (247), and it is Odysseus's discernment and planning that makes their spy mission a success as he interrogates a counterspy they catch. The core of the *Symposium* thus begins by calling in two momentous Homeric precedents, two key meetings of the Greek leaders at Troy that put in motion decisive events in the greatest of all Greek victories—and it is Odysseus each time who is the chief actor. What could the meeting at the Lenaia in 416 and Socrates' place in it be to merit such precedents?

Socrates and Aristodemus do not in fact deliberate together on what they are going to say; instead, Socrates "turned his attention to himself." He asks Aristodemus to go on ahead, ignoring the embarrassment to which this opens him of appearing uninvited at the dinner. Aristodemus obeys and is taken into Agathon's house where the others are assembled

18. *Iliad* 2.1–454.
19. *Iliad* 10.224.

and about to begin the dinner (174e). Agathon graciously removes any embarrassment by alleging that he had looked for Aristodemus yesterday to
invite him—and asks him why he hasn't brought Socrates. Aristodemus
says what he planned to say, that he had come at Socrates' invitation. So
where *is* Socrates? The arrival of Socrates becomes the little drama at the
start of the dinner as Agathon asks where he is and sends a servant to find
him and bring him in. But the servant comes back alone, reporting that
Socrates "retreated into a neighbor's portico" and was unwilling to come
when asked. "Strange," Agathon says and tells his servant to call him, but
Aristodemus overrules, reporting that it "is something of a habit with him.
Sometimes he moves off and stands stock still wherever he happens to be"
(175b)—famously public Socrates retreats into a habitual privacy just prior
to Agathon's feast. They begin the dinner, and Agathon "often ordered
that Socrates be sent for" and Aristodemus just as often "did not permit
it" (175c). Finally, in the middle of dinner, Socrates arrives, having "lingered
as long as was usual for him."

Inviting Socrates to "lie down alongside me," Agathon makes Socrates' private deliberation their topic: "By touching you, I too may enjoy
the piece of wisdom that just occurred to you while you were standing in
the portico otherwise you would not have come away" (175d). Socrates in
turn refers to Agathon's "beautiful wisdom" and its transmission to *him* by
touch. His own "may turn out to be a sorry sort of wisdom" compared to
Agathon's, which "flashed out so intensely from you while you are young,
and yesterday became conspicuous among more than thirty thousand
Greek witnesses" (175e). "You are outrageous," Agathon says and promises,
"A little later you and I will go to court about our wisdom, with Dionysos
as judge, but now first attend to dinner."

Socrates' private deliberation in the neighbor's portico takes the place
of the two Homeric deliberations with which Plato began his account of
Socrates and Agathon's party, the deliberations of Odysseus, whose thinking and acting led to the Greek victory at Troy. The Homeric precedents,
Socrates' private deliberation, Agathon's assurance that Socrates gained
the wisdom he sought there—these prominent features make the delay
in the neighbor's portico another preparation for the coming evening, another beautification for Agathon. But Plato chose to make what Socrates
prepared a puzzle: it is impossible that the wisdom gained in the neighbor's
portico is the wisdom Socrates will report at length as the understanding
of eros he gained from Diotima, for the decision to turn their evening into
a contest of speeches on Eros was arrived at spontaneously at the symposium. None of the participants could know in advance that Pausanias

would suggest that their symposium be different from the usual drinking, or that Eryximachus would then suggest a change from the usual entertainment of a girl playing the aulos to speeches they would make for their own entertainment, and that the topic of their speeches would remedy a lack that Phaedrus had complained about to him that no songs or paeans had been made in praise of the god Eros. These novelties turn Socrates' private reflection in the portico into a puzzle: What can he have been preparing in that most prominent of preparations? And what can that mean for the speech on Eros he actually does make? — for Socrates took matters into his own hands when Eryximachus proposed a series of speeches on Eros as their entertainment (176-e): he not only endorsed the proposal but ruled out any objection by others, telling the others just why each of them had to agree, and he ended by ordering Phaedrus to begin (177e).

What could Socrates' preparation in the portico be then, that pause Plato made so prominent just before the symposium as part of Socrates' preparations? The answer seems to come in two stages. First, just before Agathon gives his speech, in the only interruption in the sequence of speeches, Socrates initiates a dialogue with him about tragedy and wisdom; and second, at the end of the dialogue he makes a special promise to Agathon as a tragedian. On the first of these occasions, Aristophanes called attention to the fact that only Socrates and Agathon remain as speakers, and Eryximachus said that if he did not know that they "were skilled in erotics" he would be "very much afraid of their being at a loss for words" (193e). Socrates then sparked a little dialogue with Agathon concerning tragedy and wisdom. Beginning with the courage or fear one might experience facing the multitude in the theater or facing the few wise, Socrates moves to being *ashamed*, feeling shame before the few wise for what Agathon said to the multitude in the theater in his tragedy. The final question Socrates is permitted to pose asks, "Would you not be ashamed before the many if you believed you were doing something shameful?" Should Agathon feel shame before the wise *and* the many about his prize-winning tragedy? At that point Phaedrus put a stop to Socrates' questioning — his damaging, shocking questioning of their feted host — in order to get the evening back on track, allowing Agathon to give his speech in praise of Eros. On the second of the two occasions, at the end of the dialogue, a groggy Aristodemus reports that Socrates returned to the theme of writing tragedies. "Socrates was conversing" with Agathon and Aristophanes, the rest being asleep or gone (223c). He directed his speech at Agathon in particular because, while "compelling them to agree that the same man should know how to make comedy and tragedy," he singled out the tragedian: "He who is by art a tragic poet is also a comic poet"; the whole tragedy and comedy of life can become available to the young tragedian Agathon. These two events, the interruption on tragedy, shame, and wisdom, plus the final promise on the wisdom open to the writer of tragedy, are topics that Socrates could well have prepared in the portico for his coming meeting with the victorious young tragedian.

But if *that* is what he prepared, what about the speech he actually made on eros, the topic sprung on them only after their dinner? *That* speech needs no preparation; *that* speech is one that Socrates can always make spontaneously should the occasion arise because it concerns the only thing of which he claims expert knowledge. He gives it here because the opportunity arose in a way he could not have anticipated. It would still be a speech saved for private occasions and a select auditor, like the gifted young Agathon, whom Socrates singles out among those present, threatening to leave if he is not allowed to question him. But it would be Socrates' authentic speech, the speech most his own, the speech saved for a fit auditor, just as Parmenides saved his special speech for an audience of one whom he had tested for fitness. Socrates' speech on eros is his most important possible speech, and events have arranged themselves to make that the speech he can give this evening, not the one he seems to have prepared on tragedy and wisdom.

As Apollodorus's auditors in 399 listen to his narration of this private event in 416, names begin to trickle out that are likely known to them, names of those convicted of the religious crimes of 416–415, beginning with Eryximachus (175a). His name had been read aloud in court at the trial of Andocides a few months earlier as one of those convicted of mutilating the herms, a crime for which he had been executed.[20] And when Eryximachus mentions the name Phaedrus (175c), he adds another criminal from 415 present at the party, another whose name had been read aloud in court at the trial of Andocides, for he had been convicted of profaning the mysteries and had fled Athens.[21] Socrates' presence with these criminals makes the evening's events even more compelling than the importunate auditors could have imagined—a bonanza for potential jurors just before Socrates' trial. But where is Alcibiades, the only one Glaucon named as present? When he turns out not to be among the speakers, his absence grows all the more noticeable. And when he finally does arrive in fitting

20. Andocides, "On the Mysteries," §35. See below, "Note on the Dramatic Date," in this chapter.

21. Andocides, "On the Mysteries," §15.

spectacular fashion, the auditors will be especially attentive to his contribution to the evening's speeches, he the most notorious of the criminals of
416–415, he who dared to have the figure of Eros emblazoned on his shield.

   In determining what they will do after dinner, Eryximachus made Socrates the exception among drinkers — "He can go either way" and "will be
content whatever we do" — ruling out Socrates as one of the judges of what
they should do. Phaedrus, Eryximachus's obedient beloved, suggests they
all obey Eryximachus, who then proposes that they dismiss the aulos player
and entertain themselves with speeches of the sort he is willing to propose
(176e). He begins by citing Euripides, "The tale is not my own" (177a), for
his tale is Phaedrus's. But his quotation suggests more because Euripides
used that phrase to introduce a tale on the origin of all things,[22] a fitting
prelude for the topic he will suggest. Phaedrus frequently complained to
him that "not one person has dared to hymn Eros in a worthy manner; but
so great a god lies in neglect" (177c). Eryximachus finds it "appropriate for
those here," lovers and beloveds as all but Aristophanes are, "to adorn the
god" Eros with speeches of praise, beginning with Phaedrus, who occupied
the traditional place of highest honor, and continuing around the couches
to Agathon. Apollodorus's auditors thus learn that "the erotic speeches"
Glaucon had heard rumors about were suggested by the two lovers known
to be present who had been convicted in 415. Here they are responsible for
another profaning of mysteries, those of the god Eros.

   At this point, silenced Socrates, ruled out of the decision about making speeches, preempts the decision of all the others, asserting that no
one there would cast a vote against the proposal that Eros be the topic of
their speeches. As for him: "I claim to have expert knowledge of nothing
but erotics" (177d). This too is a different Socrates from the one who typically claimed *not* to have knowledge; here he claims not simply knowledge
but *expert knowledge* (*epistasthai*) and even repeats that claim and makes it
emphatic by claiming to know the truth about eros (198d). Having taken
charge and secured the topic, he notes his disadvantage if Phaedrus speaks
first: "It is not quite fair for those of us who lie on the last couches" (177e).
He lies in the last place on the last couch, a place he will turn to his advantage with a speech explicitly refuting the second-to-last speech, Agathon's,
and by implication refuting each of the others.

   Before continuing with Aristodemus's report on Phaedrus's speech,
Apollodorus remarks that "Aristodemus scarcely remembered all that each

22. *Symposium*, trans. Benardete, footnote at 177a.

and every one of them said, and I in turn do not remember all that *he* said."
But he will tell them "the noteworthy points of those speeches that, in my
opinion, most particularly deserve remembering" — a notice of caution at
the beginning of the speeches that the transmission is not impeccable.

After Socrates sets the speeches in motion by wishing Phaedrus good
luck (177e), he does not appear again until Aristophanes finishes and calls
attention to the fact that only two are left, Agathon and Socrates (193e)[23] —
the comment that spurred Eryximachus to say he is confident about them
because both are "skilled in erotics," thereby initiating Socrates' brief
exchange with Agathon on tragedy, wisdom, and shame. Then, after Agathon gives his speech and "all those present applauded vigorously" (198a),
it is Socrates' turn as the only speaker left. He praises Agathon's speech as
"beautiful and varied," singling out "that bit at the end" and the "beauty
of its words and phrases" (198b). Identifying the rhetoric as Gorgias's, he
uses Homer to depict his own situation: "I was afraid that Agathon in his
speech would at last send the head of the dread speaker Gorgias against my
speeches and turn me to very stone in speechlessness" (198c) — Agathon is
Persephone, queen of the underworld, and Socrates is Odysseus as "green
fear took hold" of him that Persephone would send the head of the Gorgon
Medusa to turn him into stone, the fear that drove Odysseus out of Hades
and back to his ship.[24] In his Odyssean situation Socrates is to be laughed
at for agreeing to participate in their competition of speeches in praise
of Eros and claiming to be skilled in erotics (198d), for, having heard all
their speeches, he says that he "knew nothing of the matter, nor of how
one is to eulogize anything." He was not wrong to claim expert knowledge of erotics but wrong to think that his way of praising was the same as
theirs. "In my stupidity I believed" that to praise anything "the truth had
to be told about" it and "that this was the underpinning." Knowing the
truth, he could select "the most beautiful parts of the truth [and] arrange
them in the seemliest manner possible." Socrates' way of praising eros —
his coming speech — includes a knower's suppression of the uglier parts of
the truth about it. His speech will intimate that "the truth about Eros is
terrifying,"[25] but he beautifies it, leaving that truth hidden or accessible

23. As Leo Strauss noted, when Aristophanes named only Agathon and Socrates as the
remaining speakers, he simply skipped over "poor Aristodemus," who was reclining next to
Eryximachus (Strauss, *On Plato's "Symposium,"* 152).

24. *Odyssey* 11.632–36.

25. Benardete, "On Plato's *Symposium*," 190.

only to inference from the beautiful surface. Expert knowledge of erotics combined with knowing the truth about praising anything led him to be "filled with the proud thought that I should speak well" (198d6–7). But the speeches of the others attributed to Eros "the greatest and most beautiful things possible regardless of whether this was so or not" (198e); truth didn't matter, for each speaker aimed to make Eros "seem to be as beautiful and good as possible"—to those who do not know, "for surely this is not the case for those who do know" as he knows (199a). Because he did not know "the manner of praise" that the speeches were to follow, "the tongue promised but the mind did not"—he quotes Euripides to justify saying, "Let me call it quits." Given the Odyssean setting he supplied, Socrates announces his readiness to leave this Hades.

But there is one condition under which he will stay and give a speech: he is willing "to tell the truth on my own terms, so long as my words are not to be compared with your speeches, lest I be laughed at" (199b). They spoke to please and to win; he will speak, if they grant his condition, of the most beautiful parts of the truth arranged in the seemliest manner. He calls on Phaedrus to decide whether he has "any need for such a speech too, for hearing the truth being said about Eros." He will have his own purpose, for although he says that "the phrasing and arrangement of the sentences [will] fall as they come," they prove to be expertly planned and arranged for his audience of one. For when Phaedrus and the others urge him "to speak in whatever way he himself believed he had to speak," he tells Phaedrus his condition: that he be allowed to question Agathon even though Phaedrus forbade that earlier: he will "ask Agathon about a few small points in order that, when I have got him to agree with me, I can go ahead and speak." So indispensable to Socrates' purpose is his examination of Agathon that he would give no speech at all if he is not permitted to examine Agathon—and in his examination and the expansion that follows it, he will do what he promised: shelter the true underpinnings of eros in his arrangement of its beautiful parts.

Granted permission, Socrates begins by praising Agathon, saying he made "a fine start" when he said that one had to show first what Eros himself is and only then turn to his deeds (199c). Socrates can say "I very much admire this beginning" because that's the way he begins, raising a "What is . . ." question to determine the nature of the thing. But he does not admire Agathon's answer to his "What is . . ." question, even though he calls it "beautiful and magnificent"—he shows his beautiful answer to be entirely false. The first question he poses he answers himself, giving Agathon a very elementary lesson in logic, as if this student of Prodicus was in need of basic instruction in the art of abstract thinking.[26] He asks, "Is Eros the sort that is love of something or of nothing?" (199d), immediately adding that he's not asking whether eros is "of a mother or of a father," cases in which eros would be "laughable." To explain himself he makes *father* not the object but the subject: he's asking "about this very word, father — is the father father of someone or not?" That question too he answers himself: "You would doubtless tell me, if you wanted to give a fine reply, that the father is father of a son or daughter. Isn't that so?" Agathon's "Of course" fits the obviousness of the point. Gaining agreement that "the same is true of mothers," Socrates says, "Answer me just a little bit more, so that you might come to understand better what I want" (199e) — and he asks the same question about brothers. Agathon is reduced to the simplest of roles, answering obvious questions. At last Socrates turns from family relations to eros: "Do try then to tell about eros as well. Is Eros eros of nothing or of something?" "Of course he is of something." Agathon may be getting annoyed at such simple questions but the point is both crucial and comprehensive, as Seth Benardete showed in summarizing this exchange: eros "is always in a relation," and this "relation is of a fully determined structure," a structure "independent of whatever human being it vanishes into"; "it is fully at work with its own deep structure apart from whatever superficial syntax any one of us attributes to it in our utterances."[27] Those superficial syntaxes include even the most subtle philosophic efforts to set out what is present and at work in this deep structure of eros that will turn out to be the most fundamental of all processes, the very nature of natural process.

Socrates gives Agathon a teacherly injunction, "Keep this fast in your memory, this something of which you claim he is," and asks him to "say only this much: that Eros that is the eros of something, does he desire this something or not?" (200a). "Of course he does," Agathon says. Socrates then asks the question that will lead to the critical point about desire: "And is it when he has, or does not have, that which he desires and loves, that he desires and loves it?" Agathon's answer — "It is at least likely that he does not have it" — is not good enough: "*Think*," Socrates admonishes, "is it not a necessity rather than a likelihood that the desirous thing desires what it is in need of, and does not desire unless it is in need?" He prompts the proper answer: "For in my opinion, Agathon, it is a marvelous necessity.

---

26. In the *Protagoras*, set some eighteen years earlier, in 434, Pausanias and a very young, very beautiful Agathon were sitting in a separate room with others listening to Prodicus (315d-e).

27. Benardete, "On Plato's *Symposium*," 190.

What is your opinion?" "It's my opinion too, he said" (200b). Socrates' insistence that Agathon grant that *necessity* directs desire to what it is in need of contradicts the chief claim of Agathon's speech that the appearance of Eros in the world was the changing of an age: the birth of Eros brought "the monarchy of Necessity" to its end (195c, 197b). Establishing the rule of necessity with the advocate of freedom is crucial: Socrates' rational or scientific view of necessity replaces the poet's view of freedom—but Socrates will make even necessity beautiful.

Responding to Agathon's statement that he shares Socrates' view on the necessity of desire's desiring what it needs, Socrates says, "Would anyone want to be tall if he was tall, or strong if he was strong?" Agathon recognizes that "from what has been agreed upon, that would be impossible." And Socrates confirms it: "For he surely would not be in need of those things that he already is." Socrates then makes a longer speech to ensure "that we may not deceive ourselves," offering apparent exceptions in which one "wanted to be strong being strong, and swift being swift, and healthy being healthy." "One might perhaps suppose" that these are cases of desiring what one already has. "If you have these cases in mind, Agathon, then who would desire each of these things that of necessity he has at the moment when, whether he wants to or not, he has it?" (200c). He does not allow Agathon to answer but has them answer together: "For whenever anyone says, 'I am healthy and want to be healthy or I am wealthy and want to be wealthy and I desire those very things that I have,' we should tell him"—you and I, Agathon, we would reply that he's deceiving himself in thinking he desires what he has: "'You, human being, possessing wealth, health, and strength, want to possess them also in the future, since at the present moment at least, whether you want to or not, you have them'" (200d). Socrates and Agathon together clear away the deception and show how to think about the matter correctly: "Consider then, when you say, 'I want the present things,' if you mean anything else than 'I want the things of the present moment to be present also in a future time.' Would he agree to that?" Agathon, finally given leave to speak for himself, assents and in doing so gives unknowing assent to what Socrates alone knows he is pointing to: the insatiable character of necessary desire—*having* is never enough because built into having is the desire to go on having, or, more exactly, a desire to go on desiring. For ultimately, Socrates' speech on eros will split into two accounts: one is a beautiful if unfulfillable desire to have permanently, to come to rest in satiated having; the other, Socrates' own, is true but initially terrifying and therefore not quite spoken: insatiable desire for insatiable desire. Socrates' beginning with Agathon points to the core of the speech he will make on his own.

Socrates then "draws up an agreement about what has been said." He reminds Agathon that his speech had said that the gods arranged matters through love of beautiful things, for there would not be love of ugly things—a reasonable point, Socrates judges (201a). If this is so, "Eros would be nothing else than love of beauty and not of ugliness." That near repetition leads to this: "Hasn't it been agreed that that of which one is in need and does not have one loves?" Agathon's simple "Yes" is true, for that had been agreed, but when he answers, "Of necessity," to Socrates' next statement, "So Eros is in need of and does not have beauty," he is wrong without Socrates' qualifier about not *yet* having *future beauty*. Socrates insists: "What about this? That which is in need of beauty and in no way possesses beauty, do you say it is beautiful?" "Certainly not," Agathon replies. "Do you still agree then that Eros is beautiful, if this is so?" Proud Agathon, their host and celebrated victor, is shamed into saying in front of his guests, "It's probable, Socrates, that I knew nothing of what I had said." Shamed into confessing ignorance, Agathon just made an elementary, obvious mistake: Socrates had just given instances of desiring to have what one already has—strength, swiftness, health, wealth—where the desire is to go on having in the future what one already has. Why didn't Agathon say that Eros is like that: being beautiful, Eros desires to go on having beauty in the future? He seems to have forgotten what they just said. "And yet you spoke beautifully," Socrates says, and makes the same point about the good: "Eros is in need of the good things as well" (201c). Poor Agathon says, "I would not be able to contradict you." Socrates replies that "you are unable to contradict the truth, since it is not at all hard to contradict Socrates"—it is especially easy to contradict Socrates right here, where he had just shown how to contradict his claim that eros is neither beautiful nor good. As for Socrates himself, however terrifying the truth about eros might at first be, he will judge that eros, truly understood, is both beautiful and good.

"I shall let you go for now," Socrates says, and begins the longest speech of the night, one that fits comfortably within their conditions for their night of speeches: shaming young Agathon is Socrates' precondition for making a speech at all. Socrates' beautification for Agathon includes this apparently ugly act of humiliating him in front of his guests—and with an argument he should not have assented to. If that shaming is not to be wholly gratuitous, Socrates' speech from this point on must be understood as having only one true auditor, the Agathon who admits his ignorance. For

that audience of one Socrates now performs his greatest act of beautification: he shames himself. Alleging that he once held the same view of Eros
Agathon did, he says he too was once reduced to the shameful position in
which he just placed Agathon by a wise teacher using the same arguments.
That teacher showed him the way out. Can shamed Agathon learn from his
wise teacher, as that teacher alleges he once learned from his?

3. Diotima's Myth Guides Socrates to the Third Stage of His Philosophic Education

Socrates too was once a young man in need of a teacher, and he found
one, or was found by one. That teacher, he says, first took him through the
very steps through which he just led Agathon — and took him further. His
teacher was "a woman, Diotima of Mantineia" (201d), god's honor from
a place of prophecy.[28] She was "wise in these and many other things," he
says, giving as evidence a deed she performed: "When the Athenians once
made a sacrifice before the plague, she caused the onset of the disease
to be delayed ten years."[29] This seer with magic powers "is the very one
who taught me erotics," Socrates says (201d), that one thing for which he
claimed expert knowledge (177e). Having let Agathon go, he delivers the
rest of his speech as the speech Diotima "used to make"; that speech "I
shall now try to tell you all on the basis of what has been agreed upon by
Agathon and myself."

For a chronological approach to the dialogues it matters that Plato has
Socrates himself present the events of his learning the third and final stage
of his philosophic education using the wise, publicly pious Diotima. He
had Socrates himself present the first stage too, his turn to the logoi in the
Phaedo and his discovery of transcendent forms, forms he is still using on
his dying day to prove the immortality of the soul. Through Diotima the
mature Socrates of the *Symposium* presents the steps that enabled him as
a young man to gain his mature understanding of things — which, for this

28. *Mantikos* means "seer," and *manteia* "prophesying" or "divining." Mantineia was a city
in the center of the Peloponnese. That Diotima is Socrates' invention is almost universally
agreed, as the participants in the symposium would well understand: Socrates has her speak
of "a certain account according to which lovers are those who seek their own halves" (205e)
and *that* account the participants just heard Aristophanes invent.

29. Benardete calls this a "disturbing thing about her" because if the plague had not been
delayed it would have done far less damage: rural Athenians would not have been packed
into the confined space within the city walls as they had been during the Spartan invasions
of Attica in the early war years.

highly sophisticated audience of enlightened Athenians in their thirties, omits transcendent forms except at the very end when Diotima brings in a vision of a single transcendent unchanging form as the power prevailing over all beings. As for the second and central event in Socrates' philosophic education, Plato saw to it that his *Parmenides* preserve that stage wholly outside of Socrates' reports on his becoming and have instead philosophically driven men from afar save it from oblivion. The way of Diotima, when read as the step that came after the *Parmenides*, shows a relatively young Socrates gaining a rational understanding of cause within the restraints on human intellect that Parmenides had guided him to discover, an understanding of cause that cannot include transcendent forms whose irrationality Parmenides had demonstrated to him. In the *Symposium* Socrates tells his enlightened audience how Diotima led him to a fundamental ontological psychology: the self-knowledge of the soul of the driven inquirer, that singularity among beings, permits him an inferential conclusion about the nature of all beings.

To begin his long speech Socrates tells the company that it will repeat "the speech [Diotima] was wont to make," a dialogue for the most part, but he will "try to do it on my own, as best I can," speaking both parts. What Plato writes is therefore Apollodorus's report of Aristodemus's report of what Socrates reported he and Diotima said when he was young. Socrates had started correctly, just as Agathon had, trying to find out "who Eros himself is and what sort he is and then . . . his deeds." In speaking to Diotima, Socrates says that he "came pretty near to saying the same sort of things Agathon said to me now, that Eros was a great god and was the love of beautiful things" (201e). But "she refuted me with those same arguments with which I refuted him," showing that Eros "is neither beautiful . . . nor good." His response to that refutation, however, was different from Agathon's simple surrender: he pressed Diotima with a question and went on relentlessly questioning, making new demands for answers: if the Agathon stripped of his vaunted knowledge is to follow Socrates he will have to abandon his passivity and actively question what Socrates presents as Diotima's way.

The first question Socrates says he posed to Diotima picks up the conclusion to which he had led Agathon that Eros is neither beautiful nor good: "Is Eros then ugly and bad?" Diotima's first words are "Don't blaspheme" (*euphēmēseis*), don't profane sacred matters — commanding first words that color everything she says through their whole exchange and take on added significance in the settings of 416 and 399 when the crime of profanation was an acute public concern. After her command, she asked, "Do you believe that whatever is not beautiful must necessarily be ugly?" "Absolutely," Socrates answers, presenting himself as if he were as rigid and dogmatic in his youth and as unversed in elementary logical distinctions as Agathon showed himself to be. But the *Parmenides* showed young Socrates to be in fact subtle in distinctions and well schooled in the sophisticated logical puzzles of Zeno, and not dogmatic — Socrates' reported first steps with Diotima are evidently continued guidance for Agathon. Diotima's questioning turns immediately to wisdom and its opposite as she asks Socrates if he is "unaware that there is something between wisdom and ignorance" — and the *between* becomes the crucial category for one apparently prone to think only in opposites, for Diotima gives Socrates a basic lesson about *opinion* as a between, with correct opinion lying somewhere between knowledge and ignorance (202a). She emphatically tells him not to believe that Eros, which is neither beautiful nor good, is therefore ugly and bad; Eros is instead "something between the two of them" (202b). When Socrates protests on the grounds that "it is believed by all that [Eros] is a great god," Diotima distinguishes knowers and non-knowers: "Do you mean by all those who don't know or also those who know?" Socrates insists: "No, all inclusively." Here, for the only time in their exchanges, Diotima laughs, laughs about his believing what all believe, that Eros is a great god or that Eros is a god at all: "And just how could it be agreed that he was a great god by those who deny that he is even a god?" (202c). "Who are they?" Socrates asks, as if he can't believe anyone would deny that. "You are one, and I am one," she says provocatively, implicitly inviting young Socrates to join those who know. "And I said, 'How, I said, can you say this?'" repeating himself as if he had been flustered by her accusation that he does not believe Eros is a god. Here, Diotima offers her first argument: "Don't you assert that all gods are happy and beautiful? Or would you dare to deny that any one of the gods is beautiful and happy?" "By Zeus," Socrates says, he would not dare to deny that. Determining that he means by happy "precisely those who possess the good things and the beautiful things," Diotima employs the argument that Socrates had just used with Agathon, asking, "And do you hold to the agreement that Eros out of need for the good and beautiful things desires those very things of which he is in need?" (202d). When she further asks, "How then could he who has no share in the beautiful and good things be a god?" Socrates answers, "In no way, it seems." But "has no share in"? — Socrates has his younger self commit the same mistake Agathon made when Socrates showed him that it is perfectly reasonable to desire what one already has a share in: desire to have it in the future as well (200d). Diotima draws her conclusion on the basis of this mistaken premise: "Do you see then that you too hold that Eros is not a god?" Socrates avoids directly affirming that conclusion by reverting to his dependence on opposites: "What would Eros be then, a mortal?" When she denies that and Socrates asks, "Well, what then?" Diotima can posit a *between* again: "Just as before, between mortal and immortal." When Socrates asks what this between is, Diotima, religious teacher that she is, answers, "A great daemon, Socrates, for everything daemonic is between god and mortal" (202e).

That ends the part of Socrates' report on Diotima that is directly connected to his questioning of Agathon, a part that de-divinizes eros while making it a daemonic force between gods and mortals. Learning this from Diotima ends Socrates' first effort to find out from her what eros *is*, for his next question moves to what he had said comes next, the *deeds* of eros, what it does (201e). Diotima gives a longer, non-dialectical answer to the question of eros's deeds and then, answering Socrates' next question, she gives another longer, non-dialectical response in which she in fact returns to the first issue, what eros is. In these two answers, each mythic in character, the teacher of Socrates noted for religious powers gives her answers to what eros does and what eros is; those answers show religiously outfitted Diotima to be a philosopher, for they are her initial guidance for Socrates on the two primary domains of philosophy, the nature of knowing and of being, epistemology and ontology.

When Socrates asks about eros's deeds — "What kind of power does it have?" — Diotima answers with two words, interpreting (*hermēneuon*) and carrying over or across (*diaporthmeuon*):[30] eros performs the actions of a between, interpreting one domain to the other, carrying across a boundary that nothing on either side can itself cross: "to gods things from human beings . . . requests and sacrifices," and "to human beings from gods . . . orders and exchanges-for-sacrifices." Diotima pictures eros as "in the middle of both and filling up the interval so that the whole itself has been bound together by it" — "the whole itself" (*to pan auto*) consists of two parts and active mediation between them; one part is the human, enclosed on itself, open to the other part of the whole only by mediation; likewise, that divine part of the whole can enter the human only through that mediation. Diotima's wise answer to Socrates' question of the power of eros implies a claim about the character of all human knowing; using a more or less traditional religious vision of the whole as separated into human and divine domains, she pictures all exchanges between domains as carried out by a

30. LSJ gives as secondary meanings of *diaporthmeuō* "carry a message" and "ply a ferry-boat from one side of a river to the other."

mediating power. She sketches that power using many examples of pious practice, insisting always on the complete separation of the domains except for the interpreting and carrying across of eros: "Through this occurs the whole intercourse and conversation of gods with humans while they are awake or asleep" (203a). She ends by drawing a distinction among humans: "He who is wise in things like this is a daemonic man (*anēr*)," while those wise in other arts or crafts are base or common; the wise person attains an uncommon divinity among humans, as she herself has.

Diotima puts into religious language what can be seen as an epistemological claim with serious implications for any possible ontology. Her religious terms and images invite comparison with the fundamental insight into all human awareness that Parmenides set within his logical series of hypotheses on one and many as the singular key that young Socrates would have to discover and apply to the rest: the dreaming and shadow-painting of the seventh hypothesis make all human experience mediated by a between. Diotima's religious version insists on the same point: all human experience is ineluctably mediated by an active force present in wakefulness or sleep. In the *Symposium* poetic Socrates finds a way of his own to present the fundamental insight he gained through Parmenides' guidance in the gymnastic; what Parmenides enfolded into his seventh hypothesis Socrates enfolded into Diotima's pious answer to his question of the power of eros. And he did so only after de-divinizing Eros, the god all the others praised. However the divine is ultimately understood by wise Diotima, that understanding must acknowledge the between of eros that interprets and carries across the boundary that closes all human experience within a horizon.[31]

Socrates asks no questions about Diotima's account of the powers of eros but instead moves to a different matter: "Who is his father? And who is his mother?" (203a). What are the origins of eros? Socrates has his younger self pose to wise Diotima the basic philosophic question of cause, the question that his report in the *Phaedo* made his primary question as a young man. In the *Symposium* Socrates poses the question of cause about the power that wise Diotima had just said is at work in all human experience of the whole. "This is rather long to explain," she answers, "but I shall tell you all the same" (203b); the story she tells first is quite short, but it

---

31. Such efforts by Socrates to present what he is learning in religious terms led Benardete to comment on "the quasi-religious atmosphere Socrates created around himself from the time he first met Alcibiades to the day of his death" (*On Plato's "Symposium,"* 181)—that is, through the whole of his public life.

manages to convey philosophy's most profound insight into the whole in a memorable mythos about the parents of eros.

Diotima says that on the day Aphrodite was born all the gods held a feast, and she singles out the presence of Poros (Resource), son of Metis (Intelligence). Penia (Poverty) arrived after the gods had dined; having come "to beg for something . . . she hung about near the door." After the feast, Poros went into Zeus's garden to sleep off his drunkenness, and Penia, "plotting (*epibouleuousa*) because of her own lack of resources (*aporian*) to have a child made out of Poros, reclined beside him and conceived Eros." A *plotting* Penia is a remarkable thing, a Penia who does not lack *resources* — her action shows that Penia does not wholly lack what her name alleges she lacked; she knows herself, knows what she lacks, and knows how to gain it. Seth Benardete says in interpreting this story that it is "a *mythos* and not a *logos* because it splits a single entity with an internal structure into two separate entities which then have to be recombined to recover the original."[32] The truth of Diotima's mythos depends upon that interpretive act of recombining: translated into the logos of understanding, what the mythos split into two recombines into a single entity in process: eros is *active* lack experiencing its lack, impelled to satisfy it. In depicting Eros's mother as Penia, the myth suggests that eros contains within itself all that is necessary to reproduce itself; eros is desire directed toward its satisfaction. And if eros "dies" in satisfying itself, eros is between mortal and immortal: eros rises again as desire impelled to satisfy itself. Leo Strauss was the first among contemporary readers of Plato to have recovered this understanding of Diotima's story. Poverty, he says, "must have been dissatisfied with her state and not ignorant if Eros was to be conceived at all. Eros, I conclude, resembles only her mother and not at all her father. . . . He must be always."[33] Strauss goes on to draw the implication of this interpretation of the myth: "Eros, we can say, is the heart of coming into being and perishing. Eros, we can say, is the nature of nature."[34] Diotima's mythos in answer to Socrates' question about the father and mother of Eros left it to him — as he leaves it to Agathon — to draw an awesome conclusion: interpreted rationally the mythos conveys the truth that eros, which is not

32. Benardete, "On Plato's *Symposium*," 193.

33. Strauss, *On Plato's "Symposium,"* 194. Strauss notes the precedent for Plato's account of Penia in Aristophanes' comedy *Ploutos* (*Wealth*), ll. 550–54, first produced in 388 (Strauss, 194–95). In *Ploutos* Aristophanes distinguished between the common view of Poverty as self-satisfied beggary and Poverty's own view of herself as the love of work to get out of misery.

34. Strauss, *On Plato's "Symposium,"* 196.

a god, has no parents. And *that* — "Eros has no parents" — is precisely the conclusion that Francis Bacon, profound philosophic interpreter of *The Wisdom of the Ancients*, drew from the Eros tale, an ontological sovereignty of becoming conveyed mythically. That Eros has no parents is, Bacon said, "perhaps the greatest thing of all."[35]

Diotima's *mythos* is very economical in intimating the fundamental truth about eros and she will expand somewhat on its implications in her *logos*, her argument for Socrates, which itself remains indirect, leaving to inference what the myth and the argument both imply. Like Parmenides, this teacher of Socrates entrusts the ultimate lessons to him: the things that need to be learned cannot be taught, but they can be learned. In its economy, Diotima's myth is exemplary of poetry's way with the truth: the truth that Eros has no parents had already been stated at the symposium by Phaedrus, the first speaker to define Eros and a lover of poetry. Reporting the poets' view that Eros is the oldest god, though without lingering to interpret it, he claimed that "the parents of Eros neither exist nor are they spoken of by anyone" (178b), and his proof consisted of quoting Hesiod: after Chaos came "broad-breasted Earth . . . and Eros"; and quoting Parmenides: "Genesis, first of all gods, devised Eros."[36] The truth about Eros was known to wise Greek poets and wise Greek philosophers, and a lover of their beautiful stories like Phaedrus, not himself wise, keeps the truth alive and accessible to anyone who might be driven to think about the implications of the poetic stories. For the poetic tales of poets and philosophers alike implied that the truth about the origins of becoming is that becoming has no origin. And if becoming is unlimited in time, it is unlimited in extent: *all* beings come into being and pass out of being.

Confirmation of the legitimacy of reading Diotima's myth for its ontological implications is found in Plato's *Theaetetus*: Socrates read Homer that way. Plato set the *Theaetetus* on the morning of the preliminary hearing of the capital charges that led to Socrates' execution (*Theaetetus* 210d); after the trial, in his cell, the condemned Socrates narrated that conversation to Euclides, who wrote it down and on return visits questioned Socrates about the parts he hadn't remembered in order to make sure he had everything right (142c–143a). In his conversation with young Theaetetus that Socrates acted to preserve in writing, he called Homer the great general standing at the head of the army of thinkers that constitute the tradition

---

35. Bacon, "Cupid or the Atom," in *Wisdom of the Ancients*, 122–25; White, *Peace among the Willows*, 220.

36. Hesiod, *Theogony* 116, 117, 120; Graham, *Texts*, Parmenides, 29 [F13].

of Greek wisdom (153a); that whole Homeric army holds that "all things . . . come to be from locomotion and motion and mutual mixing; for nothing ever is, but (everything) always becomes" (152d). Socrates saw that

> all the wise in succession, except Parmenides, converge, Protagoras and Heraclitus, and Empedocles, as well as the tip-top poets of each kind of poetry, Epicharmus of comedy and Homer of tragedy. Homer with the line "Ocean and Mother Tethys, the becoming (*genesis*) of gods" has said that everything is the offspring of flowing and motion.

Later, when speaking with Theodorus, Socrates elaborates on what we've taken from the ancients while also contrasting ancients and sophists: "From the ancients, who were concealing it from the many with poetry, it was that the becoming (*genesis*) of everything else happens to be streams, Oceanus and Tethys, and nothing is at rest, and from those later [the sophists] who were revealing it openly" (180d). In his commentary on this passage Benardete contrasts what Homer himself said with what Socrates made of it: the "veiled speech of Homer 'Both Oceanus and mother Tethys, the *genesis* of gods' . . . says, according to Socrates, that all things are the offspring of flowing and motion, whereas it seems to say that the gods have their origin in a male and a female god, who did not themselves become."[37] According to Socrates' interpretation then, Homer conveys a process ontology, a totality of becoming, while veiling it in a poetic theology of ostensibly immortal beings. Homer is the original master practitioner of what Socrates told Theaetetus was "the secret of the wise": they never said what they meant.[38] Socrates' Diotima belongs to that Homeric tradition of conveying wisdom poetically while not quite saying what she meant in her myth of Eros's parents: everything is flowing and motion. Unlike the sophists, she refrained from revealing openly what Homer veiled. But she also added precision to Homer's ontology of becoming: hers is an ontology in which the fundamental becoming deserves the name eros, a particular kind of active desiring that in satisfying itself is ever kindled anew.

Having told the tale of Eros's birth, Diotima uses it to explain the "nature" and "situation" of Eros (203c). "Because he was conceived on the day of [Aphrodite's] birth," Eros, her "attendant and servant," "is by nature (*phusis*) a lover concerned with the beautiful." Just how to understand eros's "concern" with the beautiful is part of Diotima's way of

---

37. Benardete, *Being of the Beautiful*, I.105.
38. Benardete, *Being of the Beautiful*, I.105.

structuring her report, for only at the end of her logos, having defined the nature of eros, will she state eros's true relation to the beautiful. As for the "situation" of Eros, being the son of Poros and Penia, "first of all he is always poor; and he is far from being tender and beautiful as the many believe"—as Agathon believed, making that the chief feature of Eros. Instead, Eros "is tough, squalid, shoeless"—as Socrates usually is—"and homeless" (203d). Diotima emphasizes Eros's homelessness by describing its consequences: he is "always lying on the ground without a blanket or a bed, sleeping in doorways and along waysides in the open air." But his homelessness is itself a kind of dwelling: "He has the nature of his mother, always dwelling in the same house (*sunoikos*) with neediness." As Benardete says, "Eros is completely at home in his homelessness. He is ever at home with neediness."[39] Eros is a perpetual condition of neediness ever-again satisfied and ever-again depleted, a mythic representation of what might be thought to be grounds for despair. But Eros, so far from despairing at that inescapable condition, is completely at home in the never-ending ebb and flood. When Diotima must after all speak of Eros's father she says "he plots to trap the beautiful and the good"; the father plots as the mother plotted in conceiving Eros: as befits the truth of his origins, all of Eros's actions befit his mother.

In her expansive list of Eros's qualities, Diotima says he is "courageous (*andreios*—manly), stout, and keen, a skilled hunter, always weaving devices, desirous of practical wisdom (*phronēseōs*), and inventive, philosophizing throughout all his life, a skilled magician, druggist, sophist." Moving to a more general characterizing of his "nature," Diotima says Eros "is neither immortal nor mortal" (203e), and she explains how the presence of one compromises the presence of the other in a perpetual sequence of dying and rising: "Sometimes on the same day he flourishes and lives, whenever he has resources; and sometimes he dies, but gets to live again through the nature of his father"—the myth's splitting of Eros is a true representation of perpetual process, a process with a structure whose polarity it pictures in mythic personages. "And as that which is supplied to him is always gradually flowing out, Eros is never either without resources or wealthy, but is in between wisdom and lack of understanding." Again, Benardete briefly supplies the essential insight: "The midpoint between ignorance and wisdom is not half-ignorance and half-wisdom but the knowledge of ignorance."[40] The mature Socrates' typical, modest-sounding claim

39. Benardete, "On Plato's *Symposium*," 193.
40. Benardete, "On Plato's *Symposium*," 194.

of knowledge of his ignorance in fact states a positive claim to the crucial knowledge: knowledge of ignorance is knowledge of the character of knowing and therefore of its limits.

Declaring, "For here is the way it is," Diotima provides a lasting image of the human character of philosophy as a between. On one side, "not one of the gods philosophizes, any more than he desires to become wise — for he *is* — and whoever else is wise, he does not philosophize either" (204a). On the other side lie "those who lack understanding"; they "do not philosophize and desire to become wise" — and this, she says, "is precisely what makes the lack of understanding so difficult." She couples this difficulty with other features of the human in order to make a telling point about the difficulty of the human situation: a person who is not beautiful or good or intelligent "has the opinion that that is sufficient for him. Consequently, he who does not believe he is in need does not desire that which he does not believe he needs." What makes the lack of understanding so difficult is the almost universal failure to recognize it as a lack. That difficulty is the reason why the mature Socrates, in order to give a speech at all that night, first had to inflict on Agathon the humiliation of recognizing and stating that he lacked the understanding of the beautiful that he thought he knew. And what Socrates had to do with his gracious host he had to do with every interlocutor he took seriously: expose him to his ignorance.

This singling out of philosophizing as a between completes Diotima's myth and provokes Socrates to ask, "Then who are those who philosophize, Diotima, if they are neither the wise nor those who lack understanding?" This is the natural question for a young inquirer: he asks, in effect, Who am I, I who experience this passion driving me to know? Diotima rightly says that "by now it's perfectly plain even to a child that they are those between them both, of whom Eros would be one" (204b). "For wisdom is one of the most beautiful things, and Eros is eros concerned with (*peri*) the beautiful" — again, as at 203c4, Diotima employs the usefully vague term *peri* because only at the end of her logos will she be able to state eros's true relation to the beautiful. Employing her myth for the last time Diotima says that "his birth is the cause" of Eros being between wise and ignorant; that "is the nature of the *daemon*." Now she can account for Socrates' false belief that Eros itself was beautiful: "You believed, as it seems to me in making an inference from what you say, that the *beloved* (*erōmenon*) is Eros, not the *lover* (*erōn*). It is for this reason that Eros appeared to you wholly beautiful" (204c). The beloved is beautiful "but that which loves has another kind of look (*idea*), the sort I just explained." In stating his acceptance of this — "What you say is fine (*kalōs*)" — Socrates addresses her as

"Stranger" for the only time.[41] The Stranger told a myth that pictured the truth about eros, allowing the young Socrates to begin to enter the third stage of his philosophic education, a stage in which he had been partially preceded by Homer and the whole Homeric army in recognizing the sovereignty of becoming. But Eros portrays that sovereignty with great precision, and Socrates now poses a new question about Eros, one that Diotima will answer in a non-mythic way, with a logos, a process of reasoning that will express the truth about eros in a more fully articulated way.

4. Diotima's Logos Guides Socrates to the Third Stage of His Philosophic Education

The question Socrates addresses to the Stranger that he said Diotima was accepts the view of eros she presented in her myth — "Being of this sort" — and asks, "What need does eros meet for humans?" This is the last major question young Socrates poses, for when she says, "It is this, Socrates, that I shall next try to teach you," she takes full charge; her way of teaching him about the need met by eros employs logos, reasoning, to make eros basic to the very way of being human, and her logos, like her myth, has implications beyond the human. But before she begins she gives summary approval to what they gained through the myth: "Eros is of that sort and was born in this way, and he is of the beautiful things, as you assert" (204d) — "as you assert" is temporizing on her part: she lets young Socrates continue to believe that eros is of the beautiful until she is in a position to teach him that it is more than that.

Diotima's first step employs a dialectical device that the mature Socrates will use effectively: she supplies a "someone" to question them both, thus uniting the two of them as co-answerers sharing a stance over against a questioner. "But what if someone were to ask us, 'What about those beautiful things of which Eros is, Socrates and Diotima?'" Expressing the someone's question "more plainly," Diotima herself asks Socrates: "He who loves (*erai*) the beautiful things — what does he love (*erai*)?"[42] The crucial discussion — Diotima's reasoned account of what eros is — begins with a questioner Diotima supplies who does not even know how to for-

41. Socrates twice calls her "Stranger" in his narration: 201e, 211d.

42. The Greek verb for "love," here *erai*, is related to the noun for "love," *erōs*. Thus, Diotima's account has a consistency and directness that English can only reproduce by translating *erōs* as "love": in Greek *erōs* can *erai* just as love can love; the choice to leave *erōs* untranslated — which seems necessary — results in a serious loss in the flow and obviousness of Diotima's argument here.

mulate his question plainly. Socrates can easily answer the question as Diotima formulated it: "That they be his." But, she says, his answer "longs for" a further question: "What will he have who has the beautiful things?" When Socrates says that he is hardly capable of giving a ready answer to that question Diotima has the someone change the query, or ask the proper question, using "the good (*agathos*) instead of the beautiful (*kalos*)" (204e). This sudden switch by the someone she supplied allows Diotima to switch from the beautiful, the topic that dominated Agathon's speech and her own until now, to the topic that will enable her to lead Socrates through the necessary steps to the fundamental insight, insight into the drive to gain the good, the comprehensive impetus to satisfaction. The someone now asks, "Come, Socrates, the lover of the good things loves: what does he love?" "That they be his" is still Socrates' answer, and it still raises the further question, "And what will he who gets the good things have?" Now Socrates "can answer more adequately: he will be happy." It is Diotima who says why this is more adequate: "because the happy are happy by the acquisition of good things and there is no further need to ask, 'For what consequences does he who wants to be happy want to be so?'" (205a). Diotima can end this line of questioning and leave the someone behind by stating that "the answer is thought to be complete"; and it *is* complete as the definition of eros that she states in her next question: "This wanting and this eros, do you suppose they are common to all human beings, and all want the good things to be theirs always?"—this definition, "All want the good things to be theirs always," is complete, but Diotima will repeat it two more times with slight variations (206a13–14, 207a2–3). The repetitions do not change the definition in its essentials, but they serve to isolate and highlight the two discussions that they frame, structuring Diotima's ultimate, complete statement on what eros is. The repetitions frame two expansions and elucidations of eros as fundamental, first on the range of eros, second on its manner and activity.

Diotima's first statement of her definition was in a question asking whether eros is common to all human beings, and Socrates responds that eros understood this way is "common to all." "Why is it then," she asks, "that we deny that everyone loves (*eraō*)—given, that is, that everyone loves the same things and always—but we say that some love and some do not?" (205b). Why is an activity, eros, that we rightly predicate of a whole class of things, everyone, and rightly say they always do, restricted in our speaking to only a subclass of that class and to what they only sometimes do? When Socrates says he too wonders at that or is amazed at it (*thaumazō*), Diotima commands him not to persist in amazement—she acts as his

intellectual conscience, as she will repeatedly (207c, 208b-c), saying in effect, replace the stupor of amazement with the activity of thinking and
find out through investigation what the answer must be — don't wonder,
think. Here she helps him think through to the answer of why we restrict
the activity eros as we do: "We detach from eros a certain species (*eidos*) of
eros and give *it* the name eros, imposing on it the name of the whole (*tou
holou*); while in other cases we employ several different names." *Eros* is an
activity of a larger class of actions than our linguistic usage would lead us
to suspect — and is at work always. Diotima's argument about the *range*
of eros is conducted under the auspices of this generalizing statement at
its opening regarding its range and constancy. Given the care with which
Greek thinkers like Parmenides sheltered their fundamental, radical insights, leaving them to inference as Parmenides did in his gymnastic for
the gifted young Socrates, Diotima's words about the range of eros, "the
name of the whole," like her words in her mythos, must be weighed carefully, thought about, for inferences that can be drawn about conclusions
she does not voice. Diotima will no more profane the mysteries of eros in
her logos than she did in her mythos, though she will make them available
to thinking.

Socrates asks about the different names that Diotima said we employ
in place of eros: "Such as what?" "Such as the following," she says, but
instead of listing such names, she offers a different example of the same
linguistic phenomenon of restricting to a subclass a word that covers a
larger class: "You know that *making* (*poiēsis*) has a wide range." And the
range she describes is wide indeed: "The cause for anything whatsoever,
in going from what is not to what is, is in its entirety a making"; "anything
whatsoever" that comes to be out of what is not is the result of a making, in Greek, a *poetizing*.[43] Diotima comes very close to giving a name
to the whole as a whole of becoming that can be understood as a totality
of *makings*. Given this implication, what Diotima goes on to say is itself a
restricting because she restricts the making of "anything whatsoever" to
that subclass of things that come to be through *human* making: "And thus
all the productions that are dependent on the arts are *makings* (*poiēseis*) and
all the craftsmen engaged in them are *makers* (*poiētai*)" (205c). Beginning
again with "You know," she says: "They are not called poets but they have
different names, and from all of making one species has been separated off,
that which is concerned with music and meters, and gets addressed by a

43. Diotima's Greek conveys her point directly as English cannot because *poiēsis* is a
word for "making": in Greek poets poetize their poems = makers make their makings.

name of the whole. This alone is called *poetry* (*poiēsis*) and those who have
this part of making (*poiēseōs*) are called poets (*poiētai*)." Diotima's example
of *making* is like *erōs* in being a case of restricted linguistic usage, but her
example too can be seen as restricting in a larger, more important, if only
implied way. The two cases, *loving* and *making*, each confine to one class of
humans, *lovers* and *poets*, what is true of all humans, but each can be understood as itself confining to all human beings what is true of all *beings*. The
ontology implied in what Diotima is teaching Socrates is that all beings are
makings, products of the making that eros is.

Applying her example of making, Diotima says, "So too in the case of
eros. In brief, eros is the whole desire (*epithumia*) of good things and of being happy, 'the greatest and deceitful eros'" (205d). This line of poetry that
Diotima quotes is now unidentifiable, regrettably so, for its source and
setting could well have cast additional light on her meaning, given that her
lesson here about the great and deceitful eros concerns the restricted application of the word *erōs* that could, like *making*, be used to designate the
most comprehensive domain possible.[44] As Plato had shown in the second
stage of Socrates' philosophic education, he learned from old Parmenides
the power of *making* built into the inescapable human processes of perceiving and conceiving—dreaming and shadow-painting; all human awareness
is a deceitful making that never betrays its activity of making but instead
compels what is dreamt and shadow-painted to come to a stand, sorted
into classes as if it simply *is* as it stands sorted.

Only now does Diotima answer the question Socrates (205b) had asked
about the different names we employ for what is actually eros. Those other
names include moneymaking, attraction to gymnastics (*philo-gymnastia*),
and attraction to wisdom (*philo-sophia*): those moved by such desires are
lovers "but are neither said to love nor called lovers" (205d). Only those
who "go along a certain single species (*eidos*) of it and are in earnest about
it get the name of the whole (*holou*), 'eros,' 'to love,' and 'lovers.'" *Erōs* is a
name of the whole that names the comprehensive condition of desire in
the being that is always desiring. Socrates had fully assented to Diotima's
example of *making*, saying twice, "What you say is true" (205c). But he alters his response in assenting to what she says here, where she reverts from
the example of making back to eros: "You run the risk of saying the truth."

44. The word translated "deceitful," *doleros*, is "not a common word in Attic prose" (Dover, *Plato: Symposium*, at 205d2). Its only other use in Plato is at *Lesser Hippias* 369c, where
Hippias says that Homer "made Odysseus *deceitful* and a teller of many falsehoods." *Doleros*
is not a word Homer used.

Socrates seems not only to recognize the truth of what Diotima is teaching him but also to have an inkling of the risk she runs in giving a "name of the whole" that makes a specific kind of desire fundamental.

At this point, having stated the comprehensive character of eros as "the whole desire of good things and of being happy," story-telling Socrates has Diotima violate the temporal span separating their party in 416 from what Diotima taught him decades ago. He has her refer to "a certain logos" that she contrasts with her own logos, the story Aristophanes just told of eros being for one's own severed half. Socrates is willing to violate the chronology of his tale in order to take explicit issue with Aristophanes: it seems necessary that the marvelous tale about eros told by the writer of comedy be refuted or at least enclosed within a larger understanding. Diotima focuses the conflict between their two logoi on Aristophanes' eros for one's own other half as opposed to her eros for the good: "My logos denies that eros is either of a half or a whole. . . . For each of them does not cherish their own, unless someone calls the good one's own and of oneself and the bad whatever is alien, since there is nothing else that human beings love (*erōsin*) than the good" (205e). Aristophanes' eros for one's own limits or confines; Diotima's eros for the good enfolds eros for one's own within a comprehensive eros: Diotima's chronology-violating contrast makes Aristophanes' view one instance of the general restriction on eros that she illustrated by the restriction on *poiēsis*. Philosophic wisdom, unlike the wisdom of Aristophanes, does not view human eros as simply unique but as a particular kind of the fundamental kind, eros, which is understood by philosophy ontologically. Aristophanes the poet views the human as too exclusive a kind; Diotima the philosopher views the human within the comprehensive whole that shares its deepest feature.

Diotima ends her reference to Aristophanes in a way that returns them to the basic issue, for she asks Socrates if human beings seem to him to love something other than the good (206a). Socrates replies with the second oath he uttered in their conversation: "No, by Zeus, not to me."[45] Diotima then didactically draws out of Socrates all the elements of the definition of eros she had already given (205a). After he assents to her question, "Is it to be said unqualifiedly that human beings love the good?" (206a), she reminds him: "Must it not be added that they love the good to be *theirs*?" And when he assents to that she reminds him that it must also be added "that it

---

45. His other oath occurred at the beginning in answer to Diotima's question whether he "would dare to deny that any one of the gods is beautiful and happy." "By Zeus, I would not," he said (202c).

be theirs *always*." And she puts it all together, repeating what she had said a few minutes earlier (at 205a): "Eros is of the good being one's own always." "What you say is most true," Socrates says of Diotima's second statement of her definition, and she moves to her second explanatory discussion of her definition. "Since eros is always this, then in what manner do they pursue it and in what activity are eagerness and intensity called eros? What in fact are they doing when they act so? Can you say?" (206b).

The *manner* and *activity* of eros in their *eagerness* and *intensity* — these are the issues Diotima addresses in her second expansion of the basic definition of eros, and here too Socrates presents himself as "amazed," as if her question about the manner and activity of eros left him wholly baffled: "If I could [answer], Diotima, then I would not, in amazement at your wisdom, be frequently coming to you in order to learn these very things" (206b). This time she simply says, "I shall tell you." The manner and activity of eros in their eagerness and intensity "is bringing to birth in beauty both in terms of the body and in terms of the soul." Her explanation thus brings back the beautiful, which Socrates had earlier said was the object of eros before Diotima had her someone change his query about the object of eros from the beautiful to the good. Her explanation focuses on *generation* as a bringing to birth bodily and spiritually. But Socrates needs more help to understand what she means: "*Divination* (*manteias*) is needed for what you mean, and I don't understand" — an act of divining is needed for him to understand what the Mantineian diviner just said. "Then I shall speak more plainly," Diotima says, but even what she says more plainly the philosophically driven young Socrates will have to divine in order to understand.

Diotima speaks more plainly by casting her explanation in explicit terms of human sexual desire: "All human beings, Socrates, are pregnant both in terms of the body and in terms of the soul, and whenever they get to be a certain age, our nature desires to give birth" (206c). Human nature (*phusis*) is her subject, and human nature desires and in acting to fulfill desire gives birth; human nature is generative. As generative, "it is incapable of giving birth in the ugly, but [only] in the beautiful. For the intercourse (*sunousia*, being together) of man and woman is a bringing to birth." Diotima elevates this process of generation to the highest dignity: "This matter is divine, and this, in the animal that is mortal [the human], is immortal, the pregnancy and the engendering" (206c). There is no permanence for individual humans; there is immortality — and divinity — only in exercising, across the human generations, the male power to engender and the female power to give birth. Diotima emphasizes the indispensability of the beautiful to this process: "It is impossible for this to happen in the unfitting;

and the ugly is unfitting with everything divine, but the beautiful is fitting"
(206d). Mutual attraction is the precondition of the generation of the new;
repulsion is not generative but is nevertheless a feature of the whole process: attraction and repulsion are basic. Diotima reverts to the language
of myth to restate her claim about beauty attending all bringing to birth:
"So Kallone [Beauty] is the Moira [Fate] and Eileithyia[46] for birth" — myth
gave fitting divine names for the powers present in perpetual bringing to
birth. Diotima describes the event of generation: "It is on account of this
that whenever the pregnant draws near the beautiful, it becomes cheerful
and in its cheerfulness becomes relaxed and gives birth and generates."
The opposite is experienced in repulsion by the ugly: "Whenever it draws
near the ugly, scowling and in pain it coils up and turns away and rolls up
and does not generate, but in holding on to the embryo has a hard time of
it." She turns back to the beautiful and generation: "It is from this source
that for the one who is pregnant and already swelling the excitement about
the beautiful becomes overwhelming, on account of its releasing the one
who has it from great labor pains" (206e) — the erotic process of desire
for the beautiful in the eagerness and intensity of its manner and action
culminates in the birth of the new. Eros is a surging for the beautiful and
a subsiding in the having that becomes another surging to have: erotic,
sexual desire turns out to be the perfect metaphor for an ever-surging need
to meet need.

Having reached the end of her description of generative attraction and
its product, Diotima can finally state just how Socrates had been wrong in
his belief about the beautiful: "For eros, Socrates, is not of the beautiful, as
you believe." Earlier she had said that eros "is of the beautiful things, as you
assert" (204d). Now, having led him through the long process of reasoning
that began with her "someone" seemingly arbitrarily changing his query
about the object of eros from the beautiful to the good, she can say what
the apparent eros for the beautiful really is: "It is of engendering and bringing to birth in the beautiful" (206e). Eros as male desire to impregnate
and female desire to give birth occurs only in the beautiful, only in mutual
attraction — and that whole process seems therefore to be what the good
is, that process whose manner and activity depend upon the eagerness and
intensity evoked by the beautiful.

The process of mutual attraction between complementary elements is

46. Benardete's footnote 16 at 203b of his translation explains that Moira and Eileithyia
"are goddesses who preside over birth, Kallone is a cult name of Artemis-Hecate."

the divine and immortal in the mortal being that makes or poetizes what comes to be. Eros is not observation or enjoyment of some beautiful external to the passion, nor does it come to rest in some external beautiful. Instead, eros simply is the drive to satisfy itself in what attracts it, to impregnate in the male, to bring to birth in the female, drives whose insatiability is the ebb and flood of always only temporary erotic satiations, drives that are productive of what itself will be fundamentally desiring. Diotima has set out the deep structure of eros as her divination of the manner and the action of eros that initially baffled Socrates. Now he can grasp that definition as the deep structure eros expresses in all its actions, and it is always acting, and its actions are productive of beings like it in kind, beings with the internal structure of eros. That is the true divine.

Socrates responds to Diotima's clarification of what he had said needed divination by saying simply, "All right." But that's not strong enough for Diotima; her conclusion is too overwhelming not to be greeted emphatically. "It is more than all right," she says, and states again her main point on the manner and activity of eros: "Why is eros of engendering? Because engendering is born forever and is immortal as far as that can happen to a mortal being." She focuses only on engendering and leaves bringing to birth aside; engendering is ever renewed as a drive to generate: that is the true immortality and is worthy of divine honor. Diotima ends her long explanation of the manner and activity of eros by stating her summary definition a third time: "Eros is of the good's always being one's own." But she adds to this last statement of her definition: "So it is necessary from this argument that eros be of immortality too" (207a). The immortality that eros is *of* is the immortality of endless engendering, and it is "more than all right" that eros be of endless engendering: the insight into the comprehensive action of eros deserves to be affirmed in the most celebratory way. This final affirmation reaches back to what Diotima's "someone" introduced when he changed his query from the beautiful to the good. The acquisition of good things makes one happy, and there is no need to ask why one wants to be happy because "the answer is thought to be complete" (204e). Here, Diotima arrives at her completed form of her complete answer: this process of eros is more than all right, it is the ultimate good; knowing that the whole is an endless becoming understandable as eros brings happiness. Learning the truth of eros from Diotima young Socrates learns both the sovereignty of becoming and the celebration of which it is worthy, for the fitting human response is gratitude, gratitude that expands and deepens as knowing the truth expands and deepens. Xenophon's *Symposium* offers a glimpse of Socrates' own response to this knowing: Socrates reports that Charmides caught him dancing alone at dawn.[47]

This is the peak of Diotima's logos, and she is content to simply stay with the human action of bringing to birth in the beautiful; she does in her argument what she did in her myth of eros's birth: leave to easy inference the conclusion that the nature of nature is universal process, a becoming that is an internal drive to fulfill itself whose product is an internal drive to fulfill itself. Diotima leaves to inference the fundamental truth she could easily have expressed less metaphorically, more starkly, stripped of the uplifting human image of engendered birth or of the pleasing mythos of Poros and Penia. But stripped that way, stated starkly as the way of all beings, it would be less true in a crucial human sense: it would seem less evidently worthy of celebration as more than all right, it would seem more bleak or terrifying, given the human propensity to long for a different kind of eternity for the divine and for the human part of the divine, the soul. Diotima, famous as a religious authority, knows that she has good reason to leave a veil on the comprehensive truth. Is Diotima guilty of anthropomorphizing nature with her view of eros? On the contrary, she is guilty of naturalizing the human.

What Socrates said the philosophers did with Homer Plato's readers must do with Diotima: the deep structure of eros exemplified in the human can become the ground for an inference about the deep structure of reality itself. Homer said, "Ocean and Mother Tethys, the becoming of gods," and the whole line of Greek natural philosophers took him to mean that "everything is the offspring of flowing and motion."[48] Socrates' Diotima says that engendering and bringing to birth in the beautiful are the structural elements of eros, and her wording too can be taken naturalistically and ontologically to mean that everything is the offspring of this kind of action, everything is a "child" of "parenting" causes driven by their nature to generate. In the *Theaetetus* Socrates made Parmenides the exception in the Homeric army, and the *Parmenides* suggests that his singularity consists in his coming to understand the place of form or fixity in the process. Nothing in the *Parmenides* suggests that this fixity is anything other than the dreaming and shadow-painting that structures all human awareness into fixities. Parmenides and Socrates, exceptions in their understanding of form, take their place in the Homeric army in the way that matters most: everything is the offspring of the flowing and motion that is erotic desire.

47. Xenophon, *Symposium* 2.17–19.
48. *Theaetetus* 152e.

The third stage of Socrates' philosophic education initiates him into an ontology based on understanding the nature of the human as eros; it is an account of beings as a whole based on acquaintance with the being most intimately knowable. As an ontology it occurs within an understanding of the limitations on human knowing, the dreaming and shadow-painting that inevitably construct the forms and particulars of human experience blocking all direct access to beings. And as Socrates' ontology it can be sheltered comfortably within a refuted teaching on irrational forms that he advocates to the end. All three stages of Socrates' becoming fit together as the becoming of the worthy heir to Homer, the poet who himself inserted the true teaching into an edifying one that inspired a high civilization to its great achievements of thinking and making.

5. Diotima Teaches Socrates What to Teach

"All these things she used to teach me, whenever she made her speeches about erotics" (207a). Socrates makes this generalizing summary statement to wrap up the series of fundamental questions he himself had posed to Diotima, questions she used as occasions for the dialectical exchanges that open onto an ontology that draws the fitting judgment that the world viewed that way is emphatically more than all right. Socrates now reports a single conversation of a different sort: *she* initiated it with a question she "once also asked," and she answered her question with a long speech punctuated only twice by Socrates' words, first because she asked him a question he couldn't answer (207c), second because he could not help expressing his amazement (208b). The shift from his questions to her question, from "whenever she made her speeches" to "once she also asked," marks a turning point in the manner of Diotima's guidance: she delivers a lecture, he passively takes it in, feeling amazed. What her lecture ultimately guides him to picture is radically different from the rational conclusions of their dialectic in many respects, but one is particularly telling: it ends not with the conclusion of a process of reasoning but with an act of the imagination. Here then, with the long speech that ends his speaking, Socrates proves that he had every right to claim knowledge of the truth about how to praise anything, how to select the most beautiful parts and how to arrange them in a seemly manner (198d): praise required that he shelter the truth about eros, the underpinning of his whole speech, in Diotima's myth and dialectic that are the center of his speech. Now, praise requires that he flaunt or put last the most edifying part of his speech, the part that looks most beautiful and thereby eclipses the terrifying truth available from its

center. What looks like a speech-long ascent is in fact an ascent to the true
pinnacle followed by a descent to the edifying.

What Diotima once asked was "What do you believe, Socrates, is the
cause of this eros and desire?" (207a). She did not wait for Socrates to answer but instead expanded the domain of erotics that she is now asking
about to animal behavior: "Aren't you aware how uncanny is the disposition of all beasts, the footed as well as the winged, whenever they desire
to produce offspring?" An erotic disposition rules them too in the desire
to generate offspring and to protect them as they grow (207b). Humans
are subject to the same disposition, and it might be thought that *we* do it
out of calculation, but the beasts, what causes this eros-driven behavior in
them? "Can you say?" (207c). He can't, so she asks, "Do you really think you
will ever become skilled in erotics if you do not understand this?" These
are the only questions she will pose to him until she ends her long speech
on three questions that remain unanswered (211e–212a).[49] Unable to answer her opening questions, Socrates pleads for the last time that this is
why he comes to her, knowing his need for teachers, and he implores her
to "tell me the cause of these things as well as of the rest that concerns
erotics." He did not say this time, as he had twice before (205a, 206b), that
he was amazed, but Diotima tells him that "if you put your trust in the
statement that by nature eros is of that which we have often agreed to,
don't persist in your amazement." What they had often agreed to is that in
the eros of the beasts, as in that of humans, "mortal nature seeks as far as
possible to be forever and immortal" (207d). Don't be amazed, *understand*
that the cause of animal erotic behavior is the same as the cause of human
erotic behavior: it is given in what living beings are that they strive to be
forever, reproducing themselves.

Diotima extends her lesson on immortality (207d), applying it to the
living individual itself as always aging: although it is said to be the "same"
through all its stages of aging, it is always being transformed in "hair, flesh,
bones, blood, and the whole body." And not only the body but the soul
too undergoes constant generation and decay in its "ways, character, opinions, desires, pleasures, pains, fears; each of these things is never present
as the same for each, but they are partly coming to be and partly perishing" (207e). The sovereignty of becoming rules in all these aspects of the
individual soul, for generation and decay apply even to the knowledges or
sciences (*epistēmai*), for "we are never the same in terms of the sciences

---

49. She poses a rhetorical question at 209a, answering it immediately herself.

either" (208a). Studying instills a fresh memory to replace a decaying one, preserving knowledge that may be thought to be the same. "Every mortal thing is preserved in this way; not by being absolutely the same forever, as the divine is. . . . By this device the mortal shares in immortality" (208a-b). To end her statement about the cause of eros and desire in all animals including the human, Diotima issues the command she had given him often: "So do not be amazed if everything honors by nature its own offshoot, for it is for the sake of immortality that this zeal and eros attend everything."

The last speech Socrates will make interrupts Diotima and does what she just told him not to do: "And when I had heard her speech I was amazed and said, 'Really!' I said, 'Wisest Diotima, is it in truth like this?'" In reporting her reply to his amazement, Socrates first says *how* she spoke and then reports a speech that runs, long and uninterrupted, to the very end of his address to the symposiasts: "And she, like the perfect sophists, said, 'Know it well, Socrates,' she said . . ." Wisest Diotima, dialogic, philosophic Diotima speaks here like the perfect sophists — which could mean like a member of the effective group of thinkers and speakers founded by Protagoras who typically made long speeches and were opposed by Socrates partly for that reason, the sheer power of well-constructed long speeches to amaze and persuade.[50] But literally a sophist is one who is wise, and Socrates here speaks of "perfect sophists" just after referring to "wisest" Diotima, praising his own teacher who, on this occasion, this "once," used the sophists' means of a well-constructed, long persuasive speech. Her speech exploits this ambiguity in *sophist*: she speaks wisely of something sophistic.

Wisest Diotima speaks like the perfect sophists to impart the last full lesson Socrates will learn from her, a lesson that moves beyond the "everything" she spoke about till now, the everything that comes into being and perishes, to a possible glimpse of something that never changes. To introduce her speech, Diotima tells Socrates that "in the case of human beings if you were willing to glance at their love of honor" — if he studied the human soul in its "eros for renown" — "you would be amazed at their irrationality" (208c). Given Socrates' repeated amazement and Diotima's repeated commands not to be amazed, it is noteworthy that his last expression of amazement (208b) does not draw her standard rebuke but instead leads her to emphasize just how amazing this last topic of hers is, human irrationality in pursuit of immortality. Still, inviting him to be amazed at it, she says it will remain amazing "*unless* you understand what I have said

50. See, e.g., *Protagoras* 329a-b and *Lesser Hippias* 369b-c, 373a-c.

and take to heart (*enthumeomai*[51]) how uncanny their disposition is made by their eros for renown 'and their setting up immortal fame for eternity'" (208c): replace amazement with understanding while taking to heart the importance of this. The mature Socrates took Diotima to heart: he not only came to understand human irrationality in pursuit of immortality; he took to heart her guidance in making rational use of it.

Diotima's speech to amaze and be taken to heart carries forward what she had said about animal and human behavior: the mortal way of sharing in immortality. Human "love of honor" (*philotimian*) or "eros for renown" drives one to run all risks, to exhaust all one's money, and even to die (208c-d). Her first examples of heroic dying are ones that Phaedrus had called on earlier, Alcestis for Admetus and Achilles for Patroclus, but Phaedrus simply honored them in amazement whereas Socrates is to understand their self-sacrifice as driven by their eros for renown. Diotima adds a local Athenian example, Codrus, traditionally the last of the Athenian kings, who died in order to ensure that his sons continue his rule (208d): like Alcestis and Achilles, Codrus believed that there would be "an immortal remembering of [his] virtue," and Athenians in fact memorialized him. Diotima draws a generalization about her three heroic examples, "I believe that all do all things for the sake of immortal virtue and a famous reputation . . . for they love the immortal" (208e). Young Socrates is to understand heroic virtue as grounded in the fundamental passion.

Diotima then speaks of pregnancy as her speech becomes a series of examples of her final definition of eros as "engendering and bringing to birth in the beautiful" (206e). First come those pregnant in terms of their bodies; they aim, through their children, to gain "immortality, remembrance, and happiness, as they believe, for all future time." She moves to those "pregnant in terms of the soul" and asks, "What is appropriate for soul?" (209a). "Prudence and the rest of virtue," she says, without waiting for Socrates to answer. The virtues she goes on to discuss are civic or moral virtues; she does not speak of wisdom, her own defining virtue, driven, like everything else, by eros, but unique in being an eros to understand. As for prudence and the rest of virtue, "all the poets (*poiētai*) and the craftsmen (*dēmiourgōn*) who are said to be inventive are their procreators and by far the greatest and most beautiful part of prudence is 'the arranging and

---

51. *Enthumeomai*, deriving from *thumos* (heart) can also mean "form a plan"; it is used in that sense by Thucydides in order to praise the thinking of "Antiphon, one of the best men of his day in Athens, who, *with a head to contrive measures* and a tongue to recommend them . . ." (8.68).

ordering of the affairs of cities and households.' Its name is moderation
and justice." Young Socrates is to understand that the civic virtues that
hold every citizen in awe and amazement are the procreated inventions
of makers driven by their version of the fundamental passion, with them
too an eros for immortal fame. Moving to the *transmission* of civic virtue,
Diotima treats that too as an engendering in the beautiful: "Whenever
someone from youth onward is pregnant in his soul with these virtues, if he
is divine and of suitable age, he desires to give birth and produce offspring"
(209b). Thus driven, he seeks out a younger man beautiful in body, cleaves
to him in body and soul, and "is fluent in speeches about virtue," educat-
ing the younger man "in what a good man must be and what he must do"
(209c). Thus do the civic virtues get passed down in reverent adherence
through generations of responsible citizens.

Focusing then on the historic founders of moral virtue, those who first
made or poetized it, Diotima speaks of "Homer, Hesiod, and the other
great poets; one envies them: what offspring they left behind!" (209d).
Their offspring, their poems, "are themselves immortal" and in turn "supply the poets with immortal fame and memory." The greatest Hellenic
poets — the founders of Greek religion and of the heroic models of virtue —
attained an enviable immortality as their poetry generated the Hellenic
peoples and sustained them through its transmission from one generation
to the next in the song and dance of collective celebration. The founding
poets enjoy the greatest human immortality, but only slightly less great is
the immortality enjoyed by the founding legislators of cities, Lycurgus in
Sparta and Solon in Athens.

What young Socrates is to understand and take to heart regarding
moral virtue and the founders of religion and cities is the genealogy of
morality: what holds a people in awe and amazement originated in the human, all-too-human, drive for immortality of poets and founders. By guiding Socrates to understand and take to heart this awesome process of the
natural generation of peoples through poetizing creators, Diotima awak-
ens a possibility for Socrates himself: *envy* the poets Homer and Hesiod
with the good envy that admires and aspires to emulate. Diotima cannot
know that the young man she is guiding is *Socrates*, the man a post-Homeric
people will look back on in awe and amazement as the creator of a new
ideal, their ideal, a maker on the scale of a Homer. Plato's *Republic*, the
dialogue devoted to the founding of new civic virtues and a new view of
cosmic order or the human place in nature, ends on an annihilating critique of Homer and Homeric virtue: they must be replaced by the virtues
and worldview Socrates advocated for Glaucon and Adeimantus and the

other *thumos*-driven, Homer-driven young men present on that night when the Athenians themselves introduced a new god. At its center the *Republic* intimated the founding character of its own fundamental deed: the philosopher must come to rule as Homer ruled. Socratic philosophic rule is grounded in belief in transcendent forms, the forms refuted for Socrates himself but nevertheless the foundational replacement of the Homeric gods as the fixed source of civic virtue for noble young men like Glaucon and Adeimantus; they and their descendants will occupy a new spiritual world grounded in new highest permanences. And on that night in the Piraeus Socrates also saw to the transmission of his new view through a new tradition of rhetoric, for present that night was a master rhetorician whom Socrates succeeded in befriending: what Socrates persuades the young men to hold can be carried forward by a new rhetoric, beginning with Socrates' new friend, Thrasymachus.[52]

Is the philosopher, is Diotima, also ruled by the passion for immortal fame? Diotima's distinctive virtue, wisdom, has its own distinctive origin in eros as an eros to understand and take to heart that she detects and fosters in Socrates. Yet philosophy is distinctive in its eros to be shared with each of the few driven by its fundamental passion. Sharing what she knows with a young Socrates, Diotima guides Socrates to emulate the poetic drive of a Homer in the midst of a great event in Greek history, the death of the Homeric gods. What Plato makes it possible to understand is that philosophy, in a Socrates, is moved to make, to poetize, not by an eros for personal immortality but by the desire to preserve and advance the highest passion, the passion to know, in the highest exemplars of humanity. And that may take, as it did in the time of Socrates, recasting the communally highest things and making those novelties believable, as the Platonic Socrates succeeded in doing.

Diotima now prepares a great novelty, a vision of what is highest that is radically different from what Homer and Hesiod had founded and radically different from what she had intimated while guiding Socrates in her dialectic, yet it fits well what Socrates will teach in the *Republic*. She tells Socrates that while he "too might be initiated into these erotics" set out so far, there remains something else, "the rites and revelations, for which the others are means, if one were to proceed correctly on the way" (210a). Is Socrates up to these new matters? "I do not know if you would be able to

---

52. A chronological reading of the dialogues emphasizes Plato's setting of the *Republic* in 429, the moment in Athenian history best suited to introducing new civic gods and virtues. See my *How Philosophy Became Socratic*.

be initiated into them." But she does what she can: "I shall not falter in my zeal; do try to follow if you are able." What Socrates is to follow is a series of steps about which Diotima says emphatically that they must be followed *correctly* (*orthōs*), a word she uses three times to introduce them and repeats three times in setting out the actual steps.[53] What he must necessarily follow — she repeats *necessary* at each step — are "rites" that if performed in the strictly correct series of steps will take him to the "revelations," the final revealing of the secret mysteries, which, in customary practice like the Athenian rites at Eleusis, are to be held in strict secrecy and not profaned, not told.[54] *Initiation, rites, proceeding correctly, revelation*, with a *zealous* speaker instructing one who is to *follow* in order to learn the strict steps he *must* perform — we are entering the domain for which Diotima was publicly famous, religion. Wise Diotima, profound guide to philosophy's difficult-to-discover truths about human nature and nature, practitioner of philosophy's method of dialectic as the proper means of inquiring into and sharing those truths, here presents herself as a religious authority able to teach in a long speech the steps that must be followed correctly if one is to be initiated into the final mysteries. Can Socrates be initiated into what she here tells him? Of course he can: he is reporting what she taught him to the symposiasts with a literalistic bare-footed follower he invited also present who will hear it and report it and help secure Socrates' reputation — Socrates sees to it that he clothe himself in the religious garb of his Diotima. Diotima knows what she's doing and she wants Socrates to know: so great is her trust in correct ritual that she repeats the order — incorrectly (211b-d). She thus tells Socrates what to do: understand this and take it to heart; the amazement is for others.

"He who is to move correctly in this matter," Diotima says, "must begin while young to go to beautiful bodies" (210a). The beginning she sets out as imperative is something she had just treated in this long speech, the lover's pregnancy with speeches for the beloved (209b-c): "First of all, if the guide is guiding correctly, [the lover] must love one body and there generate beautiful speeches" (210a). Then the lover "must realize that the

<hr />

53. Diotima had used *orthōs* twice previously, both times to describe *correct opinion* as inferior to knowledge (202a). For a detailed list of the steps Diotima sets out, see Ruby Blondell, "Where Is Socrates?," 153–55. Blondell sees eight steps in all, but her steps 5 and 6 seem to me to be a single step as do her steps 7 and 8.

54. The word translated "revelations" (*epoptika*) is the word for the secret things revealed in the final stage of the mysteries; it is not the New Testament word for "revelation," *apokalupsis*, which refers to what God is alleged to have communicated to human beings and which exists to be told.

beauty that is in any body whatsoever is related to that in another body";
believing "that the beauty of all bodies is the same," he must slacken his
attachment to the body of the beloved, believing it is petty (210b). Diotima's correct way continues with sequential "musts" through belief in
"the beauty in souls," and even if the beloved has "only a slight youthful
charm," the lover must engender "speeches that make the young better."
The lover will thereby be "compelled to behold the beautiful" not simply in souls but "in pursuits and laws" (210c). Seeing such beauty, "he will
come to believe that the beauty of the body is something trivial" and he
"must lead [the beloved] on to the sciences (or knowledges, *epistēmas*)" so
that the lover himself "may see the beauty of sciences." This will mark for
the lover "a permanent turn to the vast open sea of the beautiful" (210d);
beholding it, the lover "will give birth, in unstinting philosophy, to many
beautiful and magnificent speeches and thoughts"—philosophy becomes
the moral uplift of the beloved celebrating the world as beautiful. Then,
finally, "strengthened and increased, he may discern a certain single philosophical science which has as its object the following sort of beauty."

Diotima pauses here to issue a final injunction: "Try to pay as close attention to me as you can" (210e). Having beheld the beautiful things "suc-
cessively and correctly," she says, one arrives at "the perfect end of erotics"
and "suddenly glimpses something amazingly (*thaumaston*) beautiful in its
nature, the very thing, Socrates, for whose sake alone all the prior labors
were undertaken." This amazingly beautiful finale is different in kind from
everything she had said about eros, and the close attention Socrates must
pay will require him to treat it in the way she had consistently told him to
treat the amazing: understand it and take it to heart. As Diotima presents
it, obedience in following the correct steps of ascent leads upward to a
glimpse of something that is the contrary of eros in every respect; it "elim-
inate[es] eros entirely."[55] "First of all," Diotima says, "it is always being"
(211a)—perpetual existence as the same is the other positive attribute of
the amazingly beautiful, for what follows is a list of negations, what the
always is is not. It is "neither coming to be, nor perishing, nor increasing,
nor passing away." "Secondly," the amazingly beautiful that perpetually exists is "not beautiful in one respect and ugly in another, nor at one time so
and at another time not, either with respect to the beautiful or the ugly,
nor here beautiful and there ugly as being beautiful to some and ugly to
others." Diotima then employs a verb for the human representation of the
amazingly beautiful, *imagine*, that governs the rest of her sentence: "nor

55. Benardete, "On Plato's *Symposium*," 87.

in turn will the beautiful be imagined by him as a kind of face or hands or anything else in which body shares, nor as any speech nor any science, and not as being somewhere in something else" — it will not be imagined in any of these ways, "but as it is alone by itself and with itself" — it will be, it can only be, *imagined*.[56] Diotima presents the amazingly beautiful as a product of the imagination while at the same time depriving the imaginer of the only categories by which the human imagination could imagine it at all.

Diotima ends her sentence on this imagined something with telling words, describing it as "being always of a single form (*monoeides*) [with] all other beautiful things participating (*metexō*) in it in the sort of way that everything else comes to be and perishes, while it does not become anything more or less or undergo anything" (211b). Young Socrates is well fit to take this peak to heart because transcendent forms and participation in them by the things that change was the view of cause he first worked out on his own as a very young man and reported as the first stage of his philosophic education in the *Phaedo*. There, he spoke of the "*monoeides* being itself by itself" (*Phaedo* 78d5), and of the "*monoeides* . . . always keeping to the same condition with itself" (80b1–2), and of "the divine and pure and *monoeides*" (83e2). And as reported in the *Parmenides*, Socrates used the verb *metexō* repeatedly to set out for Parmenides and Zeno his discovery of how the changing particulars participate in the form (*Parmenides* 129a9, b3, 5, 6, 129c7, 129d1), and Parmenides then used that verb in initiating the second stage of Socrates' philosophic education by asking about his view (130b3) and refuting it (131c5, 132a9, c8, e1, 3, 133a2, d2, 134b9, c8). What Socrates depicts Diotima guiding him to at the peak of her lecture is a way that the refuted view is still of use to a Socrates who has entered the third stage of his philosophic education: knowing that ever-changing eros is the nature of things, imagine a never-changing beautiful as the edifying crowning form in which that ever-changing reality can seem to participate, and make that the ultimate "cause of this eros and desire" that she announced as the topic of her long speech (207a) — and here it is, the beautiful imagined cause of all actual causes.

With her depiction of that unchanging form of the beautiful, Diotima completes the part of her lecture that set out the steps to be followed correctly in order to glimpse that peak. Now, after providing two reminders of the necessity of "correct" following (211b5, 7), she repeats the "ascending

---

56. See Strauss, *On Plato's "Symposium,"* 236: "Everything said in this section is grammatically dependent on the word *phantasthēsetai* which means the beautiful itself will be imagined."

steps" (211c3) incorrectly.[57] She omits entirely the step from the beauty in bodies to the beauty in souls; she omits laws, mentioning only "beautiful pursuits" (211c5, 6); and then, moving from pursuits to the next step, she does not speak of the beauty of *sciences* (*epistēmas* 210c6) but instead of the beauty of *teachings* (or lessons to be learned, *mathēmata*, 211c6). Repeating *teachings* four times in the same sentence, twice in the plural, twice in the singular, she says that the teachings "end at that teaching (*mathēma*) which is the teaching of nothing else than the beautiful itself" (211c7, 8). All the steps in Diotima's long speech like a perfect sophist appear as things to be taught as distinct from the things that the dialectic could lead Socrates to learn. That dialectic led to an inferential conclusion about the whole of things that could be thought to be comfortless; the lecture leads to an edifying if refutable teaching about the fixity at the foundation of things. The distinction between what can be learned and what is to be taught carries through the rest of her speech as an unspoken but precise ambiguity: two different audiences can assent to Diotima's words while understanding in two different ways just what they are affirming.

Diotima begins to bring her intricately structured speech to a close by addressing "my dear Socrates," while Socrates, reporting to the symposiasts, speaks of her as "the Mantinean stranger" (211d). Diotima tells him that "it is here in life, if anywhere . . . where it is worth living for a human being, observing the beautiful itself" (211d). Is life worth living? That is Diotima's final topic, and she makes that question focus on the beautiful itself: "If you ever see it, it will be your opinion that it is not to be compared to gold and garments and the beautiful boys and youths at whose sight you are now thunderstruck and are ready, both you and many others, in seeing the beloveds and always being with them, neither to eat nor to drink, if it were somehow possible, but only to observe and be with." After this final declarative sentence, Diotima ends her guidance of Socrates by posing three questions that serially step away from the grammatical subject of the last part of that declarative sentence, "you and many others," first to "we," then to "you" in the singular. Her questions retain the activity the subject is engaged in — observing and being with — while extending the final topic: Is life worth living, given what we can observe and be with? All three questions replace the grammatical object of the final declarative sentence, the beloveds, with "the beautiful itself."

"What then do we believe happens to someone if he gets to see the

57. See Strauss, *On Plato's "Symposium,"* 237. Blondell also notes the steps omitted from the "reprise" ("Where Is Socrates?," 153–54).

beautiful itself in its purity, cleansed and clean, unmixed, and not filled with human flesh and colors and much other mortal nonsense, but is able to catch sight of the divinely beautiful itself as a single form (*monoeides*)?" she asks. You and I, what do we believe happens to one who sees the beautiful as it is? Diotima's "teaching" on form and the participation of things in the form showed what can happen to those who correctly follow the right series of steps up to a glimpse of that single beautiful form imagined to be the cause of all the beautiful things we experience, things that participate in it but are infected with human flesh and color. Her dialectic for Socrates, on the other hand, led to an understanding of the form of eros as a single kind of process at work in every event in nature, a way of understanding natural processes that frees itself of the infection of human flesh and color. The answer to Diotima's first question splits into two beliefs about what can happen: the imagined beautiful edifies by humanizing nature, the dialectic naturalizes the human in a way edifying to you and me.

Diotima's first question leads naturally to her second: "Do you believe . . . that life would prove to be a sorry sort of thing when a human being looks in that direction, observing that and being with it by the means he should"? (212a). *You*, not the you of you and many others but the you of you and I: do you, Socrates, believe life would be taken to be a sorry sort of thing if observed—*how*? Diotima is purposefully vague on *how* to observe and be with the beautiful. With the imagination, ascending through the correct order of steps to a revelation of the ultimate mystery as a transcendent static form? Or by a process of reasoning that leads the rational mind to infer the universal presence of a particular kind of process of generation and decay active in all events in nature? By leaving the *how* ambiguous, Diotima leaves the character of the beautiful itself ambiguous with two possible grounds for judging that life is not a sorry sort of thing. One of those grounds, the transcendent form of the beautiful, post-Parmenides Socrates could not possibly think of as true, but Diotima guides him to think of it as useful in making life worth living to the many others driven by an eros different from his: believing that life is grounded in a glorious permanence lends radiance to what is merely passing, a radiance that you and I can experience in the rational understanding of the process at work in the whole of nature.

Diotima's final words are her third question, a question that continues to focus on whether life is a "sorry sort of thing." "Or don't you take to heart . . . ?" she asks, using again the word she used at the outset of her speech like a perfect sophist (208c). There, she said that he would be amazed at human irrationality—there, the irrationality of human eros for

immortal renown — unless he understood what she said and took to heart
how uncanny that human disposition is. Here, she completes what he is to
understand and take to heart regarding what would otherwise be simply
amazing: "Or don't you take to heart that here alone it will be possible
for him, on seeing the beautiful by that by which it is visible, to give birth
not to phantom images of virtue, because he is touching on that which is
not a phantom, but to true virtue because he is touching on the truth; and
once he gives birth to true virtue and raises it, it is open to him to become
dear to the gods and if it is open to any other human being, for him too
to become immortal?" In what way is the beautiful seeable? Diotima is
again purposefully vague, allowing the two possibilities: by reasoning or
by imagining. In each case, a seeing taken as true generates true images of
virtue. The true images of virtue suitable to life as lived by you and many
others, the virtues she had mentioned of prudence and moderation and
justice, would be certified as themselves sharing in the permanence of the
beautiful itself. And the virtues suitable to the life lived by you and me,
the virtues of the inquirer, would be certified by the recognition that the
whole is open to inquiry, which can lead to an inference about its natural
character. Known for religious virtue, Diotima ends on becoming dear to
the gods and on becoming immortal as far as that is open to a human being.

Life is worth living. But affirming that depends upon observing and
being with the beautiful in two different ways; each way generates genuine virtue, which is rewarded in the ways seen to be most rewarding. The
answer to all three of Diotima's questions points to these two things that
can happen, one through her teaching, the other through her rational guidance. Her teaching leads to an edifying anthropomorphizing of nature that
secures the civic virtues; her rational guidance leads to a naturalization of
the human edifying to us.

Taking leave of Diotima with her three questions, Socrates tells
"Phaedrus and you others," "Here is what Diotima said and I have been
persuaded of; and since I have been persuaded I try to persuade everyone
else" (212b). Just what he tries to persuade them of is that "one would not
easily get anyone better than Eros for helping human nature gain this possession." This "possession" seems to refer to that highest thing he just referred to, "touching on the truth" (212a5). But "not easily get" implies that
one could, if with difficulty, get a better helper than Eros for touching on
the truth. Just what that better helper could be is hard to imagine, unless
it would be a Diotima or a Parmenides. Or, given the personal drama of
the symposium, a Socrates, offering himself to the Agathon for whom he
beautified himself from the start.

6. Alcibiades Arrives

Plato made the presence of Alcibiades in the *Symposium* decisive at the opening: Glaucon, who has no interest in philosophy, goes out of his way to track down Apollodorus in order to get a report on "Socrates, Alcibiades . . . and the erotic speeches." But Alcibiades, *expected* Alcibiades, had not yet been seen or heard or even mentioned when all the speeches were over (212c). And the evening of talk was set to continue as Aristophanes tried to say something because Socrates had challenged his speech, denying that eros "is of a half or whole" (205d). But suddenly, a lot of noise and the sound of an aulos was heard, and Agathon sent servants to find out if it was friends of theirs. Then they heard the voice of Alcibiades, very loud, very drunk, and he appeared at their door with the aulos-girl and other attendants, "thickly crowned with ivy and violets, with many ribbons on his head" (212e). That is, Alcibiades appears as a celebrant, if a drunken one, the leader of a procession like the great procession from Athens to Eleusis. And his loud shouting could sound like the cry of Iacchus, who guided the initiates on that procession, itself part of the initiation, "the departure from the everyday world" to the sacred world of Eleusis where the secret steps into initiation would occur.[58] Apollodorus's auditors in 399 — knowing that what they were hearing happened in 416 and, like all Athenians, recently reminded of the religious crimes of 416–415 by the spectacular trial of Andocides[59] — would they believe that they were about to hear an example of the shocking crime of which Alcibiades was a chief suspect, the profaning of the mysteries of Eleusis? In 415 the Athenian court had famously convicted him for that religious crime, only to have him escape and turn traitor by advising Sparta — a political crime of the highest order, as Athens' most capable strategist and general advised their enemy on how best to defeat them.

Apollodorus's expectant audience would have been jerked into alertness by what they had just heard. And they will in fact hear Alcibiades profane mysteries, not the sacred Eleusinian mysteries, but those of — *Socrates*, that mysterious, suspicious character whose trial they may be preparing for. Alcibiades believed he knew *those* mysteries better than anyone because he had been intimately associated with Socrates some seventeen years before the party, when Socrates had hunted him down, the most beautiful, most

---

58. Burkert, *Homo Necans*, 275. Walter Burkert offers an authoritative account of the Eleusinian festival (248–93).

59. See below, "Note on the Dramatic Date," in this chapter.

promising young man in Athens in the time before they served together in Potidaea.[60] Alcibiades feels no restraint in revealing those mysteries for the first time because, as drunk as he is, he is oblivious to the shame his insight into Socrates' secret mysteries cost him, a matter so shameful that he had of course, in his pride, kept it secret all these years. Now though, at Agathon's party, with this small group of enlightened friends and for the sake of winning Agathon, whom he *knows* Socrates is seducing, he can accuse Socrates of a crime against himself: Socrates *rejected* him and his youthful beauty after he made every effort to yield himself. And, he says, the Socrates who rejected him will reject Agathon and every other young beloved he seduces because of what he is at his secret core, the core from which he himself suffered such shame. Alcibiades then profanes Socrates' mysterious core: the man is rigidly, unbreakably *moral*. Socrates as a lover fails all his beloveds, and he will shame you too, Agathon, as he shamed me all those years ago. So, by Plato's artistry, Apollodorus's auditors hear what they could never have expected to hear: testimony to Socrates' *innocence* in his suspected corrupting of Athens' greatest leader and criminal, innocence proven despite its shamefulness by the very man he was famously thought to have corrupted.

As if to remove any doubt about just what events he is invoking, Plato has Alcibiades break in to his long narration of Socrates' crime in order to address the house servants just before he reached the apex of his speech revealing Socrates' secret: he looks around the room, names each of those present, and says, "You all have shared in philosophic madness and bacchic frenzy — so accordingly you all will hear" (218a). But others are present: "You house servants — and if there is anyone else who is profane and rustic — put large gates over your ears." Plato thus has Alcibiades announce that he is about to speak mysteries fit to be heard only by bacchic initiates and never to be spoken in the presence of the uninitiated, like the house servants — and it was precisely the house servants actually present at the profaning of the Eleusinian mysteries who told the Athenian court in 415 the names of the guilty, as Andocides reported in detail at his trial in late 400, some months before Socrates' trial.[61] Having identified the initiates at Agathon's house and told the house servants to block their ears,

60. Plato showed Socrates' pursuit of Alcibiades in his *Protagoras* and *Alcibiades I*, prewar dialogues set around 434; see my *How Philosophy Became Socratic*, 19–144, esp. 24–28, 36–37, 81–85, 124–30, 134–38.

61. Andocides, "On the Mysteries," §§11–14, 17–22. See below, "Note on the Dramatic Date," in this chapter.

Alcibiades reveals Socrates' most secret secrets. The two audiences Plato provided for the frame will be all ears.

Alcibiades goes into great detail about the key event, relating the actual words of their conversation some seventeen years earlier — so vivid is his memory of his shaming. It occurred after a whole series of efforts to yield himself to Socrates, his lover; finally, he arranged a private dinner after which he sent the servants away, extinguished the lamps and made his wishes clear, identifying Socrates as his "only deserving lover" and offering to gratify him in any way he wanted. His reason is consistent with everything said about him in Plato and Thucydides: "Nothing is more important to me than that I become the best possible" (218d), and no one "is more competent than you to be a fellow helper to me in this."[62] Alcibiades reports that having "shot my darts, as it were, I thought he had been wounded" (219b), and he moved to secure the advantage he believed he had won. Not allowing Socrates to say anything more, he lay beside him, wrapping them together in his own mantle, putting Socrates' threadbare cloak over them. Putting his arms around him, he lay beside him the whole night. He reports his shock: nothing more happened than if he had slept with his father or older brother. For Alcibiades there could be no greater insult: Socrates "proved so far superior to my youthful bloom and scorned and laughed at and insulted it" (219c). "Oh judges!" he says to the symposiasts. "You are judges of the high and mighty disdain of Socrates." Alcibiades "had been dishonored" (219d), yet he could not help but admire what he took to be Socrates' "nature," his "moderation and manliness," his "prudence and endurance."

Alcibiades' confession of this shameful event in his youth, his blame of Socrates in his speech of praise, receives no direct response from Socrates or anyone else at the 416 symposium. But heard from the perspective of the possible judges of Socrates that Plato supplied for Apollodorus's report, Alcibiades' blame becomes praise of a precise kind: Socrates cannot be held responsible for Alcibiades' crimes of 416–415 because Socrates' moral strictures caused an insurmountable rift between the two of them very early, for as Alcibiades said, this event that shame forced him to keep secret all his life happened "before Potidaea" (219e), before he and Socrates left on the military campaign of 433, before Alcibiades' political career began. In Plato's *Symposium* Alcibiades returns from the dead to declare Socrates innocent of the religious and political crimes he committed against

---

62. This was precisely Socrates' advertisement for himself in the first private conversation he had with Alcibiades, *Alcibiades I* 105d-e.

Athens. That innocence, Apollodorus's audiences learn, is grounded in Socrates' beautiful interior, the almost superhuman moral control that Alcibiades experienced firsthand in Socrates resisting *him*. Alcibiades' drunken confession thus counts as part of the strong indications that Plato set the frame of the *Symposium* in the thirty days between the indictment of Socrates and his trial.

Plato put Alcibiades' revelation of what he took to be Socrates' deepest interior at the end of the dialogue in which Socrates reported on the third and final stage of his philosophic education. That report placed at the core of his interior a virtue Alcibiades almost ignored: wisdom,[63] a wisdom that in this dialogue attains its deepest reach. The frame audience also expressed no interest in Socrates' wisdom, but Socrates gave his speech at the symposium on one condition alone, that he be allowed to question Agathon—to strip him of his vaunted wisdom about Eros and offer him possible entry into the interior wisdom of wise Diotima. While Alcibiades' account of Socrates' interior omits its defining feature, it is completely consistent with what Diotima taught him to teach. Alcibiades misunderstood Socrates correctly.[64]

After Alcibiades' speech, a struggle occurred for who would recline next to Agathon, Socrates or Alcibiades. Socrates won because he acted as if he would have a duty to make a speech in praise of Agathon, impelling Agathon to get up and recline next to him. The question from the very beginning of their evening together is acted out at the end: Could Socrates' interior wisdom flow into Agathon in a way that he never intended it to flow into the political man Alcibiades? Not by touch of course but by Agathon paying the closest attention to what Socrates said after stripping him of his wisdom. And possibly to the speech of praise Socrates promised: after the final arrangement of who will recline next to whom, Socrates was set to make yet another effort to encourage that transmission of his wisdom.

7. Last Words

When Agathon got up to recline next to Socrates (223b), another crowd of revelers burst in, and all order was lost. Aristodemus said that Eryximachus

---

63. "Almost ignored" because at the very end of his speech Alcibiades belatedly adds something about the exterior and interior of Socrates' speeches: opened up, he says, they alone "have mind (*nous*) inside" (222a2).

64. Benardete makes clear Alcibiades' moral misunderstanding of Socrates' beautiful interior ("On Plato's *Symposium*," 197–99).

and Phaedrus and some others left, and he himself fell asleep. When he finally woke up the cocks were already crowing, as it was near daybreak. He reports that all were either sleeping or had left except "Agathon, Aristophanes, and Socrates [who] were the only ones still awake, and they were drinking from a large cup passing it from left to right" (223c). So the final arrangement had Aristophanes recline between Agathon and Socrates with no sign of Alcibiades. "Socrates was conversing" with the other two. Aristodemus could remember only his main point, that he "was compelling them to agree that the same man should know how to make comedy and tragedy" (223d). But Socrates applied that capability to the tragedian only: "He who is by art a tragic poet is also a comic poet." Socrates' beautification for Agathon continues through to the very end, as he, a philosopher, implicitly promises the tragic poet Agathon, with Aristophanes reclining between them, a wider knowledge, one that encompasses the whole tragedy and comedy of human life. Socrates proved persuasive: "They were compelled to admit this, though they were not following too well and were nodding." Will Agathon want to follow it better when he regains full wakefulness and recalls how Socrates ended with a kind of promise to him? Will he seek out Socrates to pursue what he meant as Socrates sought out Diotima to pursue what *she* meant? For Aristodemus reports that their night's talk was over: "Aristophanes went to sleep first, and then, when it was already day, Agathon." Anything that might have passed from Socrates to Agathon as Aristophanes slept seems lost to Aristodemus.

Within this last exchange between Socrates and Agathon, where Socrates says that "he who is a tragic poet by art is also a comic poet," Leo Strauss finds something deeply radical and fully in keeping with Socrates' genuine philosophic education as guided by Parmenides. Strauss presents it with characteristic brevity, leaving the key point as an undefended announcement to be thought through and justified by the reader so inclined. Being a tragic poet "by art" and "not merely by natural gift" is crucial to the main point that Strauss presents in a single sentence: "He who by art produces tragedy, who by art can enchant men through the production of the beautiful gods, by this very fact is disenchanted and therefore also can disenchant."[65] To appreciate Strauss's first point, his equating the production of tragedy with the production of the beautiful gods, it is useful to remember that in the *Republic* Socrates made Homer the "leader" of tragedy (*Republic* 598d). As for that maker of beautiful gods being "by this very fact . . . disenchanted," Nietzsche said that "Homer is so at home

---

65. Strauss, *On Plato's "Symposium,"* 285–86.

among his gods and takes such delight in them as a poet that he surely must have been deeply irreligious."[66] Being himself disenchanted, the tragic poet "also can disenchant"—he can be a comic poet whose art of disenchantment extends even to the enchanting gods. Strauss's compact sentence helps display what a god is, for what Socrates promised Agathon can be seen to be the achievement of Plato: he wrote dialogues that are both tragedy and comedy; they succeed in their enchantment, producing the beautiful gods of transcendent forms and the idea of the Good, while also containing the comedy of their disenchantment, of seeing through the forms to the purpose they served in a post-Homeric world. As for Aristophanes, who had wanted to reply to Socrates' god-making speech, it seems that he could have no reply to Socrates' claim that only the tragedian, that enchanter, would be capable of both tragedy and comedy. For as instructive as his comedies are—and Nietzsche reported the ancient rumor that Plato slept with a copy of Aristophanes under his pillow[67]—his appeal for civic order can call in only the old gods and their old celebrants: for him, Aeschylus must defeat Euripides, the old poets must defeat the new one, the tragedian rumored to be a disciple of the philosopher Socrates.

After Agathon fell asleep, Socrates "put both of them to bed" and then "got up and went away." Apollodorus reports that Aristodemus "followed, just as he was accustomed to, as Socrates went to the Lyceum, washed up, and passed (*diatrissein*) the rest of his day just as he did at any other time, and having passed (*diatripsanta*) [the time] in this way, toward evening, at home, he took his rest (*anapauesthai*)." Heard from the perspective of the supplied, non-philosophic audiences, these last words in the report they sought out confirm the singular character of Socrates as a man to be amazed at, a teacher even of the teachers whose tragedies and comedies help educate the city, a disciplined, self-controlled man over whom even alcohol or sleep has no control. And, having learned it from Alcibiades himself, they will believe that most deeply Socrates is a moral man, not guilty of corrupting those who committed the worst of crimes against Athens. Socrates is singular but not criminal, even in private with associates who proved to be criminal.

But heard as the ending of the dialogue that transmits the third stage of Socrates' philosophic education, these last words—the odd repetition, separated by only two short words, of *diatrissō* (to pass time), and the last two words, *oikoi* (at home) and *anapauesthai* (he took his rest)—convey the

66. Nietzsche, *Human All Too Human*, §125.
67. *Beyond Good and Evil*, §28.

suggestion that the philosopher Socrates is completely at home in the natural passage of finite time that never comes to rest in anything timeless. The dialogue that presents Diotima guiding Socrates to insight into an ontology of the sovereignty of becoming, of eros-like motion and rest, ends with Socrates exemplifying the only way in which the cessation of time exists for living beings: sleep in temporary oscillation with wakefulness.

Note on the Dramatic Date of the Frame of the *Symposium*

Why now? is a necessary question for the trial of Socrates, given the many decades in which he engaged in the same kind of public speech in the marketplace and elsewhere. *Why now?* is a natural question for the frame of the *Symposium*, why this intense interest in Socrates and Alcibiades and the speeches on eros right now, on the part of two separate audiences expressly said not to be interested in philosophy? The dramatic date of the core of the *Symposium* is not disputed; the dramatic date of the frame is, with suggested dates ranging from 407 to 400.[68] What follows are considerations that favor a date just before the trial of Socrates in late May 399, during the thirty-day gap separating the hearing before the king-archon at which Meletus first charged Socrates (the setting of the *Euthyphro*) and the actual trial.[69] The considerations are less than a proof, but they do establish these thirty days as the best fit for the particulars of the frame and the religious/political temper dominating Athens at the end of the year 400 and in the first half of 399: a number of impiety trials held during that year attest to a religious fervor aimed at purifying the city; Socrates' trial on a charge of impiety was one of those trials.

The frame of the *Symposium* is intimately connected to its 416 core, as Glaucon's confusion about the date of the party makes prominent. And historically there are close connections between 399 and 416 in Athens. In 416–415 the most notorious religious crimes in the history of democratic Athens occurred, profanation of the mysteries (416–415) and mutilation of the herms (415), and trials had been held in 415 with many being convicted, attendees at Agathon's party in 416 among them, Alcibiades above all. In 399, intense revival of the memory of those crimes reinforced an

68. 407: Strauss, *On Plato's "Symposium,"* 24; 404: Nussbaum, *Fragility of Goodness*, 170; "around 402": Allen, *Symposium*, 4; c. 400: Bury, *Symposium*, lxvi; 401–400: Rosen, *Symposium*, 7; +/-400: Nails, *People of Plato*, 314.

69. This is the date determined by Christopher Planeaux in his paper "Apollodoros and Alkibiades," 30–31. Significant parts of my argument are drawn from Planeaux's paper.

already existing temper of religious purification through the prosecution of religious crimes. Three historic events in Athens led up to that 400–399 prosecutorial mood. First was the restoration of the democracy in 403 after the defeat of the Thirty in April/May 403. Because of that particularly bloody tyranny and the horrifying civil war that ended it, the restoration was accompanied by an intensified suspicion in the demos of the oligarchic and aristocratic factions of the city, and Socrates was closely associated with oligarchic and aristocratic youths, especially Alcibiades and Critias, the most notorious aristocratic criminals. Second was the general amnesty proclaimed in the fall of 403, which disallowed prosecution of crimes committed before the archonship of Euclides in 403–402, during which the democracy was restored; but ways around the amnesty were being devised in the service of the democracy's need for revenge.[70] Third was the publication of the "ancestral laws" in 400 on prominent tablets in the agora after many years of judicial effort to determine just what those laws were.[71] The upshot of these events was a period of intense religious/political focus by the democracy aimed at purifying the city in accord with the now-established ancestral laws. One of the means of purification was the prosecution of those thought guilty of crimes of impiety — and the spectacular trial of Andocides on a charge of impiety in late 400 made the crimes and trials of 416–415 vivid again for the whole population.

The Trial of Andocides (Late 400)

Andocides was a member of a distinguished aristocratic family who became notorious in 415: he was the man whose testimony at the trial for the crimes of mutilating the herms and of profaning the mysteries[72] led to the conviction of about sixty-five citizens who either fled (forty-five) or were executed (nine), imprisoned (nine), or pardoned (two).[73] The trial resulted in the recall of Alcibiades from the invasion force that was already under

70. On the amnesty and ancient and modern sources concerning it, see Munn, *School of History*, 279–80, 494n11; and Nails, *People of Plato*, 219–22. Aristotle said of the amnesty: "The Athenians appear both in private and public to have behaved before the past disasters in the most completely honorable and statesmanlike manner of any people in history" (*Constitution of the Athenians* 60.2–3).

71. Martin Munn, a historian of Athenian intellectual history, isolates these three events and gives a particularly effective and detailed account of them, relating them directly to the trial of Socrates (*School of Athens*, 258–72).

72. Thucydides reports the crimes in the midst of reporting on the Athenian plan to invade Sicily, a plan advanced and led by Alcibiades (6.27–28).

73. These figures are from Planeaux, Appendix A, 23–24.

way to Sicily; he was ordered to return to stand trial as the chief instigator both of the mutilation and of profaning the Eleusinian mysteries.[74] This recall of the architect of the Sicilian invasion, Athens' most imaginative and decisive general, contributed directly to the Athenian disaster in Sicily and caused the further disaster of Alcibiades' defection to the Spartans as he escaped the capture party escorting him back to Athens: his knowledge of Athenian strengths and weaknesses led to treasonous counsel advancing the Spartan cause decisively — a political crime of immense proportion.[75]

Andocides himself had been granted immunity from prosecution for his testimony in 415, but he left Athens voluntarily after the trial because of the anger his testimony aroused. He returned again in 403 after the amnesty. In late 400 he was charged with impiety for being present at the mysteries in Eleusis in violation of the law that forbid anyone convicted of impiety to attend festivals, a crime that fell outside the range of the amnesty. His defense speech, "On the Mysteries," reviewed in detail the great crimes of 416 and 415 and brought back memories of the outrage, stirring up the religious fervor of the democracy against aristocratic and oligarchic elements in the city. Part of Andocides' defense speech detailed the crucial event of reviewing and restoring the Athenian ancestral laws and publishing them for all to read in the agora.[76] Publication of those laws, many of them concerned with the regulation of religious practice, led "the conservative democracy" to an intense effort in enforcing these ancestral laws, "the highest authority from the past,"[77] now newly defined and published. *Why now* for the trial of Socrates in late May 399? Because it was one event in that effort of enforcement by the democracy. And the frame of the *Symposium*? That too can best be set at that time because of the two importunate audiences Plato presents, at least one of which wanted to learn of Socrates and Alcibiades and the speeches on eros. And the inquisitorial manner of that auditor in establishing Apollodorus's qual-

---

74. While the crime of profaning the mysteries was the main crime for which Alcibiades was held responsible, Thucydides says that "the affair of the Mysteries and the mutilation of the Hermae were part and parcel of a scheme to overthrow the democracy, and that nothing of all this had been done without Alcibiades; the proofs alleged being the general and undemocratic license of his life and habits" (6.28.2). The indictment of Alcibiades (quoted by Plutarch, *Alcibiades*, 22) speaks only of profaning the mysteries.

75. When Alcibiades slipped away from the Athenian state trireme, the *Salamina*, in Thurii, he went to the Peloponnese; he was living in Argos when he learned of his conviction, and, fearing for his life, he asked for asylum from the Spartans, promising to render them services if they granted it.

76. Andocides, "On the Mysteries," §§81–89; see Munn, *School of History*, 261–72.

77. Munn, *School of History*, 272.

ifications as a witness befits a time of trials. Apollodorus's narration took both of his audiences, unexpectedly, back to a time that the recent trial of Andocides had made vivid again — to a party that occurred in the time of the profanations and was attended by Alcibiades.[78]

The Trial of Nicomachus (Most Likely Summer 399)

Nicomachus was one of the *nomothetai*, the experts in Athenian law commissioned to first determine and then publish the ancestral laws of the democracy, which would secure it against treasonous actions by those who longed to establish an oligarchy. He had first been commissioned with the original group in 410, after the overthrow of the oligarchy of 411; they worked until the defeat of Athens in 404 and the establishment of the Thirty. Nicomachus was recommissioned with others in 403 after the defeat of the Thirty and the reestablishment of the democracy.[79] The trial of Nicomachus most likely occurred a few months after the trial of Socrates, in the summer of 399, and it too attests to a mood of religious fervor in Athens at this time. While the exact charges against Nicomachus are not known, his is clearly an impiety trial, for its concern is the very laws on the basis of which piety and impiety were determined in Athens, the laws defining the calendar of public sacrifices. In making his case against Nicomachus, his accuser states that it was the faithful practice of the ancestral laws that brought the favor of the gods and made Athens "the greatest and most blessed city in Greece; so it is fitting for us to perform the same sacrifices as they did."[80] He accuses Nicomachus of not reestablishing the ancestral sacrifices properly but of introducing new ones and failing to establish some of the old ones. While in this case the accusation focuses on errors in reestablishing the ancestral laws, and in the case of Socrates' trial the accusation focused on not acknowledging the gods of Athens and

78. Three of those present at the symposium were found guilty of the crimes, Eryximachus (mutilation) and Alcibiades and Phaedrus (profanation), but many others associated with Socrates had been accused of one or other of the two great crimes. Critias, a leader of the Thirty and famous as the leading Athenian sophist, had also been a close associate of Socrates in his youth. Nails lists sixteen people associated with Socrates who were implicated in the crimes (Nails, *People of Plato*, 18, Excursus I, "The Sacrilegious Crimes of 415").

79. At his trial Andocides directed that the decree reestablishing the commission in 403 be read aloud ("On the Mysteries," §§83–86). That decree explicitly stated that the Athenians were to be governed in the interim before the ancestral laws were determined and published by "the laws of Solon . . . and the ordinances of Draco," the two early formulations of the democratic laws of Athens.

80. Lysias, *Against Nicomachus* 18.

introducing new ones, the same conservative rigor is present, demanding adherence to the ancient practices. The trials of Andocides, Socrates, and Nicomachus and the fervor against impiety that they attest to suggest that Plato set the frame of the *Symposium* at the time of Socrates' trial in order to indicate that he too fell victim to this time of intense enforcement of religious orthodoxy.

The Trial of Socrates

A particularly strong indication that Plato set the frame of the *Symposium* between Socrates' indictment and his trial is the fact that both of the audiences he supplied seek out Apollodorus. Despite Glaucon's urgency to discover the truth about the speeches on eros involving the dead Alcibiades, the departed Agathon, and the still living Socrates, neither he nor today's audience sought out Socrates himself, a public man easy to find and given to talk. Why not? Apollodorus himself had checked some of the details with Socrates: Why didn't the others simply go directly to him rather than to one of his followers? The answer is obvious if Socrates is himself the issue, indicted and about to go on trial before five hundred judges and a crowded court of interested onlookers: the truth about *him* is what the supplied audiences want to learn, and who better to ask than a well-known, unrestrained blabbermouth closely associated with him?

Plato provided indispensable background to the religious setting of the trial of Socrates in the *Euthyphro* and to its political setting in the *Meno*; these dialogues are therefore highly relevant for the dramatic date of the frame of the *Symposium*. Plato set the *Euthyphro* on the day of the pretrial hearing in which Socrates was called to respond to the indictment against him.[81] The *Euthyphro* introduces yet another religious trial at this time, a trial in which Euthyphro, a young religious fanatic, accused his own father of a crime.[82] "What's new?" are the first words of the *Euthyphro* as Euthyphro asks Socrates why he is in this unusual place for him, the Royal Stoa or the Porch of the King, a prominent public building opening onto the northwest corner of the agora, where the king-archon, the chief reli-

81. Planeaux sets the date on which Meletus formally charged Socrates as April 22, 399, or shortly after; that "judicial summons" by Meletus had to be made to the accused personally in the presence of at least one witness, and it had to occur at least four days before the pretrial hearing in the Porch of the King, where the *Euthyphro* took place.

82. Euthyphro and the trial of his father are not otherwise attested in the surviving records. However, given Plato's customary practice of referring to actual historical personages and events, it is possible that these persons and events are historical.

gious official of Athens, held office and, among other duties, conducted preliminary inquiries on cases charging impiety.[83] "What's new?" deepens in meaning as both Socrates and Euthyphro are shown to be innovators in religion, with 399 being a time in Athens particularly hostile to religious innovation, given the recently completed recodification and publication of the ancestral laws, that project of religious orthodoxy and democratic ascendancy. *Why now* for the trial of Socrates? Because now his innovations in religion can be demonstrated to be criminal in the face of clearly defined orthodoxy, and because now the new conflicted directly with the intense public demand for what's old, ancestral custom in religion to help secure the democracy against oligarchic threat.[84] The long-simmering suspicions about Socrates teaching oligarchs and aristocrats can be acted on without running afoul of the amnesty because the actual indictment literally concerns only the present, with Alcibiades and Critias not mentioned but unavoidably a poison in the air. Socrates intimates the temper of 399 when he tells Euthyphro that Meletus charged him with being a "maker of gods—that I make novel gods and don't believe in the ancestral ones" (3b)—a charge especially acute in 400–399. Euthyphro thinks he knows exactly what Meletus meant: Socrates' claim that "the *daimonion* comes to you on occasion." And he too attests to the Athenian temper of 399, for he claims to be like Socrates, "making innovations concerning the divine things" and sharing with him the fate of an innovator, for innovations in religion "are easy to make slander about before the many." Euthyphro's case also concerns purification, but he is the *prosecutor*—and to Socrates' amazement he is accusing his own father of murder in a case that is, as Socrates' questioning brings out, extremely tenuous. Euthyphro mentions that his father's alleged crime had been committed "while we were farming on Naxos" (*Euthyphro* 4c4)—but Athenians had not been permitted to farm on Naxos since they lost the war in 404. *Why now?* is therefore a question that must also be raised about Euthyphro's trial against his father for an alleged crime that happened at least five years earlier. No answer is

83. Aristotle, *Constitution of the Athenians* 57. The king-archon, the second most important of the nine annually selected archons, also supervised the Eleusinian mysteries and the Lenaia festival; he also arranged all torch races and virtually all the traditional sacrifices.

84. Munn is particularly attentive to the outbreak of pious fervor and the purification of the city associated with the publication of the ancestral laws in 400/399; see Munn, *School of Athens*, 6, 258–61, and 273–91, esp. 288–91, and the extensive literature, ancient and modern, he cites. See also Ahrensdorf, *Death of Socrates*, 9–15, on the religious zeal to which Socrates fell prey.

supplied by the text, but the temper of the times regarding religious purification rises as the cause, for Socrates' questioning reveals that Euthyphro's real motive is not civic-minded but concerns his own *self*-purification. As a religious expert he knows "the pollution turns out to be equal if you knowingly associate with such a man and do not purify yourself as well as him by proceeding against him in a lawsuit" (4c). Young Euthyphro's need for purification in acting against his own father shows how extreme religious zealotry had gotten; in his self-righteous assurance he feels free to report that his own family is appalled (4d).[85]

The prosecutor Meletus, like the prosecutor Euthyphro, shares in the prosecutorial frenzy that gripped Athens with the publication of its ancestral religious laws and the consequent demand for the purification of the city through the prosecution of religious criminals.[86] The frame of the *Symposium*, with its two audiences intensely interested in a private event in Socrates' past concerning Alcibiades and eros, best fits this time of trials based on heightened religious fervor: What did that suspicious public man Socrates with close ties to oligarchic and aristocratic criminals say in private to his followers — Socrates, that teacher that Meletus believes to be an atheist (*Apology* 26c-e)? The concerns of the two audiences who question Apollodorus seem, however, not to be religious but rather to focus on the always underlying *political* suspicion about Socrates and Alcibiades — and it is in the *Meno* that Plato addressed the political concern about Socrates.

In the *Euthyphro* as in the *Apology* the accuser on whom the focus is placed is Meletus, the one of three accusers most responsible for the impiety charge. But the main force behind the trial is Anytus, a highly respected

85. Athenians held that there is no crime greater than accusing one's own father of a crime (Andocides, "On the Mysteries," §19).

86. The Meletus who prosecuted Socrates is not the only Meletus attested in the extant cases of religious crime from 399: a Meletus was also a prosecutor in the case brought against Andocides. Whether these are the same Meletus or not, John Burnet is right to say that "at the very least, the speech against Andocides and the reply of Andocides to it . . . are first-hand evidence for the state of some people's minds in 399 B.C. and thus help to make the condemnation of Socrates intelligible." Burnet had just described that state of mind: "The speech against Andocides is almost the only monument of religious fanaticism that has come down to us from antiquity" (*Plato: Euthyphro*, 89–90). Arguments for the two Meletuses being the same are given by Burnet (89–90 and 217), Taylor (*Socrates*, 102–3), and many others; E. de Strycker (*Plato's "Apology of Socrates"*) says, "Since the name Meletus is anything but common, it would be very curious if, in 399, two different Meletoi had each brought a charge of impiety" (94–95). A textual argument in favor of one Meletus for the two cases is given by Keaney, "Plato, *Apology* 32c8–d3." Nails, *People of Plato*, 199–202, summarizes the arguments in favor of different Meletuses.

political leader of the democracy.[87] No appearance by Anytus in Plato's writings can be incidental, so when he chose to have Anytus sit down next to Socrates in the *Meno* two or three years before the trial and have Socrates engage him in a conversation about the teaching of virtue, he must have intended their words to cast light on Socrates' trial in 399 — and Socrates' exchange with Anytus in the *Meno* also suggests that the frame of the *Symposium* is best set in 399.

Plato set the *Meno* in either early 402 or early 401;[88] Meno's imminent departure from Athens (76e) may suggest 401, for it was in March of that year that he departed as the general of the Thessalian forces in the Greek army under Cyrus for Asia Minor, where he met his death.[89] Socrates is in the middle of an argument with Meno when Anytus arrives, but he breaks it off in order to say, "And now indeed, Meno, just at the right moment, Anytus here has sat down beside us, to whom we should give a share in our search" (*Meno* 89e) — their search for teachers of virtue. With Anytus's sudden arrival, Socrates suppresses his denial that he knows any such teachers; with Anytus he affirms instead that he does know teachers of virtue: the sophists. He describes the man who will become his primary accuser as what the historical record uniformly attests of him: a political man honored by the restored democracy for his actions after the experiments with oligarchy in 411 and 404–403. Socrates controls their conversation, making the long speeches that set the topics and posing the questions Anytus is to answer. When Anytus gives more than a brief answer he reveals each time that Socrates' line of questioning has been deeply provoking to him,

87. In the *Apology* Socrates acknowledges the primacy of Anytus: he first refers to the prosecutors as "Anytus and those around him" (18b); when he names all three he puts Anytus at the center (23e); and when he refers to the possibility of the jurors letting him go he says, "if you disobey Anytus," and has them reply, "Socrates, for now we will not obey Anytus; we will let you go, but on this condition . . ." (29c; see 30b and 31a). After the verdict Socrates says that except for the accusations of Anytus and Lycon he would have been acquitted (36a).

88. It is after the restoration of the democracy in 403, because Anytus holds political office (90b); because Meno, a Thessalian visitor to Athens, wants to leave Athens "before the Mysteries" (76e), it is early in the year, as the Lesser Mysteries were held at the end of winter, whereas the Greater Mysteries, which presupposed initiation in the Lesser Mysteries, were held in the fall. I use the translation of the *Meno* by George Anastaplo and Laurence Berns.

89. See Munn, *School of History*, 282. Munn is rare among historians in respecting the historicity of Plato's dialogues; he is therefore in a position to provide detailed background for the politics and characters in the *Meno*. Xenophon shows Meno's character in his appalling betrayal of the Greek army in the belief that it would win him the favor of Cyrus (*Anabasis* 2.5.31–38; 6.21–30).

and reveals as well the suspicion in which he holds Socrates and just why he will eventually become Socrates' chief accuser.

Socrates engineers the conversation with Anytus to focus on "those whom people call sophists." Mere mention of the name sets Anytus off: "By Heracles, watch what you're saying Socrates" (91c). Socrates is in fact watching very closely what he is saying: he said what he said to provoke Anytus into his first extended speech, an expression of moral outrage: "May such madness not seize any of my own people, neither my family nor my friends, neither fellow-citizen nor foreigner." Anytus takes himself to be responsible for a very large company, managing his household and his city with careful attention, fearing that its members could be "debased by going to [sophists]." Naming the famous founder of sophism, Protagoras (91d), Socrates speaks of how "well thought of" Protagoras is, but refrains from saying that he himself did not think well of him.[90] His question about sophists' madness draws out Anytus's view that the sophists "are far from being mad"; the madness belongs to others, "the youth who give them money" (92a), "the relatives who turn them over to them," and maddest of all, "the cities that permit them to come in and don't drive them out" (92b). This denunciation is spoken to Socrates by an Athenian politician who helped lead the civil war that drove out the Thirty, whose intellectual leader was Critias, Athens' greatest sophist, well known to have been an associate of Socrates in his youth. When in his writings Plato permits Socrates' chief accuser to speak he has him speak the political hatred of an effective democratic leader of a city that had recently been ruled by a tyranny in which that sophist most closely associated with Socrates was prominent. When Socrates asks if any of the sophists had wronged him, Anytus replies, "No, by Zeus, I never associated with any of them, and I would not allow anyone else of my people to do so." Anytus, a man accustomed to permitting and forbidding, would like to forbid what he just identified as the great madness of permitting sophists to debase and corrupt Athenian citizens.

Socrates raises the question of just whom Meno should go to in Athens to gain the political virtue they have been talking about (92d-e). Anytus answers in the traditional way: to "any Athenian gentleman he should happen to meet" who themselves learned their virtue from "those who were

90. Plato's *Protagoras*, set in 434, is a concerted if necessarily somewhat veiled effort by Socrates to show his much older colleague how he does harm and that he and the Greek enlightenment generally must curb themselves in the interests of enlightenment; see my *How Philosophy Became Socratic*, pt. 1.

gentlemen before them." And he challenges Socrates: "Or don't you think
that there have been many good men in this city?" (93a). Socrates then calls
up the greatest Athenian statesmen since the Persian wars, the men most
responsible for the singular greatness of imperial democratic Athens, the
greatness that democratic political men of Athens like Anytus were at that
moment working to restore. Socrates names four, Themistocles and Aris-
tides, Pericles and Thucydides, two sets of rivals in policy, but he accuses
each of them of having failed to teach their political virtue to their own
sons. Anytus responds by saying, "Socrates, it seems to me that you easily
speak badly of people" — of the four greatest statesmen of the Athenian
democracy. For Socrates to speak this way with a leader of the recently
restored democracy is more than reckless. It can only be conscious provocation with the aim of goading Anytus into the anger to which Socrates
calls attention (95a), the latent anger with which the political man views
the investigator who treats what he most honors as something to be questioned and seemingly dishonored.

Unable to act now against Socrates because of the amnesty he helped
author,[91] Anytus can issue a warning as his last words: "I could give some
advice to be careful, if you're willing to be persuaded by me because it is
perhaps easier in other cities too to do harm to people than to benefit
them, and in this city that is certainly so" — this democracy, open even to
speaking badly about decent citizens and great leaders. "But I suppose you
know that yourself" — you who were the teacher of the intellectual leader
of the tyranny and now speak badly of the greatest democratic leaders of
our past. The great care with which Socrates conducted his philosophic
life in Athens includes a carefully constructed provocation calling forth
from his future accuser a promise to act in the future. Socrates respects the
finality of Anytus's last words, for his response is to Meno: "Meno, Anytus
seems angry to me, and I don't wonder at it; first of all, he supposes me to
be speaking badly about those men, and then, he also believes that he is
one of them" (95a). Socrates takes advantage of an Anytus withdrawn into
anger and silence to abuse him with a final insult about his own aspiration to greatness that can only reinforce his anger. Socrates trivializes that

91. Anytus was greatly respected for honoring the amnesty, as Isocrates reported in a
speech dated 402, around the time of the *Meno*: "Thrasybulus and Anytus, men of the greatest influence in the city, although they have been robbed of large sums of money and know
who gave in lists of their goods [to be expropriated by the Thirty] nevertheless are not so
brazen as to bring suit against them . . . even if . . . they have greater power than others to
accomplish their ends, yet in matters covered by the [amnesty] at least see fit to put themselves on terms of equality with the other citizens" (Isocrates, *Against Callimachus* 18.23–24).

anger, reducing it to merely personal offense, robbing it of its dignity and importance as a political man's recognition that chipping away the authority of the great men of the democracy makes them less obviously models to honor and emulate.

Anytus continues to sit with Socrates and Meno till the end, a silent, politically powerful presence with a deep interest in their words. Socrates notes his presence near the end after persuading Meno that political action is not founded on knowledge: "It is not, therefore, by any wisdom or by being wise that such men direct their cities, Themistocles and those like him and those about whom Anytus here was just speaking" (99b). Eager Meno agrees that political men are like "soothsayers or inspired diviners," and he finds it "certainly" the case that they "deserve to be called divine" (99c) and "divinely inspired, being inspired and possessed by the god" (99d). Socrates adds that "the Laconians, whenever they praise any good man, say, 'This man's divine,'" and Meno wonders if "Anytus here is annoyed with you for speaking this way" (99e). That Socrates refers to Spartan praise of good men as divine would in fact be part of what annoys Anytus, given that praise and mimicry of Sparta was a feature of Critias's policy. But as Martin Munn argues, his chief annoyance as a political man aiming to restore the ancestral constitution as foundational to the new democracy would be attributing political virtue to divine dispensation, creating a new aristocracy touched by the gods, instead of being the teachable virtue passed on by every Athenian gentleman and by great Athenian leaders of the past emulated by leaders of today.[92]

In his last words Socrates begins by stating that "virtue appears to have come to us by divine dispensation, for those to whom it may come," but we can never know if this appearance is true or not "until we first undertake to seek what virtue, itself in itself, is" (100b). And he ends the *Meno* with his chief accuser, for he commissions Meno to "persuade your guest-friend Anytus here too about those very same things that you yourself have been persuaded about." His last words say why: "so that [Anytus] may be more gentle: for if you do persuade him, you will also confer upon the Athenians a benefit." Socrates ends parading himself before Anytus, Athens' watchman, as Athens' divinely inspired benefactor, who could teach him how to benefit his city properly.

Plato's *Meno* is a daring dialogue. It allows Socrates' chief accuser to be seen as what he was, quick to anger, yes, but for the patriotic, principled reasons of a man responsible for his household and his city. Quick to anger,

92. Munn, *School of History*, 288–90.

he proved slow to act, plotting the proper moment to move against Socrates. Plato's *Meno* serves as an introduction to his *Apology* because it explains why Socrates' chief accuser is almost absent from Socrates' defense speech: he could not even intimate in public what he said in the private *Meno*. Plato moved Anytus offstage in the *Apology* but showed him in the *Meno* coiled to act when the right time came.

Why now for the trial of Socrates? Because Anytus, prepared since the restoration of the democracy to accuse Socrates of treasonous acts but restrained by the amnesty, sees that the time has come: the trial of Andocides rekindled the religious anger of the trials of 415 and opened the way for a trial not prohibited by the amnesty because it concerned religious innovation here and now. Meletus serves Anytus as a useful idiot for the long-simmering political hate of Socrates.

And *why now*, during the thirty-day gap been the indictment and the trial, for the frame of the *Symposium*? Because the expressed concerns of the citizen auditors who go out of their way to hear an authentic report of Socrates in private with Alcibiades and others best fits that brief period when an opinion about Socrates became mandatory for citizens who might have to serve as one of his five hundred judges.

Plato in a Nietzschean History of Philosophy

Plato . . . the most beautiful growth of antiquity.

Plato's invention of the pure mind and the good in itself—the worst, most dangerous, most durable of all errors so far.

—Nietzsche, *Beyond Good and Evil*, Prologue

In showing the stages of Socrates' philosophic education and what he ultimately discovered regarding knowing and being, this last book of mine is most clearly what all my books have been, an installment in the new history of philosophy made possible by Friedrich Nietzsche. In *Nietzsche and Modern Times* I set out the formal principles of a Nietzschean history of philosophy as stated in his own pronouncements: "The greatest thoughts are the greatest events," "Genuine philosophers are commanders and legislators," and "The difference between exoteric and esoteric was formerly known by all philosophers."[1] The three dialogues treated in this book put content into those claims by showing just what Socrates came to understand and just how he chose to present what he understood. The *Phaedo* shows the "heroic" or authoritative role the philosopher comes to play as a founding teacher, while also showing that the philosopher's deepest concern is understanding the causes of all things. The *Parmenides* shows the necessity that the philosopher gain knowledge of the nature of knowing, of the limits on all possible human knowing. The *Symposium* shows that

1. *Nietzsche and Modern Times*, 1–2; the pronouncements are in *Beyond Good and Evil*, §§285, 211, 30.

a philosopher, within those limits, can gain insight into the nature of all things, an ontology grounded in self-knowledge. In these cardinal matters of philosophy Socrates and Nietzsche come to light as kin.[2]

As installments in a Nietzschean history of philosophy my two books on Plato, *How Socrates Became Socrates* and *How Philosophy Became Socratic*, expand on a remarkable fact: Plato so arranged his dialogues that the two most basic aspects of Socrates' thought, philosophy and political philosophy, could be studied, watched, in their becoming. Plato chose the same authorial device to trace each of these momentous events in the history of philosophy: in each case he scattered Socrates' becoming across three separate dialogues whose relatedness and sequence had to be discovered by his reader, who, putting the three together, could learn the unspoken lessons that Socrates' becoming teaches. For a contemporary reader one of those lessons is the philosophic kinship between Socrates and Nietzsche. Given the nature of philosophy and political philosophy this kinship is not a surprise, or rather it is only a superficial or surmountable surprise grounded in the necessity that Socrates shelter the development of his true views in edifying ones—Nietzsche, on the other hand, played out his fundamental growth in public, in the books he wrote and in their trajectory as he discerned it retrospectively and then called attention to it in his autobiographical writings.

Nietzsche's two judgments on Plato quoted in the epigraphs to this conclusion are not contradictory; they express the necessary distinction in his mature assessment of philosophy and political philosophy in Plato/Socrates.[3] The first judgment expresses admiration for Plato's achievement at the peak and effective end of the genuine history of Greek philosophy, of which Nietzsche was a diligent and profound student from his university days on.[4] The second judgment expresses condemnation of Plato's

2. See my *How Philosophy Became Socratic*, 13–16, 413–17, where I also treat the important role Leo Strauss plays in making both Nietzsche and Plato understandable.

3. For purposes of brevity in this conclusion I use the names Socrates and Plato as if they were synonyms, markers for the same world-historical phenomenon that permanently redirected Western spiritual life: Plato's Socrates. I thereby ignore a matter that occupied Nietzsche from his student days through his last books: distinguishing Plato from Socrates, assigning to Socrates a historic turn in philosophy to mere moralism and to Plato the fateful inventions of the pure mind and the good in itself that prepared the way for Christianity.

4. In the history of Greek philosophy that he began writing as a young professor, Nietzsche had not yet recognized that Plato in fact fulfilled what Nietzsche at that time saw as the unfulfilled promise of the whole history of Greek philosophy: an outcome in "a *still higher type* of human" than the earlier philosophers were. See my *What a Philosopher Is*, 90–101.

political philosophy, a necessary condemnation at the point in Western cultural history that Nietzsche came to see he occupied: the nihilism attendant to the death of the Christian God.

Socrates and Nietzsche share the basic features of philosophy itself: an inquiry into being that comes to recognize the need to inquire first into the inquirer and his fitness to know — epistemology — and only then a properly prepared inquiry into being as far as it is knowable — ontology. Guided by Parmenides, Socrates arrived at a fundamental skepticism about the possibility of direct human knowledge of the world, just as Nietzsche's early study of Kant and Schopenhauer led him to an epistemological skepticism comparable in scope and radicality. That insight led Socrates, as it led Nietzsche, to a study of the human soul not only in its capacity to know but also in its fundamental passions — "Know thyself" in each case. Study of the human soul led each of them to the study of humans in groups, the "city" or culture in the broadest sense. Such study led both thinkers to a genealogy of morality, knowledge of good and evil in their rootedness in the passions. Ultimately, knowledge of the self and the human pointed each of them to an ontology that could never be more than inferential, the result of moving from the truth about human being to a posited truth about all beings, a sovereignty of becoming more exacting than mere process, an active, generative power at work in every event in nature. Call it eros, call it will to power; the names matter, but no name is completely adequate for what Leo Strauss called, in connection with Nietzsche's view, "the most fundamental fact."[5]

Socrates and Nietzsche share the basic features of political philosophy: in the course of their philosophic development each came to recognize the radicality of philosophy in its chief fields of inquiry — in ontology, "the sovereignty of becoming"; in epistemology, "the fluidity of all concepts, types, and kinds"; in psychology, "the lack of any cardinal difference between the human and other animals."[6] And each came to recognize that these insights were "true but deadly" to any social order and therefore required of the philosopher an edifying or exoteric carrier for the esoteric truths.[7] Socrates' exotericism followed the tradition of thinkers from Homer to

5. Strauss, *Studies in Platonic Political Philosophy*, 177–78; and my *Leo Strauss and Nietzsche*, 36–48. Nietzsche himself called will to power *"die elementarste Tatsache"* (KSA 13:14 [79], Spring 1888).

6. Nietzsche, *On the Use and Disadvantage of History for Life*, §9.

7. In the passage just cited, Nietzsche went on to say that if such truths "are inflicted on the people for another generation with the rage for instruction that has by now become normal, no one should be surprised if the people perishes of petty egoism, conventionalism, and selfishness, and falls apart, ceasing to be a people."

Parmenides in burying the deadly truth very deeply in a salutary teaching, with the Platonic Socrates, a teaching on transcendence that would prove all too successful. Nietzsche developed his own unique exotericism in light of the historic modern success of science and the consequent public presence of truth; those great gains of science, that product of philosophy, made it wise for philosophy to break with its historic forms of exotericism. Within reach for the scientifically schooled society of late modern times, Nietzsche judged, was a social order no longer ruled by the perversions of Christian Platonism, a misology and misanthropy that imagined a moral God rewarding and punishing immortal souls. But Nietzsche did not abandon philosophy's recognition of the need for exoteric decoration; nor did he embrace the Enlightenment fiction of a wised-up population living happy, wise, and free at the end of history.[8] Instead of denying the deadly truth as traditional exotericism did, Nietzsche's exotericism required that truth be adorned. In place of a life-denying Platonism Nietzsche devised a poetry of his own that would celebrate life as it is. The ultimate affirmation of that new poetry is his teaching of eternal return, the celebrant's song that *this* is what I want, this life, just as it is, an infinite number of times. In his mature writings Nietzsche pictured an ebb and flood of truth and art; because of the insurmountable difference between the philosopher and non-philosopher that ebb and flood would be lived consciously by the thinker, whereas the population at large would live primarily within the art of earthly celebration of mortal life.

That all of these conclusions of philosophy and political philosophy are shared by these two philosophers at the beginning and end of our specific tradition suggests that they are more than *their* conclusions: they are the conclusions of philosophy itself, of the application of reason to the highest problems of being and knowing and to the problem of philosophy's healthy existence in a healthy social order.

Beyond what Socrates and Nietzsche share in understanding nature, human nature, culture, and philosophy, there exists a similarity between them grounded in a historical accident: each lived during a time of the deepest possible crisis of culture, to which each had to respond wisely. With Socrates too that insight into the times meant precisely what Nietz-

---

8. Nietzsche did for a time adopt that fiction as an exoteric face for his philosophic explorations, but he abandoned it in his mature writings after his fundamental discoveries in ontology and in the affirmation of the true: will to power and eternal return, respectively. See my *What a Philosopher Is*.

sche had a "Madman" say openly in the marketplace: "God is dead and we killed him."[9] Socrates, a speaker in the marketplace, never spoke openly of the death of Homer's gods, but he observed it as a historic feature of his time, attentive as he was to the experiences of a Glaucon and an Adeimantus and to the all-too-rash openness of the teachers of the Greek enlightenment. Socrates and Nietzsche each responded to the cultural disaster of their time with what Nietzsche called "great politics," action on behalf of a philosophy of the future in a culture of the future. Socrates' great politics led him to develop a public teaching that called in the very permanences that Parmenides had long since refuted for him, transcendent forms that he never stopped talking about from the time he introduced them in the *Republic* till thirty years later on his dying day in the *Phaedo*. And along with the forms as one kind of replacement for the Homeric gods, he also introduced in the *Republic* nameless non-Homeric moral gods as watchful judges delivering payoffs for good and evil behavior to be enjoyed or endured by non-Homeric immortal souls in a non-Homeric Hades. And at the peak of his transcendent forms he placed an idea of the good as the cause of the existence and being of all beings and of their being known, a kind of monotheistic ruler topping a hierarchy of gods. And he succeeded: "Since Plato and through him, religion has been essentially different from what it had been before."[10] Nietzsche understood the cultural crisis of his time to be the death of that "Platonism for the people" that he recognized Christianity to be. Nietzsche, as a-theistic as Socrates, did not live to be seventy and to trace out all the consequences of his insights and to speak on the last day of his life of what to carry to foreign places and later times. But Nietzsche did, late in the time he had, come to recognize that even though "there is nothing in me of the founder of a religion,"[11] he had to prepare the way for gods, post-Christian gods true to the earth, and prepare the way for fellow celebrants of generative nature. As a classicist steeped in the Greeks he could say, "Oh those Greeks! They knew how to *live* . . . boldly on the surface, the fold, the skin . . . to believe . . . in the whole Olympus of appearance."[12] Admiring those Greeks who lived in the still living presence of Homer and Hesiod's gods, Nietzsche prepared the way for a new surface, even calling in gods, earthly gods celebrating the fecundity

9. Nietzsche, *Gay Science*, §125.

10. Burkert, *Greek Religion*, 322.

11. Nietzsche, *Ecce Homo*, "Destiny," 1.

12. Nietzsche, *Gay Science*, "Foreword to the Second Edition," §4.

of the earth, maleness and femaleness divinized, Dionysos and Ariadne, the divine generative pair that god-making humanity could emulate and celebrate in new festivals of earthly life.

And that is the final way in which Nietzsche shared what Socrates held: he knew that the philosopher must rule if there is to be any rest from ills for humanity. When Socrates announced that necessity to Glaucon in the *Republic*, Glaucon reacted with the expected disbelief, predicting that Socrates would be attacked and have to pay a penalty in scorn.[13] Glaucon betrayed the typical misunderstanding of rule, failing to see that he and almost everyone else were ruled by their beliefs in what was noble, just, and good, beliefs authored by Homer and Hesiod. Socrates aspired to rule as Homer and Hesiod ruled, and he succeeded. Just so, Nietzsche described the genuine philosopher as a "commander and legislator" who says to a whole age, "We have to go *that* way,"[14] and, knowing what religions are good for,[15] he knew that only belief could move whole populations. When he made *Thus Spoke Zarathustra* his most important book he intimated by the very title the scope of what was now necessary: at the end of the age of the rule of good and evil founded in Persia by Zarathustra and carried into Western philosophy and religion by Greeks and Hebrews, Athens and Jerusalem, a new rule became necessary, a new good and bad established through the thinking and writing of the one who had come to understand what a philosopher is.

A Nietzschean history of philosophy understands philosophy to be the highest human gift, the attempt to understand rationally the causes of all things and to generate a social order within which that gift can prosper. It is the gift at work in the Homeric origins of our culture and throughout the history of our culture in the writings of Plato and the great Socratics schooled by Plato. Nietzsche shares with Plato the old teaching that we are not our own, that we owe our being to something infinitely greater than ourselves that we can to some degree understand. Gratitude is philosophy's fundamental response to the world understood in the only way that it is understandable. In Nietzsche that deep-running gratitude takes public form in the most extreme affirmation of this life that is at all imaginable: the passionate desire that what is eternally return just as it is.

Gratitude. We owe a cock to Asclepius.

13. *Republic* 473d–474a.
14. Nietzsche, *Beyond Good and Evil*, §211.
15. *Beyond Good and Evil*, §62.

Ahrensdorf, Peter. *The Death of Socrates and the Life of Philosophy*. Albany: State University of New York Press, 1995.

Allen, Reginald E. *The Dialogues of Plato*. Vol. 2, *Plato's "Symposium."* New Haven: Yale University Press, 1991.

———. *The Dialogues of Plato*. Vol. 4, *Plato's "Parmenides."* New Haven: Yale University Press, 1997.

Andocides. "On the Mysteries." In *Antiphon and Andocides*, trans. Michael Gagarin and Douglas M. MacDowell, 99–140. Austin: University of Texas Press, 1998.

Aristotle. *The Constitution of Athens*. Trans. H. Rackham. Loeb Classical Library. Cambridge, MA: Harvard University Press, 1961.

Bacon, Francis. *Wisdom of the Ancients*. 1857–74. In *The Works of Francis Bacon*, ed. J. Spedding, R. L. Ellis, and D. D. Heath, 13:67–171. New York: Garrett Press, 1968.

Bacon, Helen. "The Poetry of *Phaedo*." In *The Cabinet of the Muses: Essays on Classical and Comparative Literature in Honor of Thomas G. Rosenmeyer*, ed. Mark Griffin and Donald J Mastronarde, 147–62. Atlanta: Scholars Press, 1990. https://escholarship.org/uc/item/73s3f7dr.

Benardete, Seth. *The Archaeology of the Soul: Platonic Readings of Ancient Poetry and Philosophy*. Ed. Ronna Burger and Michael Davis. South Bend, IN: St. Augustine's Press, 2012.

———. *The Argument of the Action: Essays on Greek Poetry and Philosophy*. Ed. Ronna Burger and Michael Davis. Chicago: University of Chicago Press, 2000.

———. *The Being of the Beautiful: Plato's "Theaetetus," Sophist," and "Statesman."* Translated with commentary. Chicago: University of Chicago Press, 1984.

———. *The Bow and the Lyre: A Platonic Reading of the "Odyssey."* Lanham, MD: Rowman and Littlefield, 1996.

———. "On Plato's *Symposium*." In Plato, *Symposium*, trans. Seth Benardete, 179–99. Chicago: University of Chicago Press, 2001.

———. *Socrates' Second Sailing: A Reading of the "Republic."* Chicago: University of Chicago Press, 1989.

——. *The Tragedy and Comedy of Life: Plato's "Philebus."* Translated with commentary. Chicago: University of Chicago Press, 1993.

Blondell, Ruby. "Where Is Socrates on the 'Ladder of Love'?" In *Plato's "Symposium": Issues in Interpretation and Reception*, ed. J. H. Lesher, Debra Nails, and Frisbee C. C. Sheffield, 147–78. Cambridge, MA: Harvard University Press, 2006.

Bolotin, David. *An Approach to Aristotle's "Physics": With Particular Attention to His Manner of Writing.* Albany: State University Press of New York, 1997.

——. "The Life of Philosophy and the Immortality of the Soul: An Introduction to Plato's *Phaedo.*" *Ancient Philosophy* 7 (1986): 39–56.

Burger, Ronna. *Phaedo: A Platonic Labyrinth.* New Haven: Yale University Press, 1984.

Burkert, Walter. *Greek Religion.* Trans. John Raffan. Cambridge, MA: Harvard University Press, 1985.

——. *Homo Necans: The Anthropology of Ancient Greek Sacrificial Ritual and Myth.* Trans. Peter Bing. Berkeley: University of California Press, 1983.

Burnet, John, ed. *Plato: Euthyphro, Apology of Socrates, Crito.* Oxford: Oxford University Press, 1924.

——. *Plato: Phaedo.* 1911. Oxford: Clarendon Press, 1989.

Bury, R. G., ed. *The Symposium of Plato.* 2nd ed. Cambridge: Heffer and Sons, 1966.

Camp, John M. *The Athenian Agora: Excavations in the Heart of Athens.* London: Thames and Hudson, 1986.

Connelly, Joan Breton. *The Parthenon Enigma.* New York: Knopf, 2014.

De Strycker, E. *Plato's "Apology of Socrates": A Literary and Philosophical Study with a Running Commentary.* Leiden: E. J. Brill, 1994.

Dover, K. J., ed. *Plato: Symposium.* Cambridge: Cambridge University Press, 1980.

Ebert, Theodor, trans. and ed. Platon, *Werke*: I, 4, *Phaidon.* Göttingen: Vandenhoeck & Ruprecht, 2004.

——. "Why Is Evenus Called a Philosopher at *Phaedo* 61c?" *Classical Quarterly*, n.s., 51, no. 2 (2001): 423–34.

Figarette, Ann. "A New Look at the Wall of Nikomakhos." *Hesperia* 40, no. 3 (1971): 330–35.

Gagarin, Michael, and Douglas M. MacDowell, trans. *Antiphon and Andocides.* Austin: University of Texas Press, 1998.

Gallop, David, trans. and ed. *Plato, Phaedo.* Oxford: Clarendon Press, 1975.

Garland, Robert. *The Greek Way of Life: From Conception to Old Age.* Ithaca: Cornell University Press, 1971.

Graham, Daniel W., trans. and ed. *The Texts of the Early Greek Philosophers: The Complete Fragments and Selected Testimonies of the Major Presocratics.* Pt. 1. Cambridge: Cambridge University Press, 2010.

Hackworth, Robert, trans. *Plato's "Phaedo."* With introduction and commentary. Cambridge: Cambridge University Press, 1955.

Hartle, Ann. *Death and the Disinterested Spectator: An Inquiry into the Nature of Philosophy.* Albany: State University Press of New York, 1986.

Isocrates. *Against Callimachus.* Trans. George Norlin. Loeb Classical Library. Cambridge, MA: Harvard University Press, 1980.

Johnstone, Henry W. "A Homeric Echo in Plato?" *Mnemosyne* 44, no. 3 (1991): 417–18.

Kanayama, Yahei. "The Methodology of the Second Voyage and the Proof of the Soul's

Indestructibility in Plato's *Phaedo*." *Oxford Studies in Ancient Philosophy* 18 (1996): 41–100.

Keaney, John J. "Plato, *Apology* 32c8-d3." *Classical Quarterly*, n.s., 30, no. 2 (1980): 296–98.

Klein, Jacob. "Plato's *Phaedo*." In *Lectures and Essays*, ed. R. Williamson and E. Zuckerman, 375–93. Annapolis: St. John's Press, 1985.

Lampert, Laurence. *The Enduring Importance of Leo Strauss*. Chicago: University of Chicago Press, 2013.

———. "How Benardete Read the Last Stage of Socrates' Philosophic Education." In *Political Philosophy Cross-Examined: Perennial Challenges to the Philosophic Life*, ed. Thomas L. Pangle and J. Harvey Lomax, 189–203. N.p.: Palgrave Macmillan, 2013.

———. *How Philosophy Became Socratic: A Study of Plato's "Protagoras," "Charmides," and "Republic."* Chicago: University of Chicago Press, 2010.

———. *Leo Strauss and Nietzsche*. Chicago: University of Chicago Press, 1996.

———. *Nietzsche and Modern Times: A Study of Bacon, Descartes, and Nietzsche*. New Haven: Yale University Press, 1993.

———. *Nietzsche's Task: An Interpretation of "Beyond Good and Evil."* New Haven: Yale University Press, 2001.

———. "Reading Benardete: A New *Parmenides*." *Interpretation: A Journal of Political Philosophy* 44, no. 3 (2018): 403–23.

———. "Socrates' Defense of Polytropic Odysseus: Lying and Wrong-Doing in Plato's *Lesser Hippias*." *Review of Politics* 64, no. 2 (Spring 2002): 231–59.

———. *What a Philosopher Is: Becoming Nietzsche*. Chicago: University of Chicago Press, 2017.

Lampert, Laurence, and Christopher Planeaux. "Who's Who in Plato's *Timaeus-Critias* and Why." *Review of Metaphysics* 52, no. 1 (1998): 87–125.

Leibowitz, David. *The Ironic Defense of Socrates: Plato's "Apology."* Cambridge: Cambridge University Press, 2010.

Lysias. "Against Nicomachus." In *Lysias*, trans. S. C. Todd, 296–307. Austin: University of Texas Press, 2000.

Montaigne, Michel de. *The Complete Essays*. Trans. Donald Frame. Stanford: Stanford University Press, 1965.

Munn, Martin. *The School of History: Athens in the Age of Socrates*. Berkeley: University of California Press, 2000.

Nails, Debra. *The People of Plato: A Prosopography of Plato and Other Socratics*. Indianapolis: Hackett, 2002.

Nietzsche, Friedrich. *The Antichrist*. In *The Portable Nietzsche*, trans. and ed. Walter Kaufmann, 565–656. 1954. New York: Viking Press, 1966.

———. *Beyond Good and Evil: Prelude to a Philosophy of the Future*. Trans. Walter Kaufmann. New York: Vintage, 1966.

———. *The Birth of Tragedy: Hellenism and Pessimism*. In *Basic Writings of Nietzsche*, trans. and ed. Walter Kaufmann, 1–144. New York: Modern Library, 2000.

———. *Ecce Homo: How One Becomes What One Is*. Trans. Walter Kaufmann. New York: Vintage, 1967.

———. *The Gay Science*. Trans. Josefine Nauckhoff. Cambridge: Cambridge University Press, 2001.

———. *Human, All Too Human*. Trans. R. J. Hollingdale. Vols. 1–2. Cambridge: Cambridge University Press, 1996.

———. *Kritische Studienausgabe (KSA)*. Ed. Giorgio Colli and Mazzino Montinari. 15 vols. Munich: Deutscher Taschenbuch Verlag, 1967–77. Berlin: De Gruyter, 1988.

———. *On the Use and Disadvantage of History for Life*. In *Untimely Meditations*, trans. R. J. Hollingdale, 2nd ed., 57–123. Cambridge: Cambridge University Press, 1997.

———. *Twilight of the Idols: Or How to Philosophize with a Hammer*. Trans. Richard Polt. Indianapolis: Hackett Publishing, 1997.

———. *Writings from the Early Notebooks*. Ed. Raymond Geuss and Alexander Nehamas. Trans. Ladislaus Löb. Cambridge: Cambridge University Press, 2009.

Nussbaum, Martha. *The Fragility of Goodness: Luck and Ethics in Greek Tragedy and Philosophy*. Cambridge: Cambridge University Press, 1986.

Planeaux, Christopher. "Apollodoros and Alkibiades: The Settings for Platon's *Symposium* and Their Impact on Our Understanding of Sokrates' Trial." Academia.edu.

———. *The Athenian Year Primer: Attic Time-Reckoning and the Julian Calendar*. Academia.edu, 2020.

———. "The Date of Bendis' Entry into Attica." *Classical Journal* 96, no. 2 (December–January 2000–2001): 165–92.

———. "Socrates, Alcibiades, and Plato's *ta poteideatika*: Does the *Charmides* Have an Historical Setting?" *Mnemosyne* 52 (1999): 72–77.

———. "Socrates, Bendis, and Cephalus: Does Plato's *Republic* Have an Historical Setting?" In *A New Politics for Philosophy: Essays on Plato, Nietzsche, and Leo Strauss in Honor of Laurence Lampert*, ed. George A. Dunn and Mango Telli. Lanham, MD: Rowman and Littlefield, 2021.

Plato. *Meno*. Trans. George Anastaplo and Laurence Berns. Newburyport, MA: Focus Philosophical Library, 1998.

———. *Parmenides*. Trans. Albert Keith Whitaker. Newburyport, MA: Focus Philosophical Library, 1996.

———. *Phaedo*. Trans. Eva Brann, Peter Kalkavage, and Eric Salem. Newburyport, MA: Focus Philosophical Library, 1998.

———. *Symposium*. Trans. Seth Benardete. Chicago: University of Chicago Press, 2001.

Robertson, Noel. "Athena's Shrines and Festivals." In *Worshipping Athena: Panathenaia and Parthenon*, ed. Jenifer Neils, 27–77. Madison: University of Wisconsin Press, 1996.

Rosen, Stanley. *Plato's "Symposium."* New Haven: Yale University Press, 1987.

Sebell, Dustin. *The Socratic Turn: Knowledge of Good and Evil in an Age of Science*. Philadelphia: University of Pennsylvania Press, 2015.

Stern, Paul. *Socratic Rationalism and Political Philosophy: An Interpretation of Plato's "Phaedo."* Albany: State University of New York Press, 1993.

Strauss, Leo. *The City and Man*. Chicago: Rand McNally, 1964.

———. *Liberalism Ancient and Modern*. New York: Basic Books, 1968.

———. *On Plato's "Symposium."* Ed. with a foreword by Seth Benardete. Chicago: Chicago University Press, 2001.

———. *On Tyranny*. Ed. Victor Gourevitch and Michael S. Roth. Rev. ed. New York: Free Press, 1991.

———. *Persecution and the Art of Writing*. Glencoe, IL: Free Press of Glencoe, 1952.

———. *Studies in Platonic Political Philosophy*. Chicago: University of Chicago Press, 1983.

———. *Xenophon's Socratic Discourse: An Interpretation of the "Oeconomicus."* Ithaca: Cornell University Press, 1971.

Sulek, Marty. "On the Classical Meaning of *Philanthropia.*" *Nonprofit and Voluntary Sector Quarterly* 39, no. 3 (2010): 385–40.

Taylor, A. E. "Parmenides, Zeno, and Socrates." *Proceedings of the Aristotelian Society* 16 (1915–16): 234–89.

———. *Plato: The Man and His Work*. 1926. New York: Meridian Books, 1966.

———. *Socrates*. Boston: Beacon Press, 1951.

Thucydides. *The Landmark Thucydides*. Ed. Robert Strassler. Trans. Richard Crawley. Rev. ed. New York: Free Press, 1996.

White, Howard B. *Peace among the Willows: The Political Philosophy of Francis Bacon*. The Hague: Martinus Nijhoff, 1968.

Xenophon. *The Anabasis of Cyrus*. Trans. Wayne Ambler. Ithaca: Cornell University Press, 2008.

———. *Memorabilia*. Trans. Amy L. Bonnette. Ithaca: Cornell University Press, 1994.

Achilles, 31–32

Adeimantus, 91–94, 116, 119–20, 147, 196, 225

Agathon: object of Socrates' beautification, 161–72; in *Protagoras*, 156; questioned by Socrates, 168–72; shamed by Socrates, 171; in *Symposium*, 4, 153, 157–58, 172–75, 177, 181, 183, 202–4, 206–8

Ahrensdorf, Peter, 24n34, 43n68, 214n84

Alcibiades, 140; profanes Socrates' secret core, 203–6; in *Protagoras*, 156; and the religious crimes of 416–15, 157–58, 203–6, 210–12, 214–15; and Socrates, 204n60, 205n62; in *Symposium*, 153–59, 161, 165, 203–9, 213, 220

Alcibiades I, 98n14, 204n60

Allen, Reginald, 103, 109n10, 209n68

amazement, 187, 191, 194–95, 197, 201; not persisting in, 183–84, 192–93. *See also* wonder

Anaxagoras, 39, 99, 149; as the first to bring philosophy to Athens, 42–43, 44n69; on mind as cause, 43–52, 56, 57n94, 69

Anaximander, 38n54

Andocides, trial of, 155, 165, 203–4, 210–12, 215n86, 220

Antiphon, speaker of *Parmenides* core, 93–94, 95–97, 107, 119, 122–24

Anytus: in *Apology*, 215–16; in *Meno*, 215–20

Apollodorus, 3, 16–17, 80, 83, 203; as narrator of *Symposium*, 153, 155, 157–60, 166, 173

Apology of Socrates, 2, 3n2, 17, 35, 37, 39n56, 47n77, 63, 80, 83, 215, 220

Archelaus, as Socrates' teacher, 43n67, 149

Aristodemus, 159–63, 164, 166, 167n23, 173, 206–8

Aristophanes, 37n48, 38n54, 69n111, 83, 144n60, 177n33; as character in *Symposium*, 155, 156n9, 156n11, 164, 166–67, 172n28, 186, 203, 207–8

Aristotle, 210n70, 214n83

atheism, 39, 50, 215

Atlas, as cause, 50–51, 68

Bacon, Francis, 70, 87, 178

Bacon, Helen, 14n12, 73

beautiful: as edifying, 199–202; as form, 59, 62, 109; as imagined highest form (*monoeides*), 191, 198–201; safe explanation of cause, 63

Benardete, Seth, 1n1, 42n64, 47n78, 53, 86n131, 134n44, 198n55; on the deep structure of eros, 169; the enduring importance of his interpretation of the *Parmenides*, 129; his exegesis of Parmenides' gymnastic, 124–47; on Odysseus, 33n44, 46n74, 69n112; and the *Parmenides*' report on young Socrates, 91, 111, 113, 116; on the *Symposium*, 153n1, 166n22, 167n25, 169, 172n29, 177, 180, 188n46, 206n64; on the *Theaetetus*, 137nn46–47, 138n48, 179

Blondell, Ruby, 197n53, 200n57

Bolotin, David, 21, 69n113
Burger, Ronna, 24n31, 29n39, 48, 80n125
Burkert, Walter, 203n58, 225n10
Burnet, John, 19n25, 25n35, 29n39, 37n48, 38n53, 39n56, 44n69, 62n104, 215n86
Bury, R. G., 157n13, 161n16, 209n68

cause, 31; of all things, 2, 8, 96, 99; dreaming and shadow-painting as, 128–32, 144, 176, 185, 191; eros as, 141, 169, 177–80, 187–91, 223; of generation and destruction as a whole, 8, 34, 36; inward basis of, 90; material and efficient, 41; mind as ordering, 43–52; safe understanding of, 54–55, 63–66, 75–77, 79, 81–82, 100, 115, 121–22, 147; Socrates' mature understanding of, 173; of Socrates' sitting there and conversing, 47–52; transcendent forms as sole, 42, 59
center, of *Phaedo*, 9, 18n21, 21–22, 30
Cephalus: of *Parmenides*, 3, 90–95, 97, 123–24, 129; of *Republic*, 91–92, 95
Charmides, 151, 190
Charmides, 1, 14n12; dramatic date in relation to *Republic*, 19n22, 27n37, 150–51
chronology of the dialogues, 1–2, 50, 53–54, 61, 71. *See also* dramatic date
Cicero, 148–51
Clazomenae, men of, 4–5, 53, 90, 92–93, 95, 99, 108, 119, 146
comedy, 156–57n11, 177n33, 186, 207; and tragedy, 164–65, 207
Connelly, Joan, 96n10, 97
courage, 73n120, 164; Socrates', 85
Critias, 210, 212n78, 214, 217, 219
Crito, 9, 12, 17, 81–84, 86

danger: of argument, 67n108; of misology, 18, 47; of natural science, 54, 61, 69, 71, 100; Simmias's view of, 19, 52n88; of skepticism, 119; of sophism, 67n108, 132
Descartes, René, 70, 134n42; on gratitude, 87
Diotima, 155, 175; final definition of eros, 183–84, 188–90; image of philosophy, 181; lecture on what to teach, 190–202; logos of, 182–91; myth of, 172–82; and ontology, 179; as philosopher, 175; as religious authority, 172, 173–76, 190, 202
Dover, Kenneth, 185n44
dramatic date, 1; of *Charmides*, 19n22, 26n36, 150; of *Parmenides*, 90n2, 92n5; of *Protagoras*, 153; of *Republic*, 19n22,

26n36, 92, 150; of *Symposium* core, 209; of *Symposium* frame, 154–55, 161n15, 162, 203–4, 209–20. *See also* chronology of the dialogues
dreaming and shadow-painting, 128–29, 131–32, 135, 144, 176, 185, 190

Ebert, Theodor, 17n19, 20n26, 36n47
Echecrates, 9, 14, 16–17, 18, 20–22, 24, 67, 80
edifying: in *Parmenides*, 91, 94, 147; in *Phaedo*, 2, 19, 54, 68, 80, 84, 86; in *Symposium*, 191, 199–202
Empedocles, 38n54, 50, 179
enlightenment: Greek, 4, 94, 153, 217n90, 225; modern, 152, 224; sophistic, 147, 156
epistemological skepticism, 40, 89, 91, 133–34, 146, 147, 223; warning against by Parmenides, 58, 132. *See also* epistemology
epistemological turn, 133
epistemology, 166, 175–76, 223. *See also* epistemological skepticism
eros: as active force, 176; akin to will to power, 134, 152, 223; and the beautiful, 173–74, 179–83, 187–91, 194–95, 197–202; as cause, 169, 177–80, 188–90, 223; as comprehensive, 186; deeds of, 175–76; deep structure of, 189; as drive to gain the good, 183; as a god, 154, 166, 169, 173–74; and happiness, 183; in Ibycus' poem, 124; as name of the whole, 184; as "the nature of nature," 177; as not a god, 174–75; ontology of, 30, 223; origins of in Diotima's myth, 177–82; and the sovereignty of becoming, 178, 182, 189, 209, 223
Eryximachus: in *Protagoras*, 156; in *Symposium*, 156n9, 164–67, 206, 212n78
esotericism. *See* exotericism
Euthydemus, 82–83
Euthyphro, 63, 209, 213–15
exotericism, 5, 152, 221; in Greek philosophy, 47n78; in *Parmenides*, 61, 102–3; in *Phaedo*, 61, 68–70, 79–80, 86; in Socrates and Nietzsche, 221, 223–34

festivals: Athenian, 95–98, 203n58, 213–14; Delia in *Phaedo*, 14–16; Great Panathenaea in *Parmenides*, 95–98, 108, 115; Lenaia in *Symposium*, 154, 162
first stage of Socrates' philosophic education, 108, 199; as Odyssean tale, 37–52; permanent importance of, 71; reported

by Socrates, 4, 153, 172–73; as turn to logoi, 52–71
form: Socrates' mature view of, 134–38, 190; Socrates' three stages and, 199. *See also* transcendent forms

Gallop, David, 37n51, 57n95, 65n106
Garland, Robert, 9n6
generosity, 87
Gerber, Gustav, 133n40
Glaucon: in *Republic*, 61, 66, 91, 92–94, 116, 119–20, 142, 145, 147, 195–96, 225–26; in *Symposium*, 158, 160, 165–66, 203, 209, 213
God, death of, 70, 223, 225. *See also* gods
gods: death of Homer's, 68, 196, 225; in *Parmenides*, 109, 114–16, 117, 142–43, 150; in *Phaedo*, 19–20, 32, 51–52, 68, 70, 77–79; in *Symposium*, 171, 174–77, 178–79, 181, 190, 202, 207, 212, 214, 219; tragedy and, 207
good as form, 59, 62, 66, 109–10, 114, 118, 120–21, 145
Gorgias, 51n87
gratitude, 83–86, 87, 226; in Greek religion, 85; Nietzsche on, 85, 226
"greatest evil." *See* misology
Great Panathenaea. *See* Panathenaea, Great
gymnastic, Parmenides'. *See* Benardete, Seth; *Parmenides*

Hades, 16, 20
Hartle, Ann, 7–8n1, 21n27
Heraclitus, 38n54, 47n78, 179
Herakles, 7, 7–8n1, 11, 14, 18; Socrates as, 23–26, 29–32, 84
Herodotus, 23n30, 150
Hesiod, 45n71, 47n78, 50n86, 178, 195–96, 225
Hippias, 156; in *Lesser Hippias*, 31–32, 96n11, 185n44
Homer, 7, 27n37, 45, 47n78, 84, 87, 146, 150, 223, 225; description of Odysseus, 31, 33; and the gods, 207–8; head of an army of thinkers, 178–79, 182; and Homeric religion, 150; *Odyssey*, 11, 12n10, 18; and ontology, 179; in *Parmenides*, 108, 109, 146; in *Phaedo*, 11–12, 18, 31–36, 45, 50, 52–53n88, 68, 78, 84, 87; in *Symposium*, 150, 161–63, 167, 178–79, 182, 190–91, 195–96, 207; in *Theaetetus*, 27n37, 178–79, 190; and virtue, 150. *See also* Homeric gods

Homeric gods: death of, 68, 108, 196; replaced by forms, 196, 225
honor, love of, 102, 193
How Philosophy Became Socratic (Lampert), 1, 5, 12n10, 19n22, 26n36, 34n45, 61n101, 68n110, 92n6, 96n11, 151n71, 155n8, 196n52, 204n60, 217n90, 222
Hydra, 18, 23, 26

Ibycus, 123–24
ideas. *See* form; transcendent forms
ignorance. *See* knowledge of ignorance
Iliad (Homer), 32, 40n59, 161–62
immortality of the soul, 85n129; arguments for, 15–16, 19, 21; belief of the "true philosopher," 20n26; in *Charmides* and *Republic*, 19n22, 20n26, 26n36; irrationality in pursuit of, 193; in *Phaedo*, 11, 19, 20n26, 28, 36, 67–68, 84; as Pythagorean innovation, 34; and Socrates' last argument, 71–80; in *Symposium*, 172, 187, 188–89, 192–96
impiety, 43, 209–15. *See also* piety
inquiry, philosophic, 30–31, 55, 60, 61, 79, 118–19, 121, 127, 202, 223; limits on, 110, 120; into nature, 37, 38, 79, 99, 123, 125, 131–32, 147
intentions: of Anaxagoras, 45, 46–47; of a philosophic writing, 2, 7; of Socrates' in *Phaedo*, 100; of Zeno and Parmenides, 53, 95, 100–104, 108, 122

Johnson, Samuel, 129
justice: in *Parmenides*, 109, 111, 118n27, 119, 140–41, 145; in Parmenides' poem, 140n54; in *Phaedo*, 10, 47–48, 61, 62, 87; in *Republic*, 34n45, 92, 141n55; in *Symposium*, 157, 195, 202

Kanayama, Yahei, 52n88
Kant, Immanuel, 59n99; Nietzsche's debt to, 133, 223
kinship of Socrates and Nietzsche: on ontology, 133–34, 152; on philosophy, 222–26; on skepticism, 90
Klein, Jacob, 15
knowledge of ignorance, 60, 85; as a knowledge claim, 132–33, 180–81
"know thyself," 123, 131, 223

Laches, 24n32
Leibowitz, David, 3n2

Lesser Hippias, 31–32, 51n87, 96n11, 185n44, 193n50
lie and lies, 45; "On Truth and Lie in the Extra-moral Sense" (Nietzsche), 89, 133
logoi, 17, 27–28, 148; in *Parmenides*, 100, 107–8, 111, 116, 118–19, 120, 131, 134, 138–39, 148n67; taking refuge in, 55; turn to by Nietzsche, 133; turn to in *Phaedo*, 52n88, 55–57, 65–66, 71, 84, 90, 96, 99, 107–8, 111, 172

Meno, 63, 213, 215–20
mind, 28, 206n63; as active ordering, 56, 59n99, 133; and Anaxagoras, 43–44, 45n72, 47n76, 57; as cause, 45–51; dignity of (Strauss), 85; and Odysseus, 45; pure mind in Plato, 221, 222n3; rational, 201; young Socrates', 107. *See also* dreaming and shadow-painting
misanthropy, 24–26, 84; Platonism as, 224. *See also* misology
misology, 24–30, 47, 53, 54, 61, 81, 84, 100; as "greatest evil," 23, 26; Platonism as, 224. *See also* misanthropy
moderation, 195, 202, 205
Montaigne, Michel de, 61
morality, 9, 70; genealogy of, 195, 223; knowledge of, 140–41, 149n70; nature and, 140–41n54
Munn, Martin, 210nn70–71, 211nn76–77, 214n84, 216n89, 219

Nails, Debra, 9n4, 9n6, 93nn7–8, 156n9, 209n68, 210n70, 215n86
natural science, 37n48, 56n93; in Bacon and Descartes, 70; dangers of, 54, 61, 65, 69, 99–100; limits of, 52, 79; in *Parmenides*, 100; Platonic strategy toward, 70–71
nature, 2, 100; and Greek religion, 85; and human nature, 2, 31, 108, 125, 149n70, 187, 191, 197, 200, 202, 224; investigation, 4, 42, 68–70, 100, 149n70; knowledge of, 123, 146, 173; in *Parmenides*, 133, 140n54; in *Phaedo*, 8, 82; in *Symposium*, 173, 179–80, 190, 192; as a whole, 8, 128, 175, 190, 199, 222, 223
Nicias, 69
Nicomachus, trial of, 212–13
Nietzsche, Friedrich, 5, 7, 8n2, 71n118, 85, 221–26; blame of the Platonic Socrates, 150; brought close to Plato, 146; on the

death of God, 225–26; and epistemological skepticism, 89–90, 133–34, 223; exotericism of, 152, 224–25; on gratitude, 85, 226; on Greek religion, 85, 207–8; judgment on Platonism, 70–71, 222–23; judgment on Socrates, 71n118, 85–86; as kin to Socrates, 90, 133–34, 152–53, 221–26; ontology of, 152; "On Truth and Lie in the Extra-moral Sense," 133–34; philosophical education of, 89–90; on transcendent forms as "decorative," 147; turn to the logoi, 133–34
Nietzsche's new history of philosophy, 5, 70, 87, 133, 146, 221–26
Nussbaum, Martha, 209n68

Odysseus, 7, 12n10, 18, 34n45, 52n88, 87, 140–41n54, 167, 185; and divine guidance, 45–46; in first words of *Phaedo*, 11–12; in first words of *Symposium*, 162–63; in *Lesser Hippias*, 32n41, 96n11; named only once in *Phaedo*, 33–34; as polytropic, 32–34; Socrates as, 31–34, 36–37, 45–46, 52, 54, 62, 71, 87
Odyssey (Homer), 11, 12n10, 18, 31–34, 46n74, 50n86, 52n88, 140–41n54, 167n24
one and many, 105–6, 110, 138, 176
ontological psychology: in *Parmenides*, 91, 131, 135, 139, 143–44; in *Symposium*, 152, 173. *See also* eros; ontology; third stage of Socrates' education
ontology, 70, 113, 123, 131, 135, 185, 222–23; of eros, 30, 50, 134; and the highest being, 144; and Homer, 178–79; in Nietzsche, 224n8; in *Parmenides*, 125, 131; of permanence, 30; and self-knowledge, 222–23; as "sovereignty of becoming," 27, 142, 178, 182, 189, 192, 209, 223; in *Symposium*, 152, 175–82, 185, 191; as third stage of Socrates' becoming, 191; of will to power, 134, 223. *See also* eros; will to power
opinion, 149, 160, 220; as a between, 174; and the highest being, 144; indisputable character of, 129, 135; in *Parmenides*, 110, 115, 142, 143–44, 145n62; in *Phaedo*, 39, 77; in *Republic*, 142; Socrates and "the opinions of human beings," 110–11, 115, 119; in *Symposium*, 157, 169–70, 174, 200; and the way things are, 111; of what is best, 48

Panathenaea, Great, 38, 90, 92n5, 95–97, 107

Parmenides, 1, 3–4, 5, 45, 49, 58, 60, 173–74, 190, 221; Adeimantus and Glaucon as auditors of, 91–94, 116, 119–20, 147; analysis of the arts in, 138–40; Antiphon as narrator of, 93–94, 95–97, 107, 122–23, 124; Benardete as interpreter of, 91–94, 116, 124–47; and Cebes, 96, 115, 121, 130, 147; Cephalus as narrator of, 3, 90, 91–93, 95, 97, 108, 123, 124, 129; dramatic date of frame and core of, 90, 92, 95–96, 119; "dreaming and shadow-painting" in, 128–32, 136, 144; epistemological skepticism in, 91, 132–33, 146–47; first words of, 91–95; Homer in, 108–9, 146; its gymnastic as performed for Socrates, 125; lacking Socrates' framing, 4, 53, 90; last words of, 146–47; men of Clazomenae as auditors of, 4, 90, 92–94, 98–99, 108, 119, 146; no need for safe view of cause in, 54; Odysseus in, 140–41n54; ontology in, 113, 123, 125, 130–31, 133–35, 138; Parmenides' gymnastic in, 57–58, 60, 67, 71, 91, 112, 116, 118–19, 120–46, 176, 184, 185; Parmenides' observation of Socrates in, 114, 118; Parmenides' one demythologized in, 127; Parmenides' refutation of transcendent forms in, 108–20; and *Phaedo*, 54, 59, 90–91, 99–100, 107–8, 119, 120–21, 130, 147; Pythodorus as narrator of, 93, 95, 97–98, 99, 101, 106–8, 115, 118, 123, 124; reading philosophic writings in, 95, 99–103; second stage of Socrates' philosophic education in, 90, 124, 134, 146; setting at the Great Panathenaea, 90, 92n5, 95–97, 107; seventh hypothesis as key to gymnastic in, 127–29, 131–33, 135, 146; Socratic turn in, 90, 116, 148–51; and *Symposium*, 90–91, 125–26, 131, 140, 147; transmission of Socrates' philosophy in, 94–95, 108; unique in form and content, 95; uniqueness of seventh hypothesis in, 127–34; Zeno in, 90, 93, 95–109, 117, 120–24, 125, 135

Parmenides as historical figure, 85, 148, 178, 184, 190, 202, 224; first to think through the question of being, 125

Parmenides in Plato's *Parmenides*, 4, 38, 40, 42, 45, 47, 53–58, 95–98, 100–101, 165, 176, 178, 185, 223; admiration of young Socrates, 60, 95, 120; destroys Socrates' view of forms, 34, 52, 60–63, 71, 108–20, 201, 225; and the problem of skepticism, 119; as Socrates' guide, 67, 106–8, 119, 173, 176, 185, 199, 207, 223

participation of particulars in forms, 59; how it occurs, 62; problems with, 111–12

Pausanias: in *Protagoras*, 156, 169n26; in *Symposium*, 156n9, 163–64

Penelope, 33

Pericles, 43, 46, 218

Phaedo, 9, 11–14, 18; admiration of Socrates, 22, 87; as eye and ear witness, 11; as Iolaus, 18, 23, 26, 53–54; as narrator of *Phaedo*, 3–4, 9, 24; recruited by Socrates, 23–24; on the relatedness of pain and pleasure, 13

Phaedo, 1, 3–5, 109, 221, 225; Anaxagoras in, 38n53, 39, 42–51, 56, 69, 102; being "shaken up" in, 16–18, 20–21, 27, 62, 73–75, 79; Cebes in, 9, 15, 17, 19–20, 33n43, 34–37, 39–42, 46–49, 51–52, 54, 56–59, 61–79; center of, 18, 22–33; despair at reason in, 20–23, 27, 68, 73, 75; divine accounts in, 19–20, 52n88; Echecrates in, 9–11, 14, 16–17, 18, 20–22, 24, 27, 32–33, 67, 80; first stage of Socrates' philosophic education in, 37–52, 71; first words of, 10–13; frame of, 1, 5, 9, 17; genuine use of forms in, 65–67; Herakles in, 7, 11, 14, 18, 23–26, 28–31, 84; holding tight to forms in, 62–65, 67, 73; Homer in, 11, 12n10, 18, 27n37, 31–35, 45, 50, 52n88, 68, 84, 87; immortality of the soul in, 15–16, 19, 20n26, 21–22, 28–30, 34, 36, 68, 84, 85n129; Iolaus in, 11, 18, 23–24, 26, 29, 53–54, 58, 84; justice in, 10, 48–49, 61, 87; last argument of Socrates' life in, 28, 30, 34, 67, 71–82; last words of, 87; limits on human knowing in, 24, 26, 56–57, 79; manly objector in, 73–75, 79, 80–82, 84; mention of Plato in, 17, 80; mind as cause in, 43–52; misanthropy in, 24–26, 84; misology in, 24–28, 29–30, 47, 53–54, 61, 79, 81, 84; Odysseus in, 11–12, 18, 31–34, 36, 45–46, 52n88, 87; Parmenides/*Parmenides* in, 57–58, 59–63, 66–67, 71–72, 79, 85; Phaedo as narrator of, 10, 11–12, 18, 23, 80; Phlia as setting for, 9, 11, 14, 18, 21, 24, 27, 29, 37n48, 55, 68, 84; piety/impiety in, 16, 20, 43, 71, 78, 85; pleasure

Phaedo (*continued*)
     and pain in, 13, 16, 62n103, 86; Pythago-
          rean elements in, 9, 11, 19–21, 22, 33–34,
          35–36, 37, 65, 72, 78; rhetoric of fear and
          safety in, 55, 61, 63–66, 72, 74–75, 77, 79;
          Simmias in, 9, 15, 18, 19–21, 22n29, 23,
          28, 29, 33–35, 48n80, 52n88, 58, 62n103,
          63–64, 67, 73, 74n122, 75, 78–79; Socrates'
          autobiography in, 4, 35, 53, 58–59, 71;
          Socrates' display speech in, 51, 54, 66, 67;
          Socrates' last words in, 82–88; *Symposium*
          in, 49, 50, 85; Theseus in, 7–8n1, 14–15,
          18, 31; transcendent forms in, 10, 34, 42,
          45, 51, 59–61, 63–68, 71–72, 74–75, 79, 82;
          transmission of Socrates' philosophy in,
          3, 9, 11, 34, 53, 81, 85; trust in reason in,
          19, 20–22, 24–26, 29, 30, 52n88, 54, 68, 75,
          78–79, 84; turn to the logoi in, 52, 54, 55–
          57, 66, 71; wonder in, 13, 16, 22, 41, 68, 80
Phaedrus: in *Protagoras*, 156; in *Symposium*,
          156, 164, 165–66, 168, 178, 194, 202, 207,
          212n78
Phaedrus, 47n76
Philebus, 139
Philolaus, 9, 19
philosophy: and Bacon, 70, 87, 178; and
          Cicero, 148–50; danger of/to, 7, 18,
          23, 39, 69; and Descartes, 70, 87; and
          gratitude, 87, 226; as inquiry into nature,
          37–38, 69–70, 96, 197; Nietzsche's new
          history of, 5, 70, 87, 146, 221–23, 226; and
          Odysseus, 7, 12n10, 18, 31–34, 36, 45, 87,
          140–41n54, 163; in *Parmenides*, 92–93, 94,
          98–99, 101, 106, 108, 110, 125, 136–37; in
          Phaedo, 3–4, 8–9, 34, 79; and Plutarch,
          69–70; politics of, 61, 70, 79, 102, 116,
          133, 147, 196, 222, 224–25; rule of, 31, 70–
          71, 87–88, 116, 142–43, 148–49, 196, 226;
          Socrates' defense of, 3, 26, 30, 36, 48;
          transmission of, 3, 9, 11, 34, 53, 81, 85–86,
          94–95, 108, 195, 206. *See also* epistemo-
          logical skepticism; ontology
Phlia, 9, 14, 17, 18, 21, 24, 27, 68, 84
piety, 34n45, 71; of Phaedo, 16; of Simmias
          and Cebes, 19–20, 78, 115; of young
          Socrates, 114–15. *See also* impiety
Planeaux, Christopher, 15n14, 90n2, 92n6,
          96n11, 153n2, 155n7, 161n15, 209n69,
          210n73, 213n81
Platonism, 63, 82, 86–87, 151, 224; "for the
          people," 70; Nietzsche's judgment on,
          224–25; and "Platonic metaphysics," 145

Plutarch, 15n13, 148n68, 150–51, 211n74; on
          Plato's success, 69–70
political philosophy, 1, 5; in Homer,
          140–41n54; and *Republic*, 149n70; and
          Socrates and Nietzsche, 222–24; tran-
          scendent forms as part of, 61
Potidaea, 19n22, 26n36, 61n101, 150–51, 155,
          204–5
Protagoras, 69, 179; epistemological skep-
          ticism of, 132, 136; in *Protagoras*, 156; and
          sophists, 193, 217
Protagoras, 1, 51n87, 132, 153, 155–56, 169n26,
          193n50, 204n60
prudence, 194, 202, 205
Pythagoras, 4, 22, 36, 148
Pythagoreans, 4, 9, 19, 21, 65, 147; Cicero
          on, 148; image of the soul, 21, 22; view of
          soul as immortal, 19, 34–35
Pythodorus, 93, 95–98, 99, 106, 115, 118, 124

reason: despair at, 20–21; trust in, 54, 68, 84.
          See also misology
religious crimes of 416–15, 154–55, 165, 203,
          209–20. *See also* Andocides, trial of
Republic, 1, 19n22, 24n32, 26n36, 48n82, 61,
          66, 68n110, 116, 151, 225–26; critique
          of Homer in, 195–96; dramatic date in
          relation to *Charmides*, 150–51; dramatic
          date of, 92; relation to *Parmenides*, 91–92,
          94, 109, 119–20
Rosen, Stanley, 157n13, 209n68

Schopenhauer, Arthur, Nietzsche's debt to,
          133, 223
science. *See* natural science
Sebell, Dustin, 37–38n51, 39n57, 40n60,
          41nn62–63, 48n83, 52n88, 56n93, 59n98,
          66n107
"second sailing," 34–35, 46n74, 49, 51, 52n88,
          96, 99, 120; Socrates' report on his, 52–71
second stage of Socrates' philosophic
          education, 90, 108, 199; as epistemolog-
          ical skepticism guided by Parmenides,
          124–96; intended for the philosophically
          driven, 146; not reported by Socrates,
          90, 173; recovered by the men of Cla-
          zomenae, 90, 153
shaken up, 16–18, 20–21, 27, 62, 73–75, 79
skepticism, 40, 145n62, 147. *See also* episte-
          mological skepticism
Socrates: afterlife of, 14; at age nineteen, 53,
          90, 120; Alcibiades' report on his secret

core, 203–6; attributes false intentions to Zeno, 100–103; autobiography of, 2, 4, 35, 53, 58–59, 71, 108; beautification for Agathon, 161–72, 207; and epistemological skepticism, 90–91, 132, 146; expert knowledge of erotics, 165–68, 172; final argument of, 7–8, 34, 71–79; on gratitude, 81, 83–87, 226; as Herakles, 18–31; as heroic, 3, 7–9, 11, 16, 18, 22, 31, 35, 48, 53, 69, 81, 84, 221; how he read Homer, 178–79; initial inquiry into nature, 37–39; as kin to Nietzsche, 90, 133–34, 152, 221–26; last words of, 8, 81, 82–88, 206–9; mature view of form, 130–31; as Odyssean, 12n10, 32, 34, 36, 37–82; Parmenides' admiration of, 60, 95, 107, 120; piety as a youth, 114–15; as reader, 44–46, 100–103; and the religious crimes of 416–15, 165, 209–20; second sailing of, 51, 52–71; spiritedness of, 102, 107, 123; as Theseus, 7, 7–8n1, 14–18, 31; trial of, 15n14, 209–20; turn to the logoi in *Parmenides*, 90, 96, 99–100, 111, 118–19, 121, 130–31, 134, 138–39, 148; turn to the logoi in *Phaedo*, 55–58, 66, 71, 107–8, 172. *See also* Socrates' becoming; Socratic turn

Socrates' becoming, 1; as autobiography, 2; *Parmenides* and the second stage of, 108, 133–34, 146; *Phaedo* and the first stage of, 37–52, 108; private and public tales of, 2–3; and the *Republic*, 92, 116; *Symposium* and the third stage of, 125–26, 131, 152, 155, 172–91; three stages of, 4, 49. *See also* Socratic turn

Socratic turn, 90, 116; what is unique to Socrates in, 148–51

sophist, 27, 31, 51, 131–32, 134, 136, 141, 217; Diotima as perfect, 193, 201; in *Meno*, 216–17. *See also* Protagoras

Sophist, 134n44

sophistic enlightenment, 147, 156

soul: as "deathless and imperishable," arguments for, 35–37, 59, 61, 72, 76–78; death of, 19; in Descartes, 87; knowledge of, 132–34, 139, 173, 223; in *Parmenides*, 112–13, 127–31, 136, 138, 140, 145; in *Phaedo*, 26, 34, 73, 82, 86, 193; Pythagorean doctrine of, 19–20, 33, 72; in *Republic*, 92; in *Symposium*, 187, 190, 192, 194–95, 199–200. *See also* immortality of the soul

sovereignty of becoming, 27, 142, 178, 182, 189, 192, 209, 223

stages of Socrates' philosophic education. *See* Socrates' becoming

Statesman, 116

Stern, Paul, 41n63, 42, 49, 57n95, 59n99, 62n104, 65n106, 66n107

Strauss, Leo, 1n1, 3nn2–3, 65n105, 69n112, 85, 107, 209n68; on *Symposium*, 153, 155, 167n23, 177, 200n57, 207–8, 223

Sulek, Marty, 24nn32–33, 153n2

Symposium, 1–2, 3, 5, 49–50, 221–22; Agathon in, 153, 161, 163–65; Alcibiades in, 153–54, 157, 159–61, 165, 203–8, 209–11, 214–15, 220; Apollodorus as narrator of, 153; Aristodemus in, 161–64; Aristophanes in, 155, 156n9, 156n11, 164, 166–67, 177n33, 186, 203, 207; the beautiful in, 168, 171, 173–74, 179–90, 194–95, 197–202, 207; Benardete as interpreter of, 169, 177, 180; chronological structure of, 154–55; Diotima in, 155, 163; Diotima's final definition of eros in, 183, 187, 189–90; Diotima's logos in, 182–91; Diotima's myth in, 172–82; Diotima teaches what to teach in, 191–202; dramatic date of core, 209; dramatic date of frame, 154–55, 161n15, 203, 209–20; eros as ontology in, 30, 50, 169, 176–78, 185–86, 188–90, 201; Eros the god in, 152, 154, 164, 166–70, 171, 173–75, 176–82; Eryximachus in, 156, 164–66, 167, 206; first words of, 159–61; frame audiences of, 154–55, 160, 165; Homer in, 150, 161–63, 167, 178–79, 182, 190–91, 195–96, 207–8; immortality in, 187–89, 192–96; last words of, 206–9; Odysseus in, 162–63, 167–68; ontology in, 152, 173, 175–79, 185, 186, 191; Parmenides/*Parmenides* in, 153, 165, 176, 178, 184, 185, 190, 199, 201–2, 207; Pausanias in, 156, 163; *Phaedo* in, 153, 172, 176, 199; Phaedrus in, 164, 166, 168; *Protagoras* in, 155; religious crimes of 416–15 and Socrates in, 154–55, 173, 203–6; *Republic* in, 195–96, 207; Socrates' beautification for Agathon in, 161–72; Socrates' expert knowledge in, 165–66; Socrates questions Agathon in, 168–72; sophists/sophistry in, 156, 179–80, 193, 200–201; as third stage of Socrates' philosophic education, 172, 182, 191, 199; tragedy and wisdom in, 164–65; transmission of Socrates' philosophy in, 159, 167, 195, 206; trial of Socrates as setting for, 161, 210–13, 219–20

Taylor, A. E., 95, 215n86

teleology, 47, 49, 51–52, 70

Theaetetus, 27n37, 42n66, 65, 105, 119n28, 132, 137n46, 138n48, 139, 190; and how Socrates read Homer, 178–79

Theseus, 7, 14–15, 18; Socrates as, 15–16, 18, 31; and the "twice seven," 14–15

third stage of Socrates' education, 125, 131, 136, 172–91, 199, 208; in Diotima's logos, 182–91; in Diotima's myth, 172–82; its kinship with Nietzsche, 152; as ontological psychology, 131, 152; as rational inference about beings as a whole, 134, 182–91; reported by Socrates, 90, 153, 172–73; setting for, 156; as Socrates' mature understanding of cause, 173; in *Symposium*, 172–73, 191, 199

Thrasymachus, 143; as Socrates' new friend, 196

Thucydides, 93n8, 98nn13–14, 154, 194n51, 205, 210n72

thumos, 7, 28, 150, 194n51, 196

tragedy, 156n11, 159, 164–65, 167, 179, 207–8; and comedy, 164, 179, 207; and the gods, 207

transcendent forms, 5, 8, 10, 34, 137, 150, 172, 196, 199, 201, 225; as "decorative," 148; highest form as imagined, 191, 199, 201; holding tight to, 63, 65–67; as *monoeides*, 199, 201; omitted in *Symposium*, 173; Parmenides' destruction of, 104–20, 124, 126; participation in, 59, 61–63, 81–82, 103–5, 112–13, 115–17, 126, 199, 201; in *Phaedo*, 34, 42, 49, 52, 57, 60, 81–82; as politics, 61, 196; rationale for, 68; as rationally untenable, 5, 34, 91, 122, 173; refutation of and the gods, 114–15; refutation of in *Parmenides*, 60, 63, 71, 96, 100, 103, 108–20, 121, 124, 126; replace material and efficient cause, 68; replace the gods, 52, 68, 196, 208, 225; as safe view, 63–65, 75, 79, 81, 121–22; Socrates' use of in *Parmenides*, 90, 96, 99–100, 102, 103–9; as sole cause, 45, 58–59, 61, 64; use of in Socrates' last argument, 71–74, 79

transmission: of Socrates' philosophy, 3, 9, 11, 34, 53, 81, 85, 94–95, 108, 208; of *Symposium* core, 159

trust: in argument/reason, 19, 20–22, 24–27, 29, 30, 54, 68, 75, 78–80, 84; in Diotima's religious rites, 197–98; in divine accounts, 45–46, 52n88; and Odysseus, 32, 45–46; in Socrates, 25; in Socrates' last argument, 79–81

truth about all things, 4; as deadly, 8, 30, 86, 223

unnamed objector in *Phaedo*, 73–75, 79–82

victory-loving, 28; Socrates as, 29, 34–35; Zeno as, 102

virtue/virtues, 70, 202, 216; civic, 2, 34n45, 196, 202; founders of, 195; in *Meno*, 216, 217, 219; phantom images of, 202. *See also specific virtues*

White, Howard, 178n35

will to power, 224n8; akin to eros, 134, 152, 223; as ontology, 134, 152

wisdom, 28, 180–82, 219; Agathon's, 163; Diotima's, 174, 179–81, 187, 194, 197; Homer's, 178–79; as inquiry into nature, 37, 108; Odysseus', 12, 18, 33–34; Parmenides', 123; Socrates', 163–64, 170, 205–6; sophists', 67; in *Symposium*, 164–67, 185–86, 205

wonder: Diotima's instruction about, 183–84; dumbfounded by, 13; in *Parmenides*, 103–7, 115–16, 120; in *Phaedo*, 13, 22, 41–42, 46, 68, 80; at Socrates, 22, 92. *See also* amazement

Xenophon, 9n3, 15n15, 17nn18–19, 65n105, 189, 216n89

Zalmoxis, 150

Zarathustra, 226

Zeno, 4, 45, 47, 53, 55, 95–98, 109; friendship with Parmenides, 100–103; intention in writing, 104–5; on the intentions of a philosophic writing, 45, 95, 99–102; young Socrates' judgment on, 106, 120–22